INDEPENDENCE IN READING

Distributed in the U.S.A.
by
HEINEMANN EDUCATIONAL BOOKS, INC.
70 Court Street
Portsmouth, New Hampshire 03801

Independence in reading
a handbook on individualized procedures

SECOND EDITION

Don Holdaway

Visiting Lecturer in Special Education
Adelaide College of the Arts and Education

Educational Consultant
Ashton Scholastic

ASHTON SCHOLASTIC
SYDNEY AUCKLAND NEW YORK TORONTO LONDON

Holdaway, Don.

Independence in Reading.

Index
Bibliography.
ISBN 0 86896 114 0.

1. Reading (Elementary) 2. Individualized instruction
I. Title.

372.4147

First published in 1972. Second edition 1980 by Ashton
Scholastic Pty Limited (Inc. in NSW), PO Box 579, Gosford
2250. Also in Brisbane, Melbourne, Adelaide, Perth and
Auckland, NZ.

Reprinted in 1983, 1985, 1987 and 1988.

The text of this book was set in Century Schoolbook with
Olivette for the headings.

Typesetting by S.A. Typecentre, Adelaide.
Printing by Bridge Printery, Sydney.

12 11 10 9 8 7 6 5   8 9 / 8 0 1 2 3 / 9

Contents

Preface

This book was first published as a guide to the *Scholastic Core Libraries* which present a structured introduction to individualized procedures in the teaching of reading. The use of the guide by many teachers as a general handbook on the teaching of reading indicated that a need existed for a brief classroom resource book of this kind. The appendices in particular were found useful in planning classroom programmes and in guiding individual diagnostic and remedial programmes. The present edition makes this material available in a more suitable form and is addressed to the teacher of reading in classroom or clinic, the planning or teaching team within a school, and the student of reading instruction.

In revising the handbook to meet this wider purpose, I have endeavoured to retain and enhance the qualities of a useful classroom resource which teachers obviously appreciated. The format has been enlarged and an index has been added. Thus, although much of the material is organized under the individualized reading model, helpful advice on operating a lively recreational reading programme or using children's literature in a language arts programme may be readily located. Detailed analysis of research and lengthy argument on current issues in reading have been avoided, and the text has been kept free from footnotes. Nevertheless, scholarly responsibilities have not been neglected. I have attempted to present practical ideas in a sound theoretical framework and in responsible relationship to current research. A select bibliography for more detailed study of particular issues has been provided in an appendix.

The emphasis of the handbook is on those procedures of teaching and organization which facilitate the development of independence in reading, allow the use of a wide range of children's literature in the teaching of reading, and support individual, diagnostic and developmental teaching. There is already a wealth of practical material available to teachers on the provision of basic instructional programmes based on grouping procedures, and no attempt has been made to duplicate this material. However, teachers will find many suggestions here to enrich and extend basic programmes, particularly in the development of higher level, interpretive skills, the study skills, and creative extensions. Considerable emphasis has also been given to the use of reading within wider language arts and related arts programmes.

The utility of the material is not dependent on running an individualized reading programme as such. Most of the ideas have proved themselves useful to classroom and remedial teachers for many years. The original versions of *Appendices B and C* have been in circulation for over a decade in cyclostyled form and the steady demand, amounting to several thousand copies, indicates their utility beyond question. Much of the material in *Appendix D* is of much more recent origin but arises from the same concern to provide soundly based practical guidelines regardless of the pattern of organization used by the teacher.

'Individualized Reading' threatens to become a new fashion in the teaching of reading. The tendency for new trends to be adopted with superficial and uncritical enthusiasm is perhaps inevitable in any field, but those who would control the tendency by ignoring the trend defeat their own purpose. The 'band-wagon effect' is best controlled by facilitating the flow of information and encouraging the processes of experiment, discussion, and criticism. Furthermore, it is better to understand and master a trend, forcing it to deliver the best of what it has to offer, than to expend valuable energy in opposing it. There are always powerful forces which give energy to a new educational trend, and the day-to-day practice of education is always short of energy. The present handbook is not an attempt to create a trend but to inform it and provide a proper basis for criticism.

Of course it is true that thoughtful teachers have always shared many of the objectives and procedures associated with individualized programmes. However, a clearcut and thorough going organization of these procedures into a workable programme for shorter or longer periods of time has many advantages. Simple patterns of organization which can be understood and controlled by both teachers and children are often more realistic than ambitious programmes which attempt to combine several approaches. For many years I have been a cautious advocate of individualized reading as a simple and powerful means of organizing a classroom for periods of time to achieve some objectives which are difficult to achieve, or are even subverted, by other approaches. However, my main concern is the development of a range of professional skills which will bring us closer to the developmental, diagnostic, and preventive styles of teaching required to ensure a gladly literate society.

D.H.
August, 1972

Preface to the Second Edition

A great deal has happened in the world of reading since the publication of *Independence* eight years ago and the temptation has been to engage in a fairly massive revision of the handbook. However, I see little reason for changing the basic emphasis and oganization of a book which has proved helpful and readable up to this point. And indeed, the causes which motivated it may be said to be even more central and urgent in the present climate of schooling. Children continue to be engulfed by instruction of an ever more complex kind, and though children's literature is becoming ever more rich, I fear that too often they are denied the time or the motivation to read. No system of instruction can replace the act of reading itself — independent, satisfying, joyful reading — as the fundamental means of learning to be literate. In terms of style, my initial aim was to avoid academic or obscure terminology and the erudite manner — dangerous as that may be in certain respects — and to seek to represent sound research in simple ways. I think this emphasis should be retained, although by the addition of a small section of Notes at the end of this edition I have attempted to be more explicit about my sources for those who are properly curious.

Clear statements of the psycholinguistic model of reading which underlies the structure of this book can be found in a number of readily available texts, (e.g. Hittleman 1978; Goodman 1976; Smith 1975 and 1978 a & b) including my own recent book, *The Foundations of Literacy* (1979). Many of the practical suggestions which have been included in this edition have arisen from classroom implications of the developmental and psycholinguistic models. However, I believe that these additions form a single coherent body of ideas within the revision — they simply clarify, or take a step further, those insights from which the book first took its direction.

I had considered excluding the Informal Prose Inventory from this edition in favour of the more accurate and refined procedures of miscue analysis and cloze testing. However, the Inventory does provide an economic format in which to monitor and record reading behaviour when time is at a premium, and I have been persuaded to retain and revise it despite the obvious limitations of using short extracts rather than whole stories or selections. Any procedure which facilitates the careful observation and recording of actual reading behaviour has an important place among our classroom instruments.

I have yet to see a better instrument for testing and teaching basic sight vocabulary than the contextual approach embodied in *Appendix B*. By encouraging children to use a mindful, independent, semantic strategy to identify and remember these difficult but crucial items in the automatic competence of fluent readers, central strategies of processing in reading are reinforced rather than destroyed — as they so often are in isolated item drills. I would continue to recommend such an approach for retarded readers in the strongest terms. As general guidelines to sensibly sequential teaching, the structures of *Appendices C & D* remain sound in the face of recent research. They embody an integrated, developmental approach to teaching in a meaning-centred way.

An important addition has been the inclusion of simplified psycholinguistic techniques of diagnosis and evaluation in the chapter *Developing Reading Skills and Strategies*. The developmental material on stages of development in reading in the chapter *Levels of Operation and Stages of Development* is also new. It attempts to disturb the unjustified faith we place in standardized tests and other single-criterion judgements, and to encourage a more precise and informed observation of reading *as process* at different stages of development.

The book remains centrally a practical handbook for use in the classroom rather than a coherent exposition of a point of view. Behind it, as is the case in my advocacy of Shared Book Experience at earlier levels, lies the desire to make it possible for teachers to use a wide and rich open literature at the *centre* of instruction in reading. The cause of literacy is dependent on print being deeply functional to children from the earliest stages. The books are there but the majority of children are still not getting to them — instruction at one and the same time crowds out real reading with *ersatz* activities, and makes certain that children will choose *not* to read beyond the prescribed quota.

It is my sincere hope that this revision will further assist teachers to open books to children in natural, powerful, and joyful ways. Only then can they learn to read, as *we* all did, by reading.

Don Holdaway
Adelaide
October, 1979.

Common Sense in Teaching Reading

The Language-Learning Environment

Reading in modern life

Despite the popularity of newer media such as radio and TV, no person can reach full human stature in our society without competence in reading. Ten years of compulsory failure at school can be crippling enough for the poor reader without the continuing experience of deprivation which he faces in a society based on the expectation of literacy. The written word influences modern living more deeply every day. Print is persistently increasing its impact on the lives of ordinary people, and in much more complex ways than it influenced a literate minority in the past.

While it has become topical to predict a decline in the usefulness of print and its ultimate replacement by the more direct and vital messages of electronic media, print has been enjoying its own electronic revolution. Recent inventions such as off-set printing, computer setting, and instantaneous copying have greatly increased the impact of written language on our daily lives. Several of these inventions have served a new and powerful alliance between print and other visual forms such as pictures and colour. To a large extent it is the unique flexibility that print has displayed in association with other media which accounts for the unprecedented use of printed materials today.

Books are no longer the major domain of print. The magazine, the greatly enlarged newspaper, the brochure, and the professional journal have come into their own — not to mention the plethora of forms, advertisements, and newsletters that have made their silent ways into the ordinary home. Print is certainly not in retreat: it is engaged in the most aggressive offensive of its long history. We may deplore many of the popular uses to which print has been turned, but the most important implication is the new dominance of ordinary life by printed materials of many different kinds.

The reading skills that are required to deal with the vast quantity and variety of materials in modern society are much more complex and difficult to acquire than the skills of literal decoding, although there are some bonuses in ease and pleasure to be derived from the mixed media approach. Even to be able to determine speedily and accurately what should be read, and what should not, is in itself an important reading skill today. Many of the new uses of print communicate in subtle and devious ways, and their easy style often invites an uncritical reception. While the schools still struggle to achieve basic literacy for the majority, modern life demands competence in higher level, critical and integrative skills for all members of society.

For anyone undertaking study or working in a profession where the welfare of others is at stake, the failure to acquire an adequate range of reading skills is more than ever disastrous today. Such a person must process an increasing quantity of written material to keep himself up to date, and to bring his own parochial experience within a proper international and cosmopolitan context. The ordinary person has the right to demand that the guidance provided by a specialist will be as reliable as recent international knowledge in the field allows, and a dated certificate of professional competence is no longer a satisfactory guarantee that such will be the case. To some extent there is a need for every member of a modern society to continue the practice of scholarship throughout life if he is to participate fully in change, enjoy his leisure, and find it possible to communicate with his own children. To be capable of the careful, laboured reading usually taught by the school as the only proper form of reading is not adequate preparation for reading in modern society.

The disadvantaged reader

Many children are denied the opportunity to master even the most basic skills of reading by social and educational conditions which favour certain cultural groups at the expense of others. Our schools have not succeeded in providing equal opportunity to master literate skills simply by opening their doors to everyone. Indeed, they have often *accentuated* the differences between the advantaged and the disadvantaged by squandering the rewards required for individual learning on those who are already competent, and by magnifying the inferiority of the disadvantaged with a ceaseless barrage of correction and disapproval aimed as much at the cultural differences as at actual difficulties in learning. Too often the major impact of school learning on the less competent is the destruction of self-respect and the will to strive. The school itself has become an instrument of educational disadvantage. (Holt 1964; Silberman 1970; de Lacey 1974.)

The advantaged reader

On the other hand, children who learn to read with ease are usually advantaged from the beginning. Immediately they start to operate as readers they become doubly advantaged. The world of books gives their experience a new dimension in which they can operate independently and at will. The world of children's books has become, in the last twenty years, a rich and fascinating field for exploration even at the earliest levels. (Butler and Clay 1979.)

One very gratifying result of the revolution in print technology has been the creation of an entire literature for children to read independently at each stage of development. The best of these books are comparable at their own levels with the great moments in adult literature. The alliance of print with visual art, often of great depth and beauty, has made possible a new type of literary experience which is especially appropriate to the intellectual style of young children. For the advantaged reader, this literature provides an enormous expansion of experience, particularly in language, and contributes, stage by stage, to personal development. (Huck and Kuhn 1976.)

The best form of reading programme for these children is one in which they have the opportunity to explore the widest range of books possible. To tie their experience to a limited selection, processed at a group rate, is to limit their development of reading skill quite unnecessarily, and to risk producing aversion to a skill in which they are already competent.

The teaching problem

Learning to read continues to be a difficult and distasteful task to a large proportion of our children who nevertheless display ample potential for learning. Reading is a closed book for far too many children, even for many who do in fact learn the basic skills without too much difficulty. Despite research on a massive scale and impressive changes in methods and materials, we have not met the challenge of producing a functionally literate generation, let alone one which delights in reading. The outstanding educational phenomenon of our time is the drop-out.

This is not a problem that is likely to be solved by panic measures, by crash courses of remedial instruction, by fancy methods, by the perfect series of readers, or by an extravagant technology. It is a problem which demands sober common sense above all else.

Too often we become confused by the *complexities* of teaching reading and find it hard to see the wood for the trees. If we provide for the most sensible and obvious things first, we may refine what we do as the opportunity arises, but if our priorities are wrong in the first place, nothing we do is likely to work out right.

What *are* the simple and obvious things? What *is* common sense in teaching reading? Perhaps we could agree as a starting point that reading is a language activity and that *anything we do in the teaching of reading should be consistent with the nature and purposes of language*. Most importantly, reading is the accomplishment of full, accurate and satisfying meanings.

Common sense in learning language

Language is the most complex behaviour that we ever learn. And yet, most of us master the primary speech forms of our native tongue at a very tender age. Parents undertake the major task of teaching their children the oral language with unswerving confidence and with astounding success, no matter what their race or culture or educational background. They require no advanced course in the nature of language in order to provide a favourable learning environment for their children. They rarely suffer anxiety over the process. Indeed, they enter into it with joyful expectation — one might almost say, with blissful ignorance. The remarkable thing is that they almost invariably succeed.[1]

Most parents know little about language in abstract terms and even less about the complexities of learning, yet their children rapidly master a working vocabulary, distinguishing with almost perfect discrimination between the phonemes of the language, mastering the complexities of grammatical structure, and using intonation patterns with perfect control. If only the learning of reading could proceed with the same assurance. For a few fortunate children it does, and we need to be more attentive to the experience of these children in planning reading situations for the majority.[2]

The outstanding feature of the learning environment in which children master the spoken language is the solid common sense and the abounding affection which guide the process at all stages. It is true that children could be taught to speak in much more scientific ways by teachers who had expert understanding of the processes they were communicating. But even if such teaching were to avoid the risk of becoming self-conscious and laboured, how extravagant and wasteful it would be of expensive expertise. This is not to suggest that expert knowledge would be wasteful in the teaching of reading — which is another matter — but rather to suggest that the learning of a complex process is not *dependent* on expert instruction. It is when *natural* learning processes break down that expert instruction becomes necessary.[3]

The environment of learning to speak
What are the characteristics of this natural language-learning environment which operates so efficiently in pre-school mastery of oral language? In the first place, the children are allowed to develop in their own way, at their own rate, using the living language *functionally* to meet their own needs. The parents are very positive and rewarding in their reception of almost any response that their children attempt. They model the language perfectly but they leave ample room for gradual trial and approximation without overbearing criticism and correction. They have tremendous faith in their children, never doubting that they will in fact master the language. If the child says 'la-la' for 'bottle', they don't become overwhelmed with anxiety or despair. They don't call such responses wrong. They are prepared to wait for a year or eighteen months for the final, perfect response to be mastered.

Most puzzling of all from our point of view as teachers is the almost complete absence of competition. Parents compare baby's performance today with what he was doing yesterday or last week — they rarely make close comparisons with the baby next door until the children bring home their first readers from school. Pre-school learning is a good example of the efficiency of non-competitive learning in producing a hardy competence which stands up very well to later competition when necessary.

All of the baby's learning goes on in meaningful situations which support the language being learned. Each of the baby's senses provides constant confirmation and clarification of the language around him: he is engaged in situational learning.

Babies are normally given clear models to emulate, and because they find the process so rewarding, they spend much of their time in voluntary practice of a highly repetitive kind. They are never set exercises or drills, but they programme themselves. From the very beginning they operate independently with whatever language they have at the time, and they rapidly learn to monitor their own responses in self-corrective ways. All of these things are simple and natural in themselves but they allow for the child's own complex system to structure complex behaviour without formal instruction.[4]

In all of this babies are supported by interactive adults who model the skill both by purposeful use in their normal living and by deliberate patterning. Willing and patient help is always ready at hand. Under the best circumstances the result of an honest question is a sympathetic answer.

Developmental learning
To sum up, developmental learning has the following important characteristics — and many more:
1. It occurs 'naturally' in an environment in which the mature skill is being used by everyone with obvious functional success.
2. It allows for gradual approximations towards final accomplishments. It begins in the learner role-playing him or her self as a user of the skill.
3. It is supported by sympathetic, interactive adults who praise often and punish very seldom. Correction is positively presented only for 'mistakes' which are inappropriate to the stage of development. It occurs in a most secure social environment resonant of optimism for the learner's ultimate

success.
4. It is constantly clarified by clear relationships to a total, meaningful environment of people and things — it is clamped tightly to sensory experience.
5. It is self-programmed and self-paced. Massive self-motivated practice and repetition occur on self-selected items or sequences which the learner is determined to master.

School learning

The traditional school, with its large classes and institutional limitations, provides an unnatural learning environment compared with the home. It stands to reason that we must take these restrictions into account when we discuss ways of handling the teaching of reading. We may talk about catering for individual differences as an ideal, but we are simply not in a position to provide individual programmes. However, that is *not* what comon sense suggests. And it would not be a desirable ideal even if it were possible.

In the ideal pre-school situation parents do not provide individual programmes. What they *do* provide is ideal conditions for learning and using language, allowing each child to *programme himself*. They engage in a considerable amount of incidental teaching to meet an obvious need or to provide a correct model, but no preconceived programme is imposed and no predetermined pace is set. If it is possible for us to apply this principle to the teaching of reading, even in part, we may find ourselves less imprisoned by the problem of numbers,and more able to compensate for the artificial limitations of the school environment.

It is clearly impossible for any teacher to *determine* the right level, content, pace, and style of learning for each child, each day — let alone *programme* for them. The best he can do is to make a clumsy approximation which will be wide of the mark for each child in some respect all of the time. Almost invariably, however, each child's own system is capable of determining and programming for appropriate level, content, pace and style of learning more accurately than the teacher, *provided favourable conditions for learning have been set up*. It would seem sensible to provide opportunities for each child to programme himself for at least part of the time. (Smith 1975.)

Favourable environment comes first

Whatever decision we make as to the extent of external control we will impose on the programme of each child, we can agree that provision of a favourable environment for learning is of the first importance. Reading should be learned in an environment which encourages and rewards the exploration of print by *every* child. This is sensible to the point of being obvious, but the conditions of schooling are such that sensible principles like this are seldom put into practice. Institutional things like competition, grading, and control or finance, space, and timetables, usually take precedence over common sense. Much of our teaching energy is spent on compensating for an unfavourable environment. It would be far more sensible to use our energies *first* on the environment itself.

Print should be rewarding

It is difficult to provide natural motivation for reading in an environment where books are things you work through rather than things you come to depend on for special pleasure and enlightenment. Written language requires very much more energy both to produce as writing or print, and to decode into sound and meaning, than does spoken language. In return for this extra effort it offers opportunities to select, preserve, and refine the fleeting experiences of speech. Written language is *valuable* language — or it has no right to exist.

Apart from certain obvious practical functions, printed language should be a record of the most *memorable* language. Paradoxically, the materials we often use for teaching reading are not memorable in any way — they verge on the ridiculous. In order to control vocabulary, or phonetic structure, or common background of experience, the language of many typical school readers records nothing that is worthy of attention. Imagine what would happen to pre-school children learning to speak if they were set exercises as stupid as many of those used in teaching reading. Instead, they normally see people all around them using speech effectively for its proper purposes. The child who is to be motivated towards literacy should see people all around him using written language for *its* proper purposes — to record what is memorable and make it available at will.

The only justification for the use of print — the most permanent and expensive form of written language — lies in the special qualities of experience which it makes available for wide dissemination. If the purpose is to give pleasure, print should provide it to an abundant degree; if the purpose is to give information, print should give it with special clarity and truth. The materials we make available to children for learning the skill of reading should be above all else worthy of their attention and labour, and the quality of life in the classroom should be constantly enriched by all that is precious in print.

If we observe the behaviour of children who rapidly become active readers, we see that they come to school with *high expectations of print*. Their background of experience with books provided them with lively insights into the special pleasures of written language. Books have been associated with some of their most precious experiences for several years — experiences which could have been communicated to them in no other way. A high expectation of reading is more important to progress at any level of development than the skills which can be taught directly, for these expectations energize and direct each skill.

If motivation is to be adequate for learning to read, then, children should find the language of print *more* interesting and *more* relevant than spoken language. They should enjoy the special bonuses of print each day — the freshness, the vitality, the euphony, the deep, sustained excitement and fulfilment that come from a fine story or poem; the stimulus to thought, and the enlargement of experience which come from a clearly worded and sharply focused exposition. They should discover the unique way in which books reflect the entire range of human concerns and contribute something relevant to whatever current interest may arise.

The fact that the language of books differs in certain respects from conversational language presents a special problem in learning to read. For many children, written language constitutes a new dialect which must be heard and spoken before it can be read effectively. Children who have been brought up in an actively literate environment can respond naturally and immediately to book language. Those who lack this background often feel disorientated by the language of books and experience difficulty in correcting and confirming their own responses. Oral experience of the written dialect is an essential part of an effective reading programme throughout both primary and secondary schooling.[4]

Functions of language

Language fulfils many human purposes in addition to the obvious and vital communicative functions. The message sending and receiving often carries a component of empathy which makes people feel at one with each other — language goes beyond communication to what might be called *communion*. Much of our thinking is in language and we are often grateful for the impenetrable privacy of our meditations.[5]

Our experience as *readers* may also be enriched by these special dimensions of intimacy or privacy. The reader may enter into a relationship with the author which is quite different from personal contact. Often the words of the author become more an expression of the reader's own thoughts and feelings than a communication, expecially in reading poetry or fiction. There is also a pure sensory element in language — the sensation of hearing or of producing sound, the visual impact of a page of print or the sensation of a sliding ballpoint pen. If these sensations are pleasing in themselves, as for instance in rhyme or assonance, the total language experience is enhanced. If these sensations are unpleasant, as is often the case in controlling a pencil, the total language experience is less effective.

Reading to children is important

The most direct way of communicating the special qualities of written language to children is through reading to them. If the children's personal reading is to develop fully, they must become familiar with all the special devices of the written dialect in the primary spoken forms of the language which they symbolize. Children need to experience the deadness of print being brought to life in the lively tones of the human voice. Their own attempts to reconstitute print into real language must be patterned on the reading they hear. If they hear little, or if what they hear is of a poor quality, their own reading is sure to suffer.

The language of early reading is much closer to ordinary conversational speech than is the highly wrought and formal language of the written dialect in its mature forms. Expository prose or mature imaginative writing uses language forms which never occur in normal speech. Children need to be helped to interpret and respond to these new forms by hearing them take life in tuneful sounds. Intonation breathes life and meaning into dead words — it adds a vitalizing dimension to new formal structures and literary devices.

Reading to children in as skilled a way as possible should be a dominant feature of the environment in which children learn to read — it should be a fundamental part of any reading programme. This is as true of the later stages of development as of the earlier. To stop reading to children is to deny them one of the most basic and continuing motivations to literacy. With older children this may be achieved with tape recorder or listening post bringing a wealth of voices into the classroom.

Early language is situational and concrete

The child learning to understand spoken language is surrounded by a host of clues which help him interpret the speech he hears. The things going on around him provide sensory meanings which support, clarify, amplify and confirm the language meanings. Facial expressions, gestures and intonations of the speaker provide further clues. The pre-school child is seldom in the position where he is absolutely dependent on pure language to gain meaning — he has a multitude of complementary sensations to aid comprehension and learning. He is usually unwilling to commit himself to any action on the basis of language communication alone — he looks for sensory confirmation before he acts.

Written language usually lacks situational support — the conditions which gave rise to a written statement are seldom present when it is read. This accounts for some of the difficulty of learning to read — especially for children whose language is still basically situational — and it explains the need for clear illustrations in children's books. Copious pictures are required during the years that the written dialect is being mastered. Pictures are not just an added interest — they are a fundamental part of the language transaction. The good illustrator is intuitively aware of the subtle linguistic unity of text and picture.

A supportive environment for reading will provide even more than good illustrations — which are only one form of situational enrichment. It will provide occasions for total sensory involvement, such as role playing or dramatization centred on the language of the text. Every medium which promises to externalize and give concrete form to the abstractions of written language should be brought to the reading environment in order to compensate for the situational poverty of the classroom environment. This is one of the reasons why the related arts are central to the reading programme.

All of this is particularly important for children who are disadvantaged or retarded in language and experience. The major difference between the so-called *elaborated* and *restricted codes* centres around the extent to which the language is complete or self-contained, without reference to the situation in which it occurs. Restricted code constantly points outside itself to things in the situation in which it is taking place — 'This boy — he give him a hit like this, see?' Elaborated code is comparatively independent of a non-linguistic content — 'David gave Gerry a rabbit punch on the back of the neck.' There is a greater need for situational content accompanying language learning for such children in the early years, and the process of weaning from sensory reinforcement onto pure language will be a much longer one than for the child who comes to school already familiar with the formal dialect and the special devices of book language.

The environment should be non-competitive

For every child who profits from competition in learning to read, there are several who are harmed by it. There is no greater source of inefficiency in school methods of teaching language than the dependence on competition as a motivator. The real business of learning is concerned with performing better today than yesterday or last week: it has absolutely nothing to do with performing better than someone else. Children want to learn any developmental task in order to be *the same* as their peers, not better than them. Certainly young children watch older children and adults, and wish to emulate them, in order to achieve the next stage of development, and they need such models. But emulation is not competition.

There are great personal differences in walking and talking ability, even among adults, but imagine how disastrous it would be if we made these skills competitive during the learning stages. It is even less sensible for reading to be competitive because it is *not* a performance skill like walking and talking — it is a *thinking* skill like listening. Some of the most unnecessary disabilities in reading are caused by the unnatural slant towards performance brought about by oral reading at sight and other such competitive perversions of the skill.

If we wish to teach all children to read well, we must abandon competition in *learning* to read, or at least limit its impact as much as possible within the crowded environment of school learning. The mastery of any skill within a developmental process like reading is dependent on constant and progressive success which greatly outweighs moments of setback. This can occur in walking or talking because there are no unrealistic standards set up by competition against which the bumbling successes of the infant look like failure. Competition constantly forces children to try to operate several stages beyond the one they are at. It redirects energies which are adequate to the *appropriate* tasks into hopeless engagement with unrealistic tasks represented by the performance of children several stages ahead.

Children often attempt tasks which are too difficult for them in a non-competitive environment, but their failures do not crush or demean them. They can say 'swim-swimer' for 'windscreen wiper' without triggering a response of ridicule; they can over-reach and fall without feeling deep personal failure or inadequacy. Furthermore, these occasional failures occur in a context of massive success stemming from the intensive use of the skill at the appropriate level. The child controls his own task aspirations in such a way that rewards are *almost* invariably at a high level — or in the words of educational psychology, he sets up for himself ideal reinforcement contingencies.[6]

Competition, on the other hand, feeds punishment to the majority. If winning, or being better than the others, is what provides the rewards, there can be few who receive them. For every reward that competition bestows, it metes out a number of undeserved punishments. It would be difficult to think up a more wasteful or unjust system of reinforcement, especially for learning a task in which it is vital for *all* learners to achieve. The results of such a system are predictable — precisely the high failure rate that we are getting.

Children should want to learn to read in order to be fully human — to be *like* other people, not to be *better* than them. Only then can they control their own aspirations in a healthy and *effective* manner, obtaining continuous satisfactions which sustain their learning on realistic tasks appropriate to their levels of development. The environment for such learning should be as free as possible from distorting comparisons. The aspirations to read springing from competitive pressures distort both the child's concept of the appropriate level upon which to concentrate his efforts, and also his concept of the task itself. Reading is not a performing skill, and children should not be led to think it is.

What I have said on this matter may not look like common sense to many teachers. We live in a competitive society and the school reflects and prepares children for that society. However, there are two considerations which should give us pause in making such a sweeping rationalization. The first is that the homes in which we help our children to learn vital developmental tasks are also part of our society and they are *non*-competitive. The second is that our adult society enjoys competition in all the performance skills, yet it has failed to devise reading competitions — for the simple reason that reading is not a performance skill. It is only during the years of schooling that this responsive thinking skill is twisted into a ludicrous parody of its true functions.

Reading should not be painful

Teachers do not set out to teach children to hate books and reading, but many of the things which happen in reading programmes produce aversion quite directly. Children are always learning and teachers are always teaching: whatever goes on in the reading period is part of the instruction. Children cannot learn to hate and fear books without being *taught* to do so — that is, without some form of compulsion or intervention in their experience. It is inconceivable that a child reading something of his choice, at his own level, and at his own pace, and for his own rather than for someone else's satisfaction, could come to hate and fear the activity.

We could define teaching as the direct instruction given, together with the compulsory requirements made on the learner's behaviour. Sometimes the instruction itself produces aversion. It may be pitched at the wrong level, be too abstract, or be lifeless and boring, and so on. More often, however, it is the compulsion on the learner to attempt inappropriate behaviour which produces aversion. The child is forced to perform at the wrong level where he must make many mistakes; on material outside his interests; before a critical audience of peers; or at a pace which is too fast or inflexible. Since we are responsible as teachers, both for direct instruction and for compulsory tasks, we must be prepared to see ourselves as the major agents of aversion to reading. It is no excuse to blame the child's background or intellectual limitations, or his laziness. We are responsible for the child operating at the wrong level whether he is bright or retarded. And the child who fails to learn to read because he is lazy — if there is such a child — could not develop aversion to books because of his laziness, but only because of the compulsion applied to deal with the laziness. My point is that we are as accountable for teaching aversion as we are for teaching competence and a love of reading. In no logical way can this be placed on the child's account.

A favourable environment for reading will include nothing which will make children hate or fear the printed word. It would be better to avoid teaching reading altogether, at least for a time, than to teach it aversively. The personal harm done to individual children, and the social harm done to the community by teaching children to hate literacy is truly awesome. A teacher should be as careful in using an aversive procedure as a doctor is in prescribing a poison, especially in the context of reading. The belief that successful teaching entails forcing children to do what they don't want to do is one of the most dangerous old-wives tales that continue to distort teaching — it stands conclusively discounted along with bleeding and witchcraft.

It is significant that among all our standardised tests and informal checklists we have no way of measuring the aversion we teach. We need to become more interested in these negative effects of our teaching. As children face the tasks of reading in the environments we provide, we should observe them sensitively for growing aversion, and act with prompt determination when a deterioration of attitudes becomes apparent.

We often feel forced to make an unfortunate decision for the good of the majority. So much the more reason for getting our priorities right in setting up the environment, and establishing procedures which give us the freedom and flexibility to match developmental tasks to individual needs.

The common sense environment

What are the characteristics, in summary, of a favourable environment in which to learn and to teach reading?
1. There should be a wide range of materials worthy of the children's attention and serving their life interests.
2. The printed word should bring enrichment and joy to every child.
3. The deadness of print should be reconstructed daily into the lively tones of speech by the skilled reading of the teacher and others.
4. The written language should be given situational support by pictures which do justice to the nuances of the language, by exploration of the real concrete world, by other media, and by the opportunity for externalizing experience through dramatic modes.
5. The children should enjoy social support and stimulus in their striving, but without any sense of competition.
6. Whenever possible, the children should be encouraged to operate independently. At least for part of their time they should be trusted to programme themelves, working at their own level and pace on material they have chosen personally.
7. Help and guidance should be readily available, but the children should enjoy the right to strive without overbearing interference or correction. They should be taught self-correction and self-evaluation from the earliest stages.
8. They should be taught the skills and attitudes required to use reading in the purposeful practice of modern scholarship.
9. Nothing should be done in the reading programme to spoil books for children.

If we compare learning to read with other developmental tasks, these are the conditions which could appear to favour natural and sound learning. Many teachers would consider this comparison both false and dangerous. They would insist that reading needs to be carefully taught before children are able to use it with enjoyment. We may agree that reading needs to be carefully taught, but *let us be clear that it needs to be taught within this favourable environment*. If we place the need for carefully organized instruction above all else, every one of these vital conditions is likely to be sacrificed.

The Teacher and Reading

The Role of the Teacher

Does all this mean that the children should be allowed to do just what they like? That would be throwing common-sense to the wind! A favourable environment is an ordered environment in which security springs in large measure from the predictable control of the teacher, sound routines, and clear-cut expectations in the behaviour of the children. (This was also the case in the pre-school home where the child mastered oral language.) When large numbers of children are brought together in a class, great skill is required to organize instruction without destroying the conditions of a favourable environment.

However, there are also important compensations in the social stimulus children experience in working together. Meeting individual needs is often best accomplished within a social framework. It is a misconception to think that individualizing learning entails each child working as an isolated individual. *Class activities and grouping of different kinds are essential to successful individualizing.*

The professional teacher regards each child as a client who depends on the teacher's special expertise to achieve personally beneficial goals. The professional relationship is one of trust — one in which the client may properly expect that everything that springs from the relationship will be turned to his or her benefit. The special power of the professional, especially that arising from intimate personal knowledge — such as test results — must never be used against the client.

As professionals, teachers face much greater difficulties than other groups of professionals in maintaining confidentiality because of the necessarily public nature of most of their relationships with their clients. The temptation is always pressing to put certain clients down in the interests of the majority, and pupils who most need security and confidentiality are most likely to be denied them. Failure in a task such as reading may be as humiliating for a child as the serious physical and mental disorders we trust our doctors to keep confidential and to cure.

Reading is highly complex behaviour which is difficult to research because of the enormous number of variables to be controlled. A few very general principles may be drawn from the increasing body of classroom research in reading, however:

1. Most striking is the accumulating evidence that the teacher is the most important variable in the reading programme — more important than method or pattern of organization. The quality of human concern and

professional skill stem from the teacher, and it is more important for us to establish sound relationships within the classroom and improve our awareness of sound reading development than to stake our faith in a particular method, or pattern of organization, or published scheme. Provided the teacher can take up an informed position of trust and sincerity with her children, differences in styles of teaching, methods of instruction, or patterns of organization do not appear to be of the first importance.

2. There are many satisfactory approaches to the teaching of reading which have demonstrated comparable results. No approach seems to suit *all* children and the search for such a panacea has proved fruitless. This is one reason for greater individualizing of instruction — provided the teacher is professionally knowledgeable about different approaches.

3. Experimental groups tend to make better progress than control groups no matter what methods or materials are under trial. This is a nightmare for researchers but should be taken up by teachers as a clear, positive guide. The heightened impact of fresh approaches or materials, and the optimism and enthusiasm of the experimental environment contribute greatly to learning. We all need to teach as if we were engaged in an exciting new experiment or exploration, and take every opportunity to develop fresh approaches, use fresh materials, and extend our expertise through this divergent experience.

Individualized programmes tend to develop differently in every classroom and their success depends greatly upon good relationships, flexible organization, and the awareness of the teacher in the field of reading. However, there is little research justification for advocating any particular approach, including individualized reading. Research which is descriptive, developmental, and longitudinal presents our most valuable insights. Such research underlines the highly individual nature of learning to read, the impossibility of controlling all of the crucial factors externally, the importance of intrinsic as distinct from extrinsic motivation, and the immense skill of genuinely motivated learners to control their own learning.[7]

Functions of teaching

It may be that in emphasizing teaching rather than learning we have traditionally narrowed instruction unnecessarily. What are some of the ways in which teachers may achieve their objectives in reading?

1. Providing a favourable environment for learning.
2. Organizing interactions to harness social motivations.
3. Guiding children to tasks on a level at which they will succeed.
4. Rewarding appropriate behaviour which demonstrates progressive learning.
5. Supporting children as they make new ventures.
6. Demonstrating skill and providing clear models for emulation.
7. Telling children what to do and how to do it.
8. Monitoring children's learning behaviour, diagnosing, and evaluating.
9. Setting limits to behaviour, keeping control, and discouraging inappropriate behaviour.
10. Being an interesting and mature person in the contrived environment of the classroom.
11. Taking the children out of the environment to new experiences.
12. Bringing interesting people into the environment.
13. Assisting parents to participate effectively in the learning experiences of their children.
14. *Inducing rather than instructing.*

This last point really sums up all that has been said so far, but it needs some clarification. Many skills taught at school, including reading, involve behaving or doing rather than applying knowledge. To teach these skills we have traditionally told children what to do and then hoped that they would apply the knowledge. A much more efficient way of teaching many skills would be to *induce the behaviour* or, in other words, **put the pupil in a situation where he cannot help doing what is required, quite naturally, and without conscious effort.**

For instance, if we wish a child to use the context to work out unknown words, we may read part of the sentence and stop before a word which is fairly obvious. The pupil will then come out with an appropriate word almost involuntarily — his own language system will *induce* the response. Suppose the sentence began, 'It went around and then came . . .', the response 'back' is almost compulsive. If we wanted the children to attend to initial letters, we could read, stop and write the initial letter, or present a text with just the initial letter of that word provided. For instance, if the sentence began, 'I like to play with my baby s . . . . .' the responses 'brother', 'kitten', etc. are precluded.

In this sort of teaching we induce rather than teach a process. Whenever it is possible to induce the desired process rather than give instructions on how to carry it out, this is the more efficient method of teaching. Where *automatic skills* are to be taught, or where skills which can be carried out by conscious strategy need to be made automatic — such as all the word recognition skills — *induction is more efficient than instruction.*

Programmes and common sense

It is likely that we will need to use several approaches or programme combinations in the long term to provide for rounded development in reading within normal classrooms. We have seen that there are advantages in freshness and variety, but there are also dangers of losing perspective and continuity in change for its own sake. The ideal programme would be sufficiently flexible to encompass variety and generate new enthusiasms over long periods of time without disturbing the natural development of individual children by sudden discontinuities of experience.

There are many effective ways of organizing a reading programme and splendid materials based on clearly defined instructional objectives abound. As we have seen, however, learning priorities too often become distorted by the anxious demands of instruction. Independence, relevance, diversity, and joy are often displaced by the urgent drive to teach skills and test performance, by the competitive pressures of lock-step systems, and by the stigma of 'remedial' segregation. Reading periods may degenerate by degrees into the tedium of written exercises based on the study of superficial extracts, and real books as such may disappear from the instructional scene. The reading programme may so easily become isolated from the life and language of the classroom.

When dangers of this kind begin to threaten healthy development in reading there is a need for procedures which restore common sense priorities and bring the richness of print back into the centre of classroom life. The type of programme which has come to be known as *individualized* or *personalized* reading offers an effective system of classroom procedures which allows for the reordering of priorities towards a more natural and healthy development of reading skills.

As teachers we need to be competent in the use of these procedures and capable of deciding under what conditions we should use them. A major objective of this handbook is to describe these procedures in sufficient detail to enable any teacher to establish an individualized programme with some confidence.

Levels of Operation and Stages of Development

Levels of operation in reading

Children learning a developmental task will normally choose to operate at a level of significant challenge where their skills are being extended in a general context of success accompanied by a certain risk of failure. When a task is prescribed by an instructor it should also be at this level of successful challenge. We could call this the **Instructional Level,** and in reading the criteria have been clearly set and ratified by many research studies. It is generally agreed that children operating at this level in reading understand at least 75% of what they read and make errors at the rate of approximately one in twenty running words.

Children learning a developmental task spend a considerable proportion of time using or practising the skill at a level of success which almost excludes challenge or failure. This is very necessary to sustain confidence and to habituate the skill until it becomes quite automatic. (Sometimes there is a need to regress even further in order to restore confidence which has been temporarily lost.) This level of success is usually called **Recreational Level** and in reading it is characterized by almost complete comprehension and accuracy. Although little new learning takes place at this level, children should spend a significant proportion of their reading time operating at this level.

Children will sometimes choose to operate at a level which is too difficult for them and leads to frequent or even continuous failure — observe a child learning to ride a bike. This is natural to learning a developmental task when motivation is extremely high and only becomes harmful when children are forced by *external pressure* to operate at this **Frustration Level.** A teacher should never prescribe reading at this level, especially over long periods of time or under the observation of any sort of audience. However, there is some support from research that highly motivated learners may profit by operating *by choice* at a high level of challenge — under these circumstances their frustration tolerance would be very high. Within an individualized programme the children have some freedom to choose the level of challenge which best fits their current needs and motivation.

In the directed silent reading situation, where a group of children read the same selection at their Instructional Level, they have the assistance of the teacher's introductory guidance and availability. In an individualized programme children must work much more independently of teacher guidance and instruction. Their most effective level of operating may, therefore, be somewhat below measured Instructional Level. For this reason the tests provided in

Appendix A, An Informal Prose Inventory, are slightly more difficult than Instructional Level for the age group. If the child is able to fulfil the criteria for a particular level, he should be capable of reading that level of graded material independently and this has been called **Independent Level.**

Whatever pattern of organization being used in a classroom, each child should spend more reading time at Instructional Level than at Recreational Level. He should have opportunities for reading outside school time at Recreational Level, and he should rarely, if ever, be required to read at Frustration Level. In a well organised individualized programme the same proportions should prevail through choice and teacher guidance, but there is likely to be some highly motivated reading by some children at what would be technically Frustration Level for them under normal circumstances.

Controlling task difficulty

The need to control the difficulty of reading tasks is one of the reasons for using a variety of approaches or procedures. In the past thirty years we have relied too heavily on the use of graded or controlled vocabulary texts and sequential published programmes to make this match. A wide variety of other procedures is at our disposal:

using children's own language capitalizes on personal meaning, familiarity, and recency in lowering task difficulty

using high impact books from the open literature mobilizes motivation to increase competence

using favourite, familiar stories which have been enjoyed several times renders rich and difficult material readable for almost all children

allowing self-selection from a wide range of materials leads children to make good matches in personally satisfying ways

All of these different techniques — and many others — make satisfying, independent reading possible for almost any child at any level. There is little excuse, considering the powerful techniques at our disposal, for children to battle at tasks beyond their control or to be bored by tasks beneath their competence. Organization is probably the greatest problem in mobilizing these resources so that all children are matched to personally manageable tasks. This will be our major concern in the middle section of the book.

Learning to read as a self-monitored process[7]

The climate of thinking about learning to read in the past decade has been greatly influenced by those who dispelled the myth that there was a perfect, best method of learning to read. How distracting that myth, and how deeply it distorted our view of evaluation. In the less cloudy climate that has prevailed since that time, research and development have been able to shift their emphasis to a proper focus on learning to read rather than on teaching reading.

A large proportion of children in all developed countries have learned to read successfully under very different regimes of method, and many recent research studies have been concerned with describing the actual behaviour of these children. Learning to read is beginning to be displayed as a series of natural, healthy progressions that look very similar in different instructional systems once the trappings of method have been taken away. Successful children are too busy forming their own destiny as literate individuals to take too much notice of what their teachers tell them to do. It is the really conscientious youngsters, those who try to stick closely with the instruction instead of supplementing it liberally with common sense, who are really at risk as readers.

We have much to learn from closer observation of successful learners, and we are more likely to help the less confident children by inducing them to operate like the successful ones than by imposing the half-truths of some methodology which we must monitor closely ourselves because the child has no earthly chance of understanding what it's all about

One of the most interesting things about successful readers is their comparative independence at all levels from extrinsic reinforcement and control. They approach reading with high motivation and self-confidence, aware from day to day of what print has to offer them, and they get from it that special sense of achievement which comes from the habit of self-monitoring.

In learning to ride a bicycle, a child will drive his body to the point of exhaustion, skin his knees, and even risk life and limb as he wobbles down the footpath. So, at appropriate times, the child who comes to reading with the right developmental set chooses his own speed, his own threshold of frustration, his own tolerance for repetition and practice as he masters each new challenge of the task. True, he gains much from sensitive and interested adults around him — especially from his teachers — just as, in his infancy, he took models for speech from his parents.

Self-regulating systems and reading

Most human skills are self-regulating, even in their earliest stages of development, and a part of mastering skills at each stage is learning how to regulate them. As a technology has been developed for constructing such self-regulating mechanisms as computers, some researchers have taken up the significance of cybernetic theory. (Kirk and McCarthy, 1961; Ruddell, 1970.) But we have a long way to go before we understand the feedback systems which control human skills and their acquisition.

Three important insights which arise from feedback theory are highly relevant to our subject. First, feedback and guidance systems are invariably more complex than the power systems they control; second, they can go wrong in a greater variety of ways than the power systems dependent upon them; and third, internal communication channels, responsive in miniseconds to changes in the power system, are vital to their function.

Now, if we see reading behaviour as a self-regulating system, we realize that self-evaluation of reading behaviour is at the same time more complex, more difficult to learn, more delicate and fragile, and more vital to success than is the response or performance side of the system. It would appear, furthermore, that in human learning, as distinct from contrived mechanisms, the feedback system fulfils a further function of reinforcing efficient behaviour and thereby implanting new levels of sophistication in the system as it is constructed. During the learning stages of a skill, this second function of human feedback may be even more important than the first of control.

A strong line of research pioneered by MacKinnon (1959) in Canada, developed in depth by people such as Goodman (1970), and represented locally by a decade of productive developmental research by Clay and her students at the University of Auckland, emphasizes the central importance of self-corrective behaviour in successful reading at all stages of development, but critically — and from a traditional standpoint, surprisingly, at the *earliest* stages.

Traditional methods and styles of teaching have tended to place the responsibility for performance on the learner, and have jealously pre-empted the roles of evaluation and reinforcement to the teacher. Such a misconception seriously distorts the natural learning of reading skills and threatens average and slow learners. They tend to receive little reinforcement and a preponderance of negative feedback from a system in which the teacher and peer comparisons dominate evaluation. In such a system, *successful* readers beat the teacher to correction and are relatively independent of extrinsic reinforcement. Even so, it would appear that, at the early stage, many of these successful readers become increasingly hooked on the extrinsic rewards that are wastefully lavished on them at the expense of those who *need* the rewards. Their skill may then be misdirected toward performance for praise or competition on low level tasks, when they may have developed higher level skills had their reading been redirected toward self-satisfaction.

Whenever we correct a child who could correct himself, we subtly interfere with the growth of that system of reward and control on which he must rely to carry out the skill independently. To virtually take over a child's control system, as so often happens in well-intentioned remedial programmes, could cripple the ability to master any reading skill.[8]

Monitoring and teaching self-evaluation

If self-evaluation at all stages of development play as vital a role in learning to read as research now tends to indicate, we must face many changes of emphasis in teaching and evaluating reading. We will favour patterns of organization and styles of teaching which foster the development of independence, and we will provide inducements for children to share more fully in the evaluation and control of their own learning.

Furthermore, since learning the strategies of self-regulation is necessary to mastery of any skill at any level, our own evaluation of children's progress must include *an evaluation of their ability to evaluate*. Techniques for recording and tallying self-monitoring behaviour should be an important part of our overall assessment procedures. The self-correction ratio provides a useful measure. (Clay 1972a and b.)

Stages of development in reading

From the developmental point of view, we would expect to find a number of clearly defined stages in the development of literate children. We would expect to find some behaviours which appeared for a time and were then superseded, and we would expect to find appropriate forms of self-monitoring present in the behaviour at each level. Recent research continues to fulfil these expectations, to the extent that it has directed our attention to the preschool experiences of high progress readers in order to observe the earliest stages of reading occurring under optimum conditions from infancy. Even in the reading-like behaviour of many preschoolers from the age of two years, we find clear evidence of self-corrective and self-regulating behaviour on the basis of syntax, meaning, sequence, picture cues, and memory for text.[9]

It is possible to organize our observation of reading development over the first six years of schooling into six clear stages, beginning for some children as early as the second year preschool and only partially completed by some children as they complete the equivalent of Grade 8.

1. Emergent reading Behaviour and the Development of a Set towards Literacy.

A very sophisticated complex of attitudes, insights, and skills needs to be developed before the actual decoding of print symbols becomes meaningful or manageable. Included, for instance, are motivational factors, such as having high expectations of books as sources of special kinds of security-centred fulfilment; operational factors, such as the ability to use language without reference to presently available sensory experience; linguistic factors, such as gaining spoken language control over a wide range of written dialect forms; and orthographic factors, such as the awareness that the message is carried and preserved in every detail by the print rather than the picture.

This fascinating stage, which peaks for the majority of our children during the first year at school (5-6 years), encompasses many reading skills or their embryonic forms. To call this level *prereading, readiness for reading*, or even worse, *preliteracy*, is to underestimate or misconstrue the importance and nature of these emergent reading behaviours.

It could be said that the strength, content, and articulation of the set directing a child into literacy determine in no small measure the success or failure experienced at succeeding stages. In her Concepts About Print test, Clay (1972a, 1980) has developed a fine instrument for evaluating many important behaviours of this emergent stage.

2. The Early Reading Stage — One-to-one Word Matching
In this crucial phase of learning, most young children acquire the range of skills set out in most beginning reading programmes — and much more. As the children begin to relate cues from different sources, carefully patterning a slow flow of language against a directionally oriented series of visual patterns, the miracle of true reading begins to occur. Cues are matched with deliberation. The finger or the voice points. Reruns and self-corrections often punctuate the performance. The active use of increasingly sophisticated strategies of self-correction and confirmation is of critical importance. These strategies help children to organize perceptions and to sustain attention on appropriate visual details for as long as is necessary.[10]

3. Fluency and the Submergence of Overt Monitoring
As children gain automatic control over perceptual skills, fluency develops and the operation of self-corrective strategies becomes covert. The child moves towards the stage where the orally verbalized crutch which has provided an eye-voice-ear link with the text is no longer needed. Silent reading gradually becomes a natural form of behaviour, but vocalization is only just below the surface and speed remains at or below the rate of speech. The efficient problem-solving strategies built up at the previous stage and centred on the concrete sensory support of vocalizing and pointing, are still accessible whenever needed. As Clay puts it rather graphically, the child reading fluently is able to 'drop to a lower gear' whenever difficulties in the text require it.[11]

This stage is a time for widening horizons in reading as perceptual tasks come under largely automatic control and the energy previously drawn off for conscious matching operations becomes available for deeper reactions and higher level operations. Evaluation procedures should now be directed more clearly to appropriate emotional response, identification, creation of sensory imagery, and the whole range of comprehension skills, from word meaning in context to critical and creative thinking.

4. Consolidation: Tension between Oral and Silent Reading Skills
As suppression of vocal responses allows rapid increase in the rate of silent reading, the child can no longer move with comfort back into the oral reading mode until he has learned a new battery of skills. When oral reading is forced on him he may bungle and stammer his way through the text, puzzled by the fact that he has no trouble when reading to himself; he cannot coordinate his responses when eye and voice are at different points in the text. Until he has received some instruction and purposeful practice in the special skills of audience reading, he is likely to report that he 'hates reading aloud', and he has reason to.

At the same time, in the private security of efficient silent reading, he is likely to be gripped by a text and begin to adjust his style of attention, rate, and comprehension to suit the widening range of materials he is now able to process. On the other hand, this may not be a period of very active reading and his skills may remain at the previous level for several years before he makes a breakthrough to real ease and pleasure in silent reading. Even the new perceptual skills which he needs to master at this level, such as the increase in sight vocabulary to cover over 90 per cent of word recognition, depend on the burgeoning of reading interests fed by the ease in comprehension of efficient silent reading.

Self-evaluation tends to be less apparent at this level and is certainly difficult to monitor. There is some evidence to suggest that the continuing emphasis of reading programmes on the evaluation of lower level skills may inhibit the natural drive toward wider interests and the desire to read.

5. Flexibility: Developing Styles of Reading for Different Purposes
A competent minority of children at age 10-11 display several mature styles of reading depending on motivation and purpose. These children tend to regard themselves as good readers and may display the same determination to master the difficult skills of audience reading as they displayed in mastering decoding skills at the second stage. In a challenging educational environment, they may develop astonishing flexibility in rate and in new perceptual strategies such as those involved in scanning, skimming, selecting, and sampling. A close study of the reading behaviour of these children may suggest ways in which we can assist the majority of children to diversify their skills at an earlier age but, currently, we cannot regard maturity at this level as characteristic of eleven- and twelve-year-old children.

6. Mature Life-Style in Reading
The outstanding feature of mature literacy is the unique relationship it displays in the lives of individuals. It has no convergent form or upper limit, but rather, constitutes a body of learning strategies which allow the mature reader to extend and develop new skills or refinements of skill to meet changing life purposes. It often becomes interest-and-vocation-centred. Rapid comprehension tends to develop first in areas of habitual preoccupation served by highly refined powers of prediction which are based on knowledge and familiarity.

What is good reading from a developmental point of view?
Value judgements about the quality of performance at any of these five stages are likely to be valid only for the particular stage being observed. What we mean by *good reading* at one stage may be very different from what we regard as good reading at the next. For instance, if we take oral reading as a parameter for evaluation over these stages, the first, third, and fifth are likely to display fast, fluent, lively reading — although not equally accurate, of course — while in the intervening stages this is unlikely to be the case. Oral reading at the second stage is likely to be slow and meticulous, even laboured, while at the fourth stage it may be erratic, bumbling, and mannered. Each of these types of reading must be considered good reading for the stage at which it appears.

Evaluative judgements about different reading skills should be specific to the stage of development so that children may be reinforced for appropriate behaviour. In general, the children themselves seem to be able to make the necessary shifts of evaluation from stage to stage more easily than teachers or test developers — both of whom are tempted to run the same rule over reading behaviour at every stage.

Evaluating Reading

Extrinsic monitoring of progress in functional reading

What are the implications of a developmental point of view for those who interact with children learning to read — the teacher, who has the most profound influence, as well as the department head, the principal, the inspector or supervisor or adviser, and the parents as they fall under the influence of the school? All these are included because together they constitute a powerful judicial force bearing down on the teacher, and hence on the children. It is often this third force which turns evaluation into a mockery of what it should be — an act of comparison or ranking rather than a sensitive measure of progress and need.[12]

Assuming, then, that the teacher is permitted to evaluate the progress of each child in a sensitive way, what priorities stem from regarding reading as fundamentally a self-regulating task?

1. Nothing the teacher does should inhibit the use of self-monitoring procedures by the children. She should reinforce the most desirable behaviours and, for learning to read, that means pre-eminently reinforcing self-regulating behaviour. The teacher's highest praise must be reserved for that critical moment of self-awareness when the child's own feedback has informed him accurately of his own success.

2. Since self-regulation is more vital, more difficult to learn, and more open to malfunction than any other part of the reading process, the teacher has a responsibility to monitor the *children's* monitoring. This may be done by using the *Informal Prose Inventory: Appendix A*. Other procedures are taking 'running records' (Clay 1980) and making a miscue analysis (Goodman and Burke 1972; Johnson 1979).

3. The full spectrum of reading attitudes, insights, and skills appropriate to the stage of development should be evaluated in a balanced and coherent way. Our standardized group tests set a bad example in this respect, since they measure only a portion of the spectrum. We need to be much more aggressive in demanding research-based procedures of evaluation covering the higher order cognitive and integrative skills of reading. Operations such as personal identification with characters, or the ability to structure alternative plot possibilities, loom large in the experience of successful readers and may contribute significantly to their success. Certainly, the affective area is of prime importance in sustaining healthy reading behaviour.[13]

4. A balanced spectrum of reading behaviours may best be evaluated by observing functional reading rather than performance reading, especially under test conditions. Teachers need techniques to assist them in observing and recording the progress of children in day-to-day reading under natural conditions. Types of organization, such as individualized reading, which readily display a wide range of reading behaviour, or opportunities for personal interaction between teacher and pupil, may facilitate this day-to-day evaluation.

The *Informal Prose Inventory: Appendix A*, sensitively applied, may be a most valuable instrument in monitoring progress in functional reading.

5. Despite the cautions sounded previously, standardized tests are essential to certain proper functions of evaluation. However, since they need to be used no more than once or twice a year to fulfil these purposes, they should not be an obtrusive feature in the reading experience of children. The Progressive Achievement Tests, recently developed in New Zealand by Elley and Reid (1969), have been provided with practical guidance and notes on interpretation of exemplary clarity, but a sampling of the use being made of the tests raises doubts as to the extent to which we can rely on advice communicated by a carefully designed manual. The potential for misapplication of standard measures seems to come from very deepseated assumptions about evaluation which persist despite being shown to be harmful. Assumptions which encourage the school to exercise a prophesy-fulfilling influence, limiting the progress of many children, seem to be among the most deeply entrenched prejudices of the school system. We need to know more about the actual uses and the real impact of standardised test results before we can have a clear idea of their place and value in guiding the development of children who are learning to read.

6. Finally, diagnostic tests and procecures need to be used more widely to monitor normal development. Too often, careful diagnosis is not used to improve the efficiency of reading in a general sense, but is used for special purposes too late in the development of progressive disorders. A diagnostic approach to evaluation is desirable from the earliest stages if preventive intervention is to be effective. The diagnosis should be sufficiently functional to suggest the most appropriate forms of intervention. More often than not, the appropriate form will include restoring healthy self-regulating functions in the total operational strategy of the individual reader. (Clay 1979.) See also *Summary* of chapter, *Developing Reading Skills and Strategies*; and *Note 16*.

Readiness
Children should not be given instruction in skills for which they are not ready. There are three simple principles of readiness:

1. Readiness to undertake a task is characterized by confident and spontaneous use of earlier stages in the task. (*Appendices C and D* provide details of the sequential stages of different skills.)
2. An essential component of readiness to undertake a task is the conscious desire to master the task. Too often we conscript children into instruction and fail to determine whether this aspect of readiness has been fulfilled. A greater use of voluntary grouping for instruction would identify children who were not ready in this important respect. We are then in a position to induce readiness for the children who lack it before we give useless or harmful instruction.
3. Following from 1. and 2. above, it is clear that readiness may be induced or taught by providing successful experience at the lower stage and providing for the development of conscious motivation.[14]

Summary

From the developmental perspective we are able to look critically at traditional assumptions about evaluating progress in functional reading. In particular, it is possible to see the inbuilt dangers in many of our accepted procedures of restricting the growth of vital, self-regulative skills in young readers, and of directing massive negative feedback into the learning endeavours of the children most in need of positive reinforcement.

We face a challenge to develop styles of teaching and procedures of evaluation which will encourage optimum development of self-monitoring strategies at every stage and over the whole spectrum of reading, and which will allow teachers to intervene more positively in the learning adventures of children who are struggling to master the skills of literacy.

Finally, classroom teachers need to be supported in every possible way to make these changes, and remove the institutional and supervisory impediments which so often force teachers to adopt harmful procedures in evaluating the progress of children learning to read.

Objectives of Development in Reading

Independence in the reading programme

All teachers agree that independence in reading is an ultimate objective of the programme. Most now agree that independence is desirable at every stage of development. Many are beginning to realise that the experience of independence is more than a final objective at any stage — it is vital to efficient day-to-day learning.

The achievement of independence at each stage of development entails building on basic instruction to fulfil personal interests and needs.

Among the skills required for this achievement are:

The ability to select appropriate materials.

The ability to persist at a personal pace which makes efficient use of current skills.

The ability to evaluate in terms of personal satisfaction, social expectation and future need.

Too few children build on basic instruction in this way. For some it is a late discovery of adolescence rather than a continually maturing process at every stage of development. For many it is never realized and reading fails to become an important part of daily living. Any child who fails to enjoy what reading has to contribute to his experience, *stage by stage*, is to that extent impoverished.

Is the recreational reading programme adequate to meet this need?

Yes. A *lively* recreational reading programme, richly provided with books and with the teacher *active*, goes far towards meeting the need for independence. Typically, however, the recreational reading programme — often known as 'free reading' or 'pleasure reading' — suffers from the loss of the teacher's influence and the stimulus of discussion.

Can the instructional programme afford to exclude free choice and pleasure?

No. But, of course, we don't *intend* to exclude pleasure from the instructional programme — it just happens. There are many reasons, apart from compulsion, for the dullness of many programmes: lack of variety; the emphasis on 'comprehension questions' of an often factual or inane kind; the small amount of actual reading and the large amount of writing; the problem of keeping up with the group for some and suffering the slow pace for others; the limitation of content to materials of which there are multiple copies; and so on.

The *permanent* division of the programme into instructional and recreational phases tends to be self-defeating. In theory it is hoped that the instructional programme will provide for basic learning in reading skills while the recreational programme will consolidate these skills by putting them to use in personally satisfying ways. In fact, the instructional programme suffers because pleasure and personal satisfaction and independence are not given the priority they are given in the recreational programme. The efficient learning which is the objective of the instructional programme cannot take place without the joy and relevance and independence which we associate with the recreational programme.

What is the place of independence in the instructional programme?
The experience of independence is vital to efficient learning at any stage of a developmental process. A child must *enjoy* the power of grasping things with his fingers before he learns to oppose his thumb to the fingers; he must stand *confidently* before walking; he must communicate *effectively* with simple structures before he learns to use complex grammatical forms. Purposeful performance at one stage is a prerequisite for efficient learning at the next.

Does efficient learning require independence?
Many of the important things we know about learning suggest that the experience of independence is vital to the learning of a development task:

> the fulfilment of real purposes for the learner provides strongest motivation
> reinforcement or reward is at a maximum in the satisfaction of intrinsic interests and needs
> learning resulting from a process of discovery is more hardy than learning stemming from direct instruction
> self-pacing is more efficient than other forms of pacing such as competition, desire to please or 'keeping up with the group'
> in large classes, individual differences may be best catered for where children have learned to operate independently.

Each of these principles has been strongly supported by research. Taken together they amount to proof of the importance of independence. We can say with reasonable assurance, then, that the experience of independence provides for the most efficient accomplishment of the tasks of that stage: it both meets the needs for personal development and sustains fundamental learning processes. This is not to say that the techniques and procedures we have come to associate with a sound basic programme in reading are unnecessary — rather that they are incomplete.

The experience of independence in reading at every level has been stated as a major objective of any sound programme and as the principal goal of an individualized reading programme. This is a fine objective, but a vague one. What does *independence in reading* mean in terms of the daily, detailed tasks of the classroom? To answer this question it is necessary to say more about reading and its component skills.

A practical way of analyzing the reading process, in the first instance, would be to observe the behaviour of a competent reader. We can all recognize good readers, and our schools produce many of them.

Characteristics of Competent Readers

Most fundamentally, every response of the competent reader displays the activity of a purposeful and comprehending human mind served by an incomprehensibly complex system of automatic responses in the organism. Readers maintain personal control of that whole, integrated system which we think of as human behaviour – they never respond mindlessly.

They are capable of accurate and lightning-fast perception, their attention moving automatically from left to right across the page, back and down to the next line without a miss. *(Visual discrimination and directional habits.)*

They recognize the majority of words 'by sight' without deliberation, and they perceive common structural elements immediately as familiar patterns. *(Sight vocabulary and structural analysis.)*

They can 'attack' unfamiliar words with confidence provided they have heard them spoken in their past experience of the language: they predict possibilities of vocabulary, calling upon a remarkably sensitive awareness of common language patterns, and upon the developing meaning of the sentence; they attend to the sound associations of letters whenever necessary in strict order. *(Word attack by the combined use of past language experience, context clues and phonetic analysis.)*

They carry out these decoding skills almost entirely at an automatic level and are therefore able to focus their conscious attention almost exclusively on the developing meaning. However, they know when to focus conscious attention on a decoding problem and they possess an adequate range of strategies for solving such problems. *(Habituated decoding skills, problem-solving strategies.)*

They exercise a critical alertness to the sense and accuracy of their own responses realizing in a flash when they have made a slip and where. *(Self-correction.)*

They are responsive to the conventions of punctuation and grammar, organizing the words into meaningful groups and recreating the intonation patterns significant to the meaning of these groups. *(Word and sentence organization.)*

They adjust the meanings of words and word groups in a wide range of different contexts deciding upon literal, figurative, idiomatic, or rare meanings. *(Use of context to determine meanings.)*

They understand and retain the meanings of what they read at least as well as they do in listening; they are aware of many implied meanings not directly stated; and they create a detailed sensory picture of whatever they are reading about, using images drawn from their own experience. *(Comprehension – literal and inferential, creation of sensory imagery.)*

They respond emotionally to what they read in appropriate ways, and are capable of identifying with some characters and situations and dissociating from others. *(Affective response.)*

They relate what they read to their own background, testing the author's ideas against their own experience, modifying their ideas whenever necessary, and assimilating new ideas. *(Integration, assimilation and critical response.)*

They sometimes display original insights about what they read in relationship to their own experience, and they often make practical use of what they read. *(Creative thinking and application)*.

They think about and evaluate what they are reading as they read, forming appropriate questions with which to probe the text. *(Evaluation.)*

They use and develop reading skills with increasing flexibility to meet the special needs of study and daily life. *(Study skills and flexibility.)*

They are able to read aloud to an audience, after preparation, in a pleasing and effective manner adding much from their own experience to present the oral message with style, cadence, and vitality. *(Audience reading.)*

They enjoy reading as an activity, often finding relaxation in continuous reading and persisting without fatigue or sensory discomfort for long periods. *(Self-reinforcement and the automatic operation of skills.)*

They are able to locate and select materials appropriate to their needs and within their range of competence as readers. *(Self-selection)*

They value books as cultural items of importance in their lives, usually use whatever library facilities are open to them, and actively seek out books to satisfy many different and changing needs as they develop. *(Using reading to meet life purposes.)*

Although this analysis may miss many of the subtleties of the reading process, and some aspects may apply more importantly to an earlier or later stage of reading development, most of us would be satisfied as teachers if a majority of the children in our classes displayed all of these qualities. Those of us who like to see things in more concrete and practical terms may use this analysis as a checklist of objectives against which we can evaluate the reading progress of children in a global way. Much more detailed guidance is presented throughout the Handbook, especially in the Appendices.

Formal analysis of the reading process

Reading itself is part of a wider body of skills — the major language skills.

Its relationship to listening, speaking and writing must be taken seriously. The language arts are mutually reinforcing and should often occur together in the same learning context. Writing is a code which uses the meaning systems of speech; 'oracy' therefore precedes literacy both in time and in importance.

An efficient and satisfying reading programme, then, will develop all the dimensions of language. *Reading should not be only a means of communication – of getting the author's message: it should be an opportunity for empathy, for thinking, for expressing, and for sensory pleasure.* When all of these are achieved in some measure together, reading becomes an aesthetic experience capable of providing the most satisfying of pleasures. A skill which begins to deliver up such rewards is soon mastered.

The reading process may be divided into two major tasks:

A. **Word recognition** — skills concerned with the decoding of print symbols, or determining the spoken language which the written characters represent.

B. **Understanding** — skills concerned with interpreting the language which results from successful decoding. This includes thinking beyond the literal meanings of the text; appropriate emotional response; integration of the meanings of the text with the reader's own background of knowledge; and evaluation of what is read.

This is the most fundamental division of reading into parts, reflected both by ordinary practice and by most expert opinion. However, this division results in three traditional misconceptions which can be seen to underlie much of the heated controversy which has surrounded the teaching of reading for a century or more:

The assumption that the two processes are so distinct that they may be taught quite separately.
The belief that one is more important than the other.
The judgement that one precedes the other and should be taught first.

The answer to these misconceptions is that **A and B are interdependent in every moment of reading.** One without the other is a travesty of the reading process:

A without B amounts to a string of meaningless noise
B without A is an empty dream — a figment of the imagination
Neither is reading: reading is both.

It is simplistic in the extreme to suggest that comprehension arises from accurate word recognition, for it would be just as true to say that accurate word recognition arises from comprehension. Fundamentally, the two processes interact at the moment of perception and neither can operate efficiently unless this fusion takes place. What the brain brings to the eye is as important as what the eye brings to the brain — indeed, what the eye brings to the brain has already been organized by the brain. (Goodman 1976; Smith 1978a, pp. 25-42.)

At the centre of this integrated act of perception will be found a highly complex pattern of expectation which *determines* what the eye will see. Prediction, or what we call 'the use of context', predigests the visual information in such a way as to render the act of perception rapid, appropriate, energy-efficient, and generally accurate.[15]

Much of the sensory information is used to confirm the solution which the brain has already presented through sampling and prediction. This is the feedback or self-corrective process which we analysed earlier. Hence, much of the reader's attention to grapho-phonic information moves from sounds in words predicted to letters which would be expected on the page, rather than, as in all classic phonics, from letters on the page to sounds which are 'blended' into words — and then comprehended. The latter, though occasionally necessary, and well within the competence of the *mature* reder, is a complex process which cannot be sustained for long without crippling fatigue and loss of meaning. (Smith 1978a, pp. 43-54.)

The practical implications of this meaning-saturated process which characterizes efficient perception in reading at all stages are worked out in the chapter on *Developing Reading Skills and Strategies*. Bearing these considerations in mind, we may accept the formal division between word recognition and comprehension as an analytic convenience without falling into any of the fallacies outlined above.

Study Skills may be seen as a third major task.

These are the specialised reading skills needed for literate enquiry and with them the reader may pursue his interest beyond the particular text being read.

Audience Reading may be seen as a fourth major task.

These are the skills required to share reading with others. Although involving many skills which are specific to it, such as reading ahead of the voice, audience reading is, nevertheless, based upon competence in A and B above.

Using reading appropriately to meet life needs may be seen as a fifth major task and as a necessary culmination of reading skills.

Only when all the skills are unified into a single process serving personal needs does true reading come into being. This implies versatility in the style and rate of reading depending on purpose and the nature of the material being read.

Summary of Reading Skills

We may look upon the sequential development of these skills as detailed objectives of the reading programme. When we come to evaluate the programme we should consider development in each area.

Word recognition

1. Sight vocabulary
2. Structural analysis
3. Use of context
4. Phonetic analysis

Because the skills of word recognition (A. above) need to be taught in a sensibly graded sequence concentrated on the first four or five years of normal reading experience, they are treated separately from the interprative skills. (For details see Appendix B: *Basic Sight Words in Context,* Appendix C: *Simplified Progression of Word Recognition Skills.)*

Understanding the text

1. Word meanings
2. Sentence and word group meanings
3. Paragraph, chapter and total meanings
4. Affective meanings — responding appropriately
5. Comparative meanings — judging and evaluating
6. Meanings of supportive symbol systems

Study skills

7. Locating information
8. Using dictionaries
9. Using reference materials.
10. Library skills
11. Using magazines, journals, etc.
12. Using supportive media
13. Mastering the vocabulary of criticism
14. Adjusting reading style and rate
15. Organizing information for presentation or recall, note-taking.
16. Carrying out a topic study.

Audience Reading (17)

Using reading appropriately to meet life needs (18)

(For details see Appendix D: *The Sequential Development of Reading Skills.)*

The Individualized Reading Programme

Introduction

Individualized reading suggests different things to different people. Although the programme takes its name and its central idea from the opportunity provided for each child to choose his own material, and read it at his own rate, it would be misleading to suggest that each child is engaged in an isolated programme of his own, receiving individual instruction. This would be not only unrealistic, but also unhealthy. One of the dominating features of the programme is the lively interaction in group and class settings which generate common interests and shared reading experiences.

The suggestion that individualized reading entails a particular *method* of teaching is also misleading — rather, it is a pattern of classroom organization within which different methods of teaching may be used depending on the needs of different children and the style of the particular teacher. Indeed, one of the outstanding advantages of these procedures is the flexibility they allow in applying different methods, strategies, learning styles, and sensory modes to meet the needs of different children.

Principles of the programme

The most important principles in the programme have often been stated as

1. **Self-selection.** Children learn to choose their own reading materials from a wide selection in a way which matches their abilities and interests. Children are encouraged to read real books and whole books rather than snippets or pre-digested extracts.
2. **Self-seeking.** Children are encouraged to develop an active determination to explore printed material and find for themselves materials that are relevant to their daily concerns.

3. **Self-pacing.** Children are able to operate at a personal pace determined by their own abilities and varied according to the purpose of their reading and the nature of the material. This permits them to make maximum development in rate, powered by their own deepest interests and freed from outside pressures — which cannot be delicately adjusted to their own right pace at any particular time.

4. **Self-evaluation.** Scope is provided for the natural interest of children to set up day-to-day goals, and gradually mature towards skilled self-analysis.

Another principle which is not usually listed because it is difficult to state should be included as fundamental to the programme. We could call this principle:

5. **Self-sharing.** Children are encouraged to communicate the personal feelings and insights from their own reading to others and to be open to the self-expression of others. They learn to handle this interpersonal communication as a welcome part of their own development — to respect and consider the views of others; to be forthright and sincere in stating their own point of view; to be tentative and open-minded in a context of differences; to tolerate uncertainties without irritation; and to channel the experience of others back into their own reading experiences. It is a mistake to think of individualized reading as a purely individual programme which creates islands of personal egotism in the classroom.

How does the programme operate?

1. The teacher makes available a wide range of individual copies of children's books. Ideally, he has considerable personal knowledge of some of these books and has access to reliable information about their levels of reading difficulty. He also has reliable information about the abilities and interests of his children and has ensured that the range of books spans the ability of all the children in the class and includes books about some of their deepest interests.

2. The reading period normally begins with a session in which the whole class shares with each other their enthusiasms about books they have read. In the first instance, the teacher plays a leading part in 'selling' books to children. During this time, children read aloud from their favourite books, give reviews or impressions, display illustrations or interest others in some activity they have engaged in as a result of reading a particular book.

3. The children choose material from the wide range provided. They will take into account the guidance of the teacher. A good deal of skimming and browsing goes on in the same way as can be observed with a group of literate adults in a public library. Nevertheless, formal ways are provided for the children to record a responsible choice committing themselves to some form of evaluation even if they fail to finish reading the material. They keep brief functional records of their own reading in a Reading Log.

4. A substantial portion of the period is given over to personal silent reading. There will normally be at least a short period every day in which the rights of readers to peace and quiet are catered for. In order to provide for this undisturbed period, it is often necessary to see that each child has two or three current reading projects.

5. As soon as the children settle to reading, the teacher begins daily conferences in which he meets perhaps five or six individual children in turn for a few minutes. During this time the children share their enthusiasms with him, perhaps read a little to him, or answer a thought provoking question or two. While this is going on, the teacher manages to check the

child's Reading Log and makes his own brief records of each child's reading progress. It is unlikely that the teacher will have time to engage in individual tuition during this conference, but he will make a note of teaching needs to be met by independent practice or small group tuition later.

6. Active reading along the lines of personal choice will provide the children with many experiences they wish to share, to express or to explore further. Provisions are therefore made for a great variety of activities stemming naturally from the reading. This will include the opportunity for expression in many different media, for research, for study, or for problem-solving stemming from issues raised during reading. Ideally, in order to persistently deepen the children's comprehension and reaction to what they read, the programme should provide some stimulus towards critical thinking in addition to the natural stimulus of discussion and debate. The use of open-ended questions, either in written or in oral form, is an important way of providing this depth experience in books.

The organization of time

Since the objectives of both instructional and recreational reading are combined in the programme, it is possible to use larger blocks of time than would be given to a purely instructional programme. A daily period of forty-five minutes would be the minimum required for an effective programme. Larger blocks of time, up to half a day, may be made available by combining the reading periods from two or three days on occasion, or by allowing the major programmes in language and expressive arts to arise from, and be integrated with, the reading programme for a number of weeks.

The period is usually divided into four major parts:

Opening Activities: The class meets briefly as a whole with the teacher to share enthusiasms about books and make daily plans. At this time reviews may be presented, brief selections may be read aloud by children or the teacher, and news about books which have just arrived may be broadcast. The teacher may, on occasion, take a brief class lesson on some aspect of skill development which is relevant for all the children. Any special plans for the day, such as the arrangement of conferences with the teacher, or group work, are finalized.

Quiet time: A quiet period of reading or study is usually essential to the development of efficient reading habits. The time will vary according to the age and ability of the children. It is also wise to increase the time gradually each week. Eight-year-old children may begin with a period of five minutes, increased to eleven or twelve minutes after six weeks. Thirteen-year-old children may begin with ten minutes and increase to twenty minutes after a few weeks, provided that this period does not exceed one third of the total daily time available.

During this time, distraction is kept to a minimum, although a wide range of profitable activities may be permitted. Many children continue reading at home and return to the programme next day impatient to undertake some follow-up activity. Provided this can be engaged in silently and without distracting, it is consistent with the spirit of the programme to permit it. However, all management matters of this kind should be discussed with the class at the beginning of the programme, and settled by discussion and agreement. The need to discuss these matters forms an ideal situation for the class to learn how to operate as a committee if such a procedure is not already well established. This time is always used for teacher conferences which may extend well into the following section.

Activity time: Approximately one quarter of the total time available should be given over to independent activities of a very varied kind. During this time children may continue to read and study by choice, but noise and movement are consistent with an activity period. Children operate in any of the expressive arts during this time to explore and clarify the experiences which have arisen from reading and thinking. Activity centres, well supplied with materials, should be set up. Children should take responsibility for the organization and, to some extent, the *supply* of materials. It has been found that the practice of dramatic activities during this time is perhaps best restricted to one or two days each week.

Closing session: At the end of the period the class comes together again as a participating audience for creative presentations, or to discuss, debate, or role play any matters of human concern that have arisen from their exploration of books. In this way the children have daily experience of the lively relevance of print to all the major human concerns which currently preoccupy them at their particular stage of development. Although only ten to fifteen per cent of the total time is spent in these terminal sharing sessions, it becomes a vital and satisfying part of the programme giving the lie to that suspicion of personal isolation which hangs around the term *individualized*.

Organization of a typical period.

Activity	Time	40 minute	60 minute	90 minute
Opening activities	**5-10%**	**3-4**	**4-6**	**7-9**
Quiet time (Teacher Conferences)	**25-30%**	**10-12**	**15-18**	**25-30**
Activity time, including reading and study (Conferences and Group Teaching)	**40-45%**	**15-18**	**25-30**	**35-40**
Closing session	**10-15%**	**4-6**	**6-10**	**10-15**

Note: A slightly different way of looking at time distribution is given in the *Overview*.

Actual reading extends beyond *Quiet Time* making up about 40-50%.

The Individualized Reading Programme

Overview

Independent Activity

Creative response
reviews, creative writing
mime, drama, puppetry
role-playing, dance
art and construction
music and song

RESOURCES
Independent ideas
Teacher's ideas
Materials for related arts

Study
related reading,
topic studies, projects,
original research

TIME
Pupil 25% - 30%

CHILD

Individual
interests
abilities
needs
aspirations

Teacher's Knowledge
awareness
diagnosis
continuous records

Personal Choice

Self-selection
active seeking
exploring new interests
extending goals
estimating difficulty

RESOURCES
Class Library
School Library
Public Library
Conference guidance

Silent Reading

Self-Pacing
in interest
in difficulty
in speed or rate
independent reference
flexibility

Self-evaluation
personal satisfaction
new interests
skills
self-correction

(A part of this period
is quiet time.)

Individual Conference

Discussion
sharing a book
checking understanding
sharing oral reading

Guidance
practice needs
level

Diagnosis
Independent Level
skills – understanding
word-recognition
study skills
interests and needs

RESOURCES
Prose Inventory

RECORDS
Teacher's Log

TIME
Teacher 60% - 70%

Sharing Time

Opening Activities
daily plans, reviews
'selling books'
audience reading

Teaching
class lessons
new skills
new interests

Closing Activities
performance,
display, debate,
discussion,
role-playing, etc.

RESOURCES
Pupil's presentations
Bulletin boards
Reviews

TIME
Pupil 20%
Teacher 20%

Understanding and Critical Thinking

Comprehension
central meanings
major concepts
judgements
comparisons
inferences
author's message
facts, details, sequence

Reaction

Teacher Guidance
individual help
guided silent reading
lessons
questioning

RESOURCES
References
dictionaries
encyclopedia
atlas

RECORDS
Pupil's Log

TIME
Pupil 40% - 50%

PERSONAL GROWTH in and through READING

Word Recognition

**Understanding the Text
Using References to
Aid Understanding**

Study Skills

Audience Reading

**Using Reading
Appropriately to Meet
Life Needs**

Skills Practice

Consolidation

Group Teaching

Special Needs
guided silent reading
skills instruction
TIME
Teacher 5% - 10%

The Children

An individualized programme is designed to provide children with an experience of independence at the level of development they have reached *both* in reading and in personal growth. Simply to provide the opportunity however, is no guarantee that it will be taken up. Success depends on the guidance and stimulation of the teacher through knowledge of the children. It is not long before this kind of programme *provides* intimate knowledge of individual children but it is in the early stages, before this new knowledge becomes available, that the children's need for guidance is at a maximum. They must *learn* independence through increasing knowledge of themselves, through self-evaluation and through self-pacing. To guide this learning process the teacher needs to marshal information about the children.

What should the teacher know before beginning the programme

Refer to the section on the Teacher's Log in *Records and Evaluation*. File the following information on each Child.

Current instructional level and results of Standardised Tests.

If additional information on Instructional Level is desirable for some children use the *Informal Prose Inventory, Appendix A*.

Interests

Since priority is given to selection in terms of interest, this information is vital. Provide books and magazines to cover as many of the children's individual interests as possible.

You may administer the following Interest Inventory in preparation for the programme or on the first day:
1. Place the headings on the blackboard and supply each child with a sheet of paper that will fit into your file.
2. Explain to younger children the sort of entry to make under each heading and insist that they complete each item before writing the next heading.

3. File this inventory with your notes on each child.

INTEREST INVENTORY:
My Family
　　Names and ages of siblings
Our Pets
　　Personal or family pets
My Hobbies
My Favourite Sport
My Clubs
My Experiences
　　Places I have lived:
　　Places I have visited:
　　Important things that have happened to me:
My Ambitions
　　Things I want to do very much:
　　When I grow up: (For young children)
My Favourite Book
Books I have enjoyed
Topics I would like to read about

Abilities — special strengths and weaknesses

Note abilities displayed in the reading field, e.g. 'very competent in word recognition'; or, 'very slow reader'. Children with strengths may act as volunteer Trouble-shooters. Note also *general* abilities — especially those that may influence the running of the programme. e.g. 'natural leader'; or, 'very dependent'. Add to this section during the programme. The Prose Inventory will be useful in diagnosing specific reading problems, especially for the children who puzzle you or who need most urgent help.

Attitudes — towards reading in particular

It is in this area that you will expect to see early growth as a result of the programme. Make an entry before beginning the programme, even if it is simply a rating on the five-point scale.

Highlights of personal development and background

This programme is concerned with personal development *through* reading as well as development *in* reading. If you note outstanding characteristics, you may be surprised at the extent and nature of changes, even in a period of a few weeks.

Personal Choice

Active searching and skilled self-selection are vital to functional literacy. Too many children read little more than what is required of them in school and this seldom includes a full book of any length. Choosing a book which is appropriate in both interest and difficulty is not a simple task, and 'getting into a book' may also prove a barrier to many children. If teachers choose all the materials that are to be read and personally control levels of difficulty, children are likely to remain dependent and immature in the use of books.

Reading and life interests

Learning to read should involve learning a way of life in which books satisfy central needs at each stage of development. Reading should become an integral part of living. If we fail in this vital aspect of teaching children to read, the new skills may become a hindrance to personal development during the school years. The complexity of reading skills threatens the mental health of too many children.

Books bring children into contact with exceptional experience at the receptive moments of growth and need. The world's finest resources are brought to the education of each child who learns to *seek* what books have to offer. A love of books encourages a constant, critical exploration of the growing heart and mind which no teacher can provide.

Both the need and the moment of need *differ for every child* — no plan of work can provide for them with any accuracy. Children's current, individual interests are the index to these needs. Direct questioning to detect interests may not always succeed — opportunity and stimulus are often required to germinate the seeds of concern into living shoots of conscious endeavour and intent.

Children's interests have always been wide and more individually varied than the resources of the classroom. Reflecting the diversity of modern society, they are becoming increasingly so. The divergent richness of human interest is moving down through the school at an astonishing rate. Any class of ten-year-olds is likely to contain at least one child who knows more about atomic physics or the care of dogs than does the teacher. The influence of mass media stimulates an even wider range of early interests. It is little wonder that for a class of forty children there tend to be four hundred consuming interests and needs.

Wider reading

An individualized reading programme should be supported by a very wide range of books. Children should be able to follow their interests through several books — by topic, by author, by type, by contrast. Classroom resources, or even school resources, are never wholly adequate for this. One of the marks of independence in reading is confidence in using libraries and request services.

Learning to Choose

Choosing wisely must be *learned* — it does not come naturally to most children. Many teachers become discouraged in the early stages of running an individualized programme because so many children seem unable to make a sound choice.

One function of the Conference is to check how appropriately each child is selecting within his range of interests and ability. The teacher should give special help to children of limited reading ability — for whom the range for selection is narrower. Sometimes he may place a child on carefully graded instructional material, perhaps designed for remedial tuition. A child reading at his own pace in material of this kind is likely to be happier in an individualized programme becaue *all* the children, to some extent, are operating in the same way as he is.

Children should learn simple ways of determining whether or not a book is suitable for them in both level and purpose. A count of words which cannot be pronounced or understood on a typical page is a useful guide. On a normal page of print — diminishing in print size as they do according to the age for which they are designed — five or more unknown words generally indicate that the material cannot be read satisfactorily.

Commitment to choice

Freedom of choice implies decision-making and commitment. The programme should provide some clear way of registering commitment to read a book. Children should have adequate time to browse, but they should be required to record their decision to read a particular book or carry out a particular study in their *Reading Log*. Having made this entry they should be clearly *committed to make some report* under that entry, even if it is only to register that they did not complete the book because it was too difficult or did not hold their interest.

Problems in the growth of independence

Like any complex learning, the development of independence is a slow and gradual process with its own difficulties, dangers and problems. Independence can only develop in an environment which provides a considerable degree of freedom — as in this programme. Children do not learn a wise use of freedom suddenly, especially if they have adjusted to restraint and dependence. They make many mistakes as they test themselves and explore the limits of their self-control. The shy or withdrawn child is likely to appear impudent at some stage in the process of achieving confidence. The child who has been over-restricted is likely to abuse a sudden freedom. The teacher must be ready to handle these clumsy experiments and false starts with tact, friendly guidance, and firmness. Clear-cut routines in the first few weeks help to sustain a sense of security out of which the children may steadily grow.

Some children may respond to the freedom of self-selection by —

reading well below their instructional level

following a narrow interest such as horse books

searching for light or humorous books only.

These tendencies are likely to be shortlived if positive guidance and motivation are provided without any suspicion of ridicule or compulsion. Some children will persistently choose books that are too difficult for them to read. Their interests and personal maturity may have outstripped their reading skill. A conference to diagnose reading needs and plan intensive remedial action is called for in these cases. For others the problem arises from peer competition — a desire to appear more competent. These children need to be shown that by remaining within their range of natural competence they can perform best in front of others during Sharing Time.

Some children respond to the freedom of self-pacing by —

avoiding continuous application

annoying others and disturbing their concentration

avoiding Conferences.

These tendencies need to be met rather more firmly because of their disruptive nature. Arrange a Conference, attempt to diagnose sources of the problem, and set firm limits and goals which may be relaxed gradually as independence grows.

The children as a whole are likely to become more outspoken and critical as a result of their growing confidence. Carefully planned discussion and debate in Sharing Time will help the children discover the secrets of *open-mindedness* and *constructive criticism*. Provided your objectives give the achievement of independence a genuinely high priority, and that you are prepared to reach these objectives slowly, you will find increasing excitement and satisfaction in the children's development. (You may even become a protagonist for bibliotherapy.) Certainly the joy and enthusiasm of the majority of children will compensate for the difficulties, solved or unsolved, that you experience with the few.

Silent Reading, Understanding and Critical Thinking

It would be an axiom of reading teaching today that reading is understanding or thinking, and an accepted corollary that the major activity of the instructional programme should be silent reading. A further implication, not so generally perceived, is that whether the reading organization deals with groups or individuals, its centre — actual reading — is an individual and intensely personal thing. We cannot speak of reading as thinking without emphasizing the individual nature of the process: groups don't think.

Why 'silent' reading?

The vital thing in instructional reading is that children should read *for personal understanding and satisfaction* — otherwise they may not be truly reading — they may be simply saying words for someone else to monitor and correct. When children are reading material which they have never seen before, while their peers listen or 'follow' in their books, a highly unnatural and stressful audience situation is set up. In this situation it is virtually impossible for them to carry out the central tasks in reading — those associated with understanding and responding in a personal way. Furthermore, children reading aloud are restricted in rate to the speed of speaking — which is usually exceeded in silent reading at about the eight or nine year level.

The important distinction, then, is not between silent and oral reading, but between reading for personal understanding and satisfaction, on the one hand, and reading for the understanding and satisfaction of an audience, on the other. It is not important for children to actually suppress audible vocalization in the early years of reading. The important thing is that they should *read to themselves* — whether orally or silently. Many children do not become capable of inaudible reading for several years, and this should not concern us unduly. When we say that instructional reading should be silent, this is simply a short-hand way of saying that in learning to read children should be engaged in reading for personal understanding and satisfaction.

Reading groups

We attempt to match children to materials at the right level by grouping according to reading ability. However, this matching can be achieved much more accurately by individualizing, and if this were the only purpose of grouping for reading instruction, it would be poor justification. The main function of grouping concerns the importance of discussion, under the influence of the teacher, both before and after reading. The guided silent reading lesson, which is discussed in the chapter, *Group Teaching*, is a powerful and essential technique in any reading programme, including individualized reading.

However, it is not a satisfactory technique when used continuously because it necessitates ability grouping.

There are serious inadequacies in the use of group procedures for silent reading over long periods and this is one reason why the procedures of individualized reading are needed to balance the total programme. What are the chief inadequacies of group reading?

a. It does not allow adequately for variations in pace: it may be wasteful of reading time for the gifted reader, and destructive of the ease and confidence of the retarded.

b. It does not allow adequately for divergence of interest and the achievement of personal satisfaction as a reward for the labour of attention in reading.

c. It tends to highlight invidious comparisons among children by teachers, by parents, by peers. If your attention is constantly on Jimmy as failing to keep up with the group, you are likely to overlook Jimmy's real interests, abilities and needs in reading.

Self-pacing

Learning to read, like the learning of any complex developmental task, occurs most effectively when the pace is just right for the individual: learning takes place when there is a delicate balance between challenge and confidence. It is very difficult to assess this pace at any given time for any given individual learning a developmental task. It may vary for the same individual even from day to day in response to a host of factors such as interest, fatigue or mood. How *should* we determine the right pace? When babies learn to crawl or run we tend to allow *them* to do the determining: we provide the situation, the motivation and guidance, *they determine the pace*.

What is involved in pace? Fairly obviously more than just rate or speed. Pacing includes *all* the pressures to perform. Interest is very important in pace, then, and self-selection has some part to play in self-pacing. If a child has no choice in what he reads, the proper pace may be nil, for to *force* him to read is likely to harm sound development.

Pacing and audience situations

One of the most powerful of external pacing pressures is the audience situation. Any requirement for performance at a given rate is multiplied by an audience — especially if there is embarrassment and the audience is thought to be critical. Children should determine for themselves when they are ready to perform before any sort of audience. They need to be *taught* how to prepare themselves, but *they* should choose *when* they are ready.

Efficient reading may also develop naturally in the programme. Children should be encouraged to push their reading rate to the most efficient level consistent with their current skills and with the purpose for which they are reading. When whole books are being read for a variety of purposes — rather than extracts being read to answer comprehension questions — children have a better chance of developing rapid reading skills.

Audience Reading

Skilled oral reading may be developed very naturally in an individualized programme because:

a. The children are provided with a real audience in *Sharing Time*, and a very special audience in the *Conference*.

b. They choose what they will read for themselves — something they both want to share and feel competent to handle.

c. Oral reading has always been preceded by silent reading.

d. The audience do not have a copy of the text and the material is usually fresh to them. They can therefore listen in the proper way.

Traditionally, reading has been taught by 'hearing children read'. In this highly paced and pressured situation many children are unable to develop healthy processes of independent reading. They often fail to develop the essential skills of self-correction and self-reinforcement without which their reading must remain at a rudimentary level — if it can be called reading at all. Hearing children read is important in diagnosing children's needs, but children do not *learn* while this is going on. The doctor's diagnosis does not cure you — the *treatment* does.

Further guidance on audience reading and the diagnostic situation is given in *Appendix D*, Section 17.

Comprehension

Comprehension is what *should* occur at the moment of reading, and the aim of any reading programme should be to produce the highest level of comprehension possible during actual silent reading. This seems self-evident, but it is a truth often overlooked or distorted by habitual testing of factual comprehension following reading.

A major aim of this programme is to achieve development over the entire range of comprehension skills. A glance at Sections 2, 3, 4 and 5 of *Appendix D* will provide an overview, and will obviate the need for a detailed analysis here.

These aims are difficult to achieve in a programme which limits itself to the study of short extracts. The development of critical thinking may be fostered in a programme in which whole books are read, discussed and compared. In particular, the understanding of total meanings — themes, major concepts, author's 'message', emotional response — follows naturally from such a programme as this. The children are stimulated to go beyond literal meanings and superficial responses to a deeper understanding in terms of their own personal background. They are guided towards new experience and insights and towards a thorough exploration of themes and topics which are important to them in their development.

Related books may be read and compared while a lively social atmosphere provides adequate opportunities for thrashing out ideas with others, becoming tolerant, tentative, sympathetic and objective. No question is asked in this programme which merely 'tests comprehension'. No activity is suggested which is mere 'busy work', especially no activity involving writing. Wherever the labours of writing are suggested, a strong motive and a clear function are provided.

When do you check basic comprehension?

Factual comprehension should be checked only when there has been a failure to achieve deeper understanding, and as an exploration and diagnosis of that failure. Only then is the achievement of accurate, factual comprehension thrown into proper perspective in the children's minds.

Traditional comprehension exercises tend to cripple development in reading by lacking point or relevance. If literal recall of detail is checked only when there has been a failure of insight, and as an essential prerequisite for full understanding, there is little chance that children will become bored with reading instruction. There is also little chance that you as a teacher will fail to detect a real breakdown at the factual level. When there has been such a failure it will often be found that the child is reading above the appropriate level for his abilities, and guidance into simpler material will usually be effective.

We believe that if a child is able to discuss the deeper meanings of a book with some insight, it may be taken with assurance that his comprehension at the factual level is adequate, if not virtually complete. Large blocks of time spent in testing factual comprehension — and in recording answers in the permanent form of writing — are unnecessary where an adequate check is being kept on critical thinking and response. When time is at a premium — as it *should* be in a vital reading programme — it is a wasteful mistake to begin with factual comprehension questions in the hope that time will be available at the end for developing critical understanding.

Cloze procedure

An efficient check on comprehension at the moment of actual reading may be made by using a cloze test constructed from a passage currently being read. This technique is particularly suited for use with *part* of a passage being read by a group engaged in a directed, or guided silent reading lesson. Delete every seventh or eighth word from the passage after the first sentence in a typescript or printed format. Children complete the gaps. A score of 50 per cent *exact* replacements indicates good comprehension. Discuss replacements with the group following the session.[16]

What about children who don't spend the reading time profitably?

The problem can usually be resolved by taking a little trouble to locate materials which are accurately matched to the interests, needs, and abilities of such children. Very often the failure to settle to independent reading is a symptom of some more deep-seated problem of personal development. If you are able to identify such a problem and tactfully present one or two relevant books, you will often achieve a striking change in reading behaviour. See also the chapter, *Personal Development through Reading*.

You probably have a fair idea which children will avoid reading and thinking before the programme begins — although you may receive some surprises. Call such children to an early Conference, and attempt to deal with the problem diagnostically.

Reading takes precedence over activities

Children should have no upper limit placed on the amount of reading they will do in the instructional programme. If they wish to read another book rather than complete an activity, this should be welcomed. It should also be possible for children to read at odd times during the day when other work has been completed or as a chosen activity. There is no doubt that the programme is stimulated by allowing the children to take books home both to read and to discuss with parents.

Self-evaluation and records

Each child should keep brief records of the books he has read, his responses to them and some comment about how he coped in reading each book.

The Individual Conference

Although the teacher spends only a few minutes with each child in conference at varying intervals of five to ten days, this experience provides unique opportunities for both teacher and child. Most of the children value this chance to have the teacher to themselves for a few minutes, to receive undivided attention, to have personal problems discussed, and more than anything else, to share an enthusiasm with the teacher, or display competence in purposeful oral reading. On his side, the teacher gains this opportunity to get to know his children in a quite different way, to be able to diagnose individual difficulties, offer brief but effective guidance and enter into the reading enthusiasms of the children.

During a successful Conference the child will feel that his own opinions and insights are valued, that he has not been expected to give correct answers pat from the book but that the experiences of his own heart and mind have added something of value to the understanding of the book. He should choose a book that has been important to him in some way — one which has excited him, has raised important questions in his mind or has stimulated some interesting activity or project. The teacher will ensure that each child has grasped the significance of the book in his own terms, has a sense of direction in making further choices, and is continuing at a high level of involvement in his reading.

Functions of the Conference

1. To give each child the opportunity to share a personal experience of reading with the most influential person in his school experience.
2. To give the teacher an opportunity to interact with each child personally, to monitor his reading experience, diagnose difficulties, offer guidance, and set practice where necessary.
3. To check the *Reading Log* of each child and make appropriate records in the teacher's *Conference Log*.

Note that where intensive diagnosis is required, this will need to be scheduled for some other time, as in any other type of programme. Such a session might involve the use of the *Informal Prose Inventory*, or other tests, and this procedure normally takes twenty to thirty minutes.

The Conference is one of the most valuable and satisfying aspects of the programme but it also tends to present the greatest difficulties. The teacher schedules to interview five or six children each day. This means spending no more than four to six minutes with each child, and most teachers find it very difficult to limit themselves in this way, especially until they have had considerable experience. There are two main reasons for this:

a. The teacher attempts to give individual instruction
b. The Conference lends itself to fascinating digressions by both teacher and pupil.

No pattern of organization can provide for long periods of individual instruction, and individualized reading is no exception. Major teaching and practice must still be organized on a group basis as described in the chapter, *Group Teaching*.

Overcoming the time difficulty

There is no need to conduct a Conference on every book that the child reads — indeed this would prove quite impossible as some children begin to read two or three books a week. Children who display good progress through the quality of their individual activities and their contributions to sharing sessions need fewer and shorter Conferences. Simply note their activity in the *Log* and find the occasion to commend them in an appropriate way.

If you get behind in seeing all the children, or wish to spend more time in other parts of the programme, there are a few ways to economize:

a. Find which children have read the same book — a number of books tend to become very popular — and hold a *Group Conference* on that book. This is an excellent way to develop critical thinking skills. Alternatively, a group of children may be brought together to discuss a central theme which rises in a number of books. See *Personal Development Through Reading*.
b. Children soon become capable of holding conferences with each other on the model that you have established. They should keep a simple record which you file in the Conference Log.
c. The Principal or another senior teacher may be interested to interview a number of children — especially those who are making enthusiastic use of their opportunities and hence need your personal help less.
d. If parents have been involved actively in the programme, some may be happy to use the Conference technique with their children at home. A brief newsletter outlining the procedure may be sent home in appropriate cases.

Steps in a Conference

1. **Rapport:** Make sure the child is at ease by some friendly, welcoming comment, or question.

2. **Sharing:** Listen as the child tells something about his response to the book he wishes to talk about. Discuss any related activity he may be pursuing.

3. **Question:** Ask one or two searching, general questions concerning the theme of the book, the author's message or point of view, or the nature of the characters.

4. **Oral reading:** Listen to the child read a short passage he has selected to share with you.

5. **Records:** Check the child's *Reading Log* and make appropriate entries in your *Conference Log* concerning progress, interests, and problems.

6. **Encourage and Guide:** Discuss plans for the future. Offer suggestions about selections of books. Set practice exercises where necessary. Suggest joining a group for special skills instruction where you see that a number of children display a similar need.

Independent activities

When reading has been effective it will create a desire for expression, for study or for further related reading. Good expression may be intensely personal or it may require careful preparation towards genuine opportunities for sharing with others.

Often the greatest desire or need will be for discussion, but any form of personal interchange is likely to be more effective if there has been some thinking and some attempt to formulate or express ideas beforehand. Interests aroused by non-fiction are likely to lead into topic study which is better for some guidance, at least until children are used to working independently. Often the most appropriate response to an enjoyable experience in reading is to repeat the experience with another book of a similar kind, about the same topic or by the same author. Sometimes a contrastive experience is called for.

Range of activities

Many reading programmes involve a great deal of writing of an unimaginative kind — answering comprehension questions or carrying out skills exercises. There is an opportunity in this programme to achieve a better balance of activities and the writing that is undertaken should be of a more purposeful and creative kind. The activities should help to deepen understanding and encourage the assimilation and integration of ideas. They should help to develop sound study habits and promote the careful, enquiring, critical, tentative attitudes which are essential to sound scholarship.

Reviews: The programme lends itself to reviewing but care should be taken not to require so much reviewing that the children become bored. Help should be given to move away from stereotype reviews towards identifying and evaluating the author's message, point of view, bias, prejudices, reliability, etc. Cumulative reviews may be built up for selected books which a number of children read. *appendix D*, Section 13, *The Vocabulary of Criticism*, may be found useful. Sections 3.7, 3.8, and 5.1 to 5.4 are also relevant.

Creative writing: The writing of verse in response to a moving experience in reading is particularly effective. Turning a story into a ballad or a play is an excellent way of developing awareness of main ideas, sequence, climax, and point of view.

Tape recording: Oral reviews, playlets, audience reading for shy children, and many other oral activities may be developed by individuals and small groups with the tape recorder. Applying interviewing techniques and developing radio or TV programmes are facilitated by the recorder and older children may actually interview people outside the school environment, or undertake simple polling procedures to establish different beliefs about controversial issues which have arisen from reading.

Drama: A wide range of dramatic modes may be used — mime, improvisation, charades, puppetry, role playing, and creative dance. Engaging in the creative activity is more important than preparing for an immaculate performance.

Music: Creating sound pictures, tunes or accompaniment for ballads, sound effects for dramatic or radio presentations, and dance rhythms help children to focus attention on mood, atmosphere, and emotional tone.

Art: Materials of many kinds should be available for visual exploration and expression. Designing alternative covers for books, cut-outs for flannel-board presentations, picture sequences for overhead transparency projection, and bulletin board displays offer purposeful variety.

Construction: Many children find three-dimensional expression the most satisfying way of expressing their ideas, and many books lend themselves to this sort of treatment.

Study: Related reading, the use of references, and library techniques develop naturally from the programme. Section 15 and 16 of *Appendix D* provide detailed suggestions. See also *Developing Reading Skills*.

Learning centres.

A modern trend, especially in open education, has been the development of Learning Centres within the classroom or other available space, and there is now quite a literature on the subject. This technique fits well into an individualized reading environment. (Barbe and Abbott, 1975, 118-148.) Learning Centres may be established to support reading in non-fictional or content areas such as science or social studies. They are based on the principles of 'discovery learning' and should provide the materials to motivate genuine problem-solving activities. After some experience, capable children in the upper primary school may be able to set up Learning Centres with a minimum of supervision from the teacher.

Problems in free activity

Difficulties are bound to arise from time to time as the children learn to operate in more free and responsible ways. Avoid the temptation to deal with these problems in authoritarian ways. Call the class together and ask *them* what they think has been going wrong. Then attempt to formulate corporate solutions. Sometimes this regulative function may be undertaken by the class 'in committee'. See *Appendix D*, 16.2.

Sharing Time

The culmination of independent and group activities is reached when the class comes together each day to share experiences. Far from isolating children from all the benefits of corporate expression as is sometimes believed, the individualized programme throws them together into lively interchange.

The children come to the Sharing Time carefully prepared — by independent reading and thinking, by planned activities and, perhaps, by the influence of a Conference — to make a personal contribution of their own choice.

They come with driving needs, interests and prejudices, knowing that their efforts are purposeful and their audience genuine.

They enter discussion and debate from a position of personal commitment and they meet the sincerity and commitment of others as an influence which stimulates self-examination, and deepens awareness of other points of view.

They are infused with new interests and enthusiasms and are driven back into reading with a new zest.

The teacher enters into the group activities with his perception of the children sharpened by insights from the Individual Conference.

He guides and controls corporate learnings with a view to both common and unique needs.

He carries the whole class into the exploration of deeper meanings, into the development of new skills and into a widening range of literate pleasures.

He meets the new spirit of independence and confidence with apprehension at times, for, as they stretch towards fulfilment, children are sometimes arrogant or self-assertive or boisterous or disturbed; but as he realises that this is what real learning looks like when it is driven by a full head of steam, he undertakes the role of guidance with growing confidence in the value of independence for the children. This is especially so as he begins to see rapid development towards maturity by a few of the children — including one or two from whom he least expected such mobility.

Certainly, there will be an increase in the proportion of time spent in various forms of discussion and debate. This will reflect, in part, the influence of certain popular books on a wider number of children.

Developing corporate activities

Discussion and Debate

Many of the independent and group activities lead through a number of books to general discussion or formal debate.

It is important to develop committee procedures early in the operation of the programme. Children should become increasingly confident in chairing sessions of various kinds and in recording corporate activity. Many opportunities arise for simple *voting procedures* and for techniques of opinion polling. See Section 16.2 of *Appendix D*.

Group Study

Early discussion or debate will often indicate a need for further exploration of topics. The teaching of general reference and study skills is given a new momentum by this purposeful study. *Appendix D*, Sections 7-16, relevant sections from *Study Skills*, will be useful in this respect. Perhaps of greatest importance in this area will be the development of *Library Skills*, and opportunities should be made for groups to work in a library as often as possible. Arrangements can often be made with a local Public Library for regular visits of groups for different purposes.

Dramatic Activity

The value of dramatic activity, especially for the participants as distinct from the audience, will be clear to all teachers. Although there may be occasions when particular performances are worthy of development for polished audience presentation, the emphasis should be on providing opportunities for *all* children to participate in satisfying ways. It is in fulfilling the need to integrate new ideas from books into the personal experience of the children that drama has its greatest value for reading. The children should be encouraged to move away from actual texts and characters as soon as possible towards the working out of central concepts in personal, everyday situations. The techniques of *role playing* are very appropriate to the working out of such themes as child-parent, child-adult, child-authority, and child-child relationships; facing fear and danger; exploring new sensation; and various types of problem solving.

Display

Even with a large area for bulletin board presentations and the rapid turn-around of material, it will soon be found that the facilities of a single classroom are rather too restrictive for the creative drive that the programme generates. Gradual expansion into other areas for special displays should be encouraged. Corridors, foyers, the library, the assembly hall — even local shop windows — provide all the additional space that may be required. See suggestions below, *Some ideas for bulletin boards*.

Audience Reading

Many corporate activities require and develop the skill of sharing reading with others. Section 17 of *Appendix D* is concerned with these skills. Here again, movement outside the classroom will often be appropriate.

For instance, arrangements should be made with infant classes for regular Story Time sessions organized and executed by older children in a spirit of independent responsibility.

Visitors and Interviews

Often, the most appropriate response to an interest or a need for further information will be to invite a visitor to the classroom to give a brief talk, display a skill, or suffer public interview by the children. Older children may move outside the school environment to gather live information using interview techniques, reporting skills and the tape recorder. *Parents* with their wide range of vocations, skills, hobbies and enthusiasms are the most appropriate group of people to call on first for visits and interviews. When skills are developed, other outsiders may be invited to assist. Provided the time of busy people is not wasted by lack of preparation or interest on the part of the *whole class*, even eminent visitors are usually glad to meet a very young audience at close quarters.

Visiting
Institutions such as the museum, the zoo, local libraries and art galleries are obvious sources of interest and information supportive of a live reading programme. As special interests develop, class or group visits to other institutions, such as the Police Department or the S.P.C.A., may be appropriate. Occasionally special interest may generate the need to visit an old quarry, an industry or a building of historical interest. Such visits stimulate further reading and bring relevant concerns back into the classroom.

Other Media
Interests aroused by books may be followed up by the use of other media such as *films, film-strips*, and *records*. Children can often be trained to use catalogues, trace sources and order suitable related material. With a little training many children are capable of handling a filmstrip projector.

Some ideas for bulletin boards

1. **Title of the Week Section** Discussion and voting, perhaps supported by the design of new dust jackets or illustrations. At the end of the programme, a *Book of the Term* or *Book of the Year* display with written submissions supporting choice.

2. **Author of the Week Section** Develop as for the former. See *Books are By People* by Lee Bennett Hopkins, or other references noted in *References and Bibliography*.

3. **Books that Make Us Laugh Section** A small group of children make a large clown's head for the Bulletin Board. When someone reads a funny book he makes a gay book jacket to become part of the ruffle around the clown's neck.

4. **Storybook Pet Show** A group designs the outline of a pet shop window. When someone reads a story about a pet he makes a cutout to display in the window. This looks splendid mounted on an actual window pane with the light streaming through a variety of materials. A development may be a Storybook Zoo.

5. **Storybook Prison** — for villains, traitors and other 'baddies' from books, with appropriate sentences brought down by a Classroom Court. The discussion arising from this activity will reflect the growing tolerance and tentativeness of children in the class — leading to suspended sentences, retrials, or even the ultimate abandonment of the prison institution.

6. **Call to Freedom Section** The need to solve social problems or remedy injustice as explored by books in current reading. (At least a more creative approach to the writing of demonstration placards may be stimulated by such an activity — it is certainly needed.)

7. **People We Respect Section** Storybook characters who have made a positive impact on the children.

Developing Reading Skills and Strategies

Mastering the skills of reading is a complex task: theory and practice in the teaching of these skills is even more complex. It is not within the scope of this guide to discuss these matters in detail. The following suggestions are intended to indicate ways in which skill development may be guided in an individualized reading programme. What do we know about the learning of reading skills?

1. Learning by doing

We know that the skills of reading develop best *through actual reading* —

    reading at the level of success — Independent Level

    reading which is interesting to the individual

    reading which is continuous and persistent

An individualized reading programme provides exceptional opportunities for the fulfilment of these requirements. However, many children will need *guidance*

    to select material at the appropriate level

    to sustain and develop established interests and to generate new interests

    to persevere with actual reading over increasing periods of time

2. Teaching at the moment of need

We know that a *few minutes teaching directed* precisely to a child's *individually felt need* is likely to be more effective than teaching to meet expected group needs. Many opportunities for this personal teaching arise in an individualized programme — especially through the Conference. When a number of children *display* a common need, group teaching may achieve the impact of personal tuition.

3. Practice makes perfect

We know that as skills are taught they need to be *practised to the point of automatic mastery*. This takes us back to 1. Actual reading of appropriate material is the most effective provision for reinforcement, consolidation and over-learning.

    Normal reading seldom presents the opportunity to practise a given skill with *sufficient frequency*, however. You will need ready access to *some* structured exercise material dealing with *crucial* learnings especially in the word analysis area. *Appendix B* will assist in the area of basic sight vocabulary. Some source material is best custom-made for a particular situation. *Appendix C* should help in suggesting materials to make. *Related language skills* help to consolidate learnings in the reading area. Oral discussion with reference back to the text, prepared audience reading, purposeful writing activities, dramatization, labelling and related reading around a topic are a few mutually reinforcing activities.

4. Attitudes and strategies are more important than formal knowledge

We know that greater efficiency in skills learning may be achieved by promoting certain *sound attitudes, understandings and procedures* — strategies if you like. Here are a few of the most important for developing reading skills.
1. An aggressive demand for meaning — an absolute intolerance of nonsense.
2. A spirit of independence — willingness to 'have a go'.
3. A confident use of helpful references.
4. General procedures for problem solving which are linguistically and psychologically sound.

Each of these is well catered for in a soundly organized individualized programme. However, because word solving problems loom largest in the early years of reading, we will make some suggestions in this area.

Guidelines in Word Recognition

Principle One
Mastery of a basic sight vocabulary

Nothing is more essential to fluency and ease in reading than a complete mastery of the basic words of the language as sight vocabulary:

some three hundred words account for over seventy per cent of running words in normal English prose

immediate recognition of the *majority* of words in a sentence is required for speed and accuracy in working out the *unknown* words

It follows, then, that a significant increase in efficiency of reading may be achieved in a short time by ensuring the mastery of a basic sight vocabulary for those children who have gaps in this area. By working persistently in this small area with effective techniques such children may experience a new ease in reading. A simple test which leads immediately to the creation of effective learning resources will be found in *Appendix B, Basic Sight Words in Context*.

Principle Two
Automatic response to an increasing range of affixes and roots — structural analysis

Closely related to the type of perception involved in sight vocabulary is the response to words which have been structurally modified by a prefix or a suffix. The recognition of the affix as a common configurational element serves to locate the root, which is likely to be a sight word. In compound words, the immediate recognition of one root as a known unit (sight word) isolates the other.

Here again, because of the high-frequency of certain affixes, the efficiency of early reading may be improved in a short time by ensuring immediate recognition of a very few such affixes.

Principle Three
Mastery of a central method of word attack

Word solving is a complex process drawing upon several skills in combination:

no single skill is reliable. The use of alternative skills singly is inefficient — 'If that doesn't work, try this.' Word solving skills operate most efficiently in combination. A few points of high reliability may be made about this process of using skills in combination:

1. The process always entails the use of context — both prediction on the basis of sentence structure and prediction on the basis of developing meaning. A secure basic sight vocabulary is essential in giving body to these predictions.
2. In attending to letter detail, as in solving any sequential task, you must begin at the beginning. The process, therefore, gives prior, heightened attention to initial letters.
3. The process always results in a sensible word for that context and one which is reasonably consistent with the total letter structure. In other words, the solution is always 'checked out' or confirmed.

Now from these highly general points we may construct a generally reliable technique of word solving — what might be called a Central Method of Word Attack:

CONTEXT focused upon
BEGINNING LETTERS
CHECKED by sense and letter detail

Why a *central* method of word attack? Because this should be an invariable, automatic, first approach which leads naturally to other techniques in appropriate situations. Furthermore, this approach may be taught from the beginnings of reading in a single progression developing from simple to complex over several years of learning. See *Appendix C, A Simplified Progression of Word Recognition Skills*.[17]

A Central Method of Word Attack in its Relationship to Other Skills

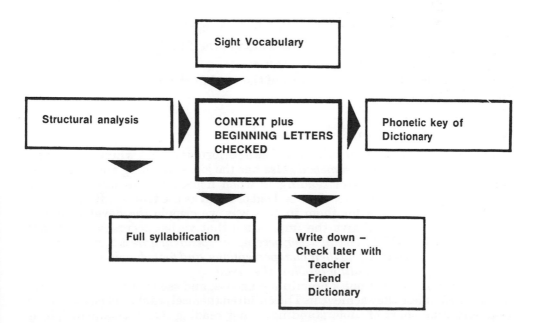

How do we get children operating like this?
Here is a suggested approach.

Say to the children
Reading is understanding what the writer of a book has to tell you. You should understand him just as clearly as if he were talking to you. If you don't understand what someone says to you, you say 'Eh?' or 'What did you say?' — you won't let him go on until you get it clear. Now when you read and don't understand what you are reading, you should do the same. If what you are reading is all nonsense to you, stop and find out why. Don't go on to the next sentence until you understand the last one. *You* are the one who has to be satisfied with what you read — not the teacher or anyone else.

You might think that's all very well, but what about the hard words? How can you understand what it's all about if you get the words wrong, or get stuck on hard words? Here's what to do.

When you come to a strange word look at the first letters without forgetting what the story is about, and think:
'What word beginning this way makes sense here?'
Usually a word will jump into your mind — a good guess. Now check that it *is* the right word by listening to the way it ends and seeing if the letters at the end of the word would fit. It might be:
'Look out. This is a w - - - cat.'
What letters would be at the end? (It ends like *child*. Were you right?)
'We will have to - - - - - him'.
(Accept several suggestions — *kill, shoot, catch*, etc.)
It begins with *sh*. What letter would you expect at the end? Yes, that's right, it ends like *boot*.

Now when you come to hard words you can work them out and be sure you've got them right without asking the teacher. Let's try it with a book. (Now choose a book above instructional level, for the children. Begin reading and stop at a 'hard word'. Ask for suggestions. Write up the initial letter or initial syllable on the blackboard. Let the children determine the word giving you the final letters or the final syllable as proof.)

Now, what do we do when we come to a strange word?

First: Think of the meaning and the sound of the first letters.

Then: Think of a word that makes sense.

But: Check that the *letters* in the rest of the word fit the *sounds* you can hear at the end of the word.

Principle Four
Mastery of independent procedures

Many children tend to think of 'reading' as a performance task wherein it is their job to say the words while *somebody else* has the job of listening and picking up the 'mistakes' — successful reading is when nobody has to interrupt. The 'somebody else' might just as often be Dad or Mum as the teacher. By doing the children's critical work for them in this way we cripple the development of independence, and also give the impression that verbal accuracy is all that counts in reading. *Children can never become independent unless they accept full responsibility for confirming their own perceptions, and for achieving an accurate and satisfying understanding of what they read.*

First then, we must put a premium on sense, and see that the children are dissatisfied unless they achieve it. The children themselves should be convinced that anything short of understanding is not reading. Once this principle is established, we can be sure that the children will use context in the governing role among their skills, and will therefore be more likely to succeed. Further, if they do not solve their word difficulties immediately, the demand for meaning will encourage them to persist, and will inform them and reward them immediately they *are* successful. Provided the text is not beyond their range, a *determination to understand will guarantee persistent and successful word attack.*

'What's this word?'

The outstanding characteristic of retarded and reluctant readers is their dependence on others for both help and assurance. They develop a remarkable range of techniques to wrest aid even from those who are unwilling to give it. This constant pressure for aid can be very disruptive in a classroom, but we are likely to intensify the problem whether we resist it or yield to it. A rebuff diminishes confidence still further, while a direct answer reinforces dependent attitudes. If we say, 'You work it out for yourself,' or worse, 'You ought to know that word,' we destroy confidence and therefore make him more dependent still. If we simply *tell* him the word, we make it more likely that he will seek help in the same way again, and if we send him to a 'helper,' this not only has the same effect but also threatens his dignity in the eyes of his fellows. What should our response be to these appeals for aid?

Encourage children to 'have a go' at a word, and then to examine their guess critically. A good classroom policy is to establish the pattern of inquiry for vocabulary assistance to take the form, 'Is this word x?' rather than the more usual form, 'What's this word?' If this policy is followed, not only are independent habits of word solving being encouraged, but also a teacher has immediate and accurate knowledge of the type of difficulty a child is encountering, and a clue as to how he is operating to solve his word problems. Here is the opportunity for the type of teaching to which children respond most fully — *an accurate question which will direct their attention* in fruitful directions.

Mistakes and Correction

But what about mistakes? Shouldn't we *hear* children read regularly so that we can correct their mistakes? Isn't it dangerous to have them working so independently in silent reading activities as they do in an individualized programme?

Children go through the experience of misreading words hundreds of thousands of times during the learning stages. This is quite natural. Indeed, the brighter readers make numerically *more* mistakes than the slow, because of the driving rate at which they read book after book. What is our normal response to misreadings and how does it contribute towards the anxiety and reluctance of children having difficulty? A child should never feel he has failed because he has misread a number of words, but equally, he should never be satisfied if the meaning of the text has eluded him.[18]

No matter how accurately or inaccurately he reads words, be uncompromising over his understanding of the text. The support and guidance of context will then always be with him, and this will make it immeasurably more likely that he will be successful when he meets difficult words. So often our comments on his misreadings direct his attention *away from* the very clues which are essential for successful operation in word attack. We should attempt to see behind a child's difficulties to whatever essential consideration he has dropped from attention, and our questions should be such as to entice his attention back to such considerations.

1. If he is reading nonsense and not bringing context to bear, we may ask, 'Does

that make sense to you?' 'Is that likely?' 'Are you happy about that?' etc. In general, interrupt only at the end of sentences, and allow the reader to locate his own error.

2. If he attempts to read words or constructions or idioms which are not in the language, he must learn to trust his awareness of common language patterns more than apparent phonetic structure, and to be intolerant of word groupings and intonation patterns foreign to English. If he reads 'journey' pronouncing the 'our' as the phonetic unit he knows, we may respond with, 'Is that a real word?' or 'That's a peculiar word isn't it?' If he reads, 'Here I am what — do you want me to do,' or 'I will come of you,' we may ask, 'Do people talk like that?' or 'What would Mum think if you started talking like that?' 'What would be a better way of saying that?'

Our questions should help him to develop a self-checking sensitivity based on a secure area of knowledge — namely his grasp of the language in its primary spoken form. To draw his attention in the first case to punctuation and in the second case to basic sight vocabulary would have involved using a confused area of experience to clarify a confusion. When he attends to the real language fact and is therefore successful, the punctuation and the confusing sight word receive the best reinforcement possible.

3. Finally, if he takes insufficient account of letter details and guesses without adequate checking, we must direct his attention to the letters in such a way that he can see the discrepancy for himself: he must check that the sounds he hears in the word guessed are consistent with the letters printed on the page. For instance, if he reads *track* for *trail*, or *jumps* for *jumped*, he should be encouraged to discover the inconsistency from his own knowledge of letters. 'What letter would you expect to see at the end of track?' 'Is it there?' 'Then, can this word be track?' And just as importantly, if he reads *rejoice* for *rejoice* he should achieve immediate confirmation and security that he is right, *from his own knowledge* of meanings and letter possibilities.

Aim to achieve an outgoing attitude on the part of the children avoiding the word-fear which forces so many children to withdraw from the problem of reading. Encourage them to suggest possibilities and probabilities, teaching them how to select the correct reading and ratify it beyond any shadow of doubt. One way of doing this is to write a story on the blackboard or overhead projector leaving spaces for words and phrases of different kinds. Let the children write or suggest several possibilities for the missing words and discuss these, determining favourable possibilities on the grounds of context and sentence structure. Now write in one, two or three letters for each word showing their place in the series by dots representing the missing letters.

(Concentrate on initial letters in the first instance). Let the children complete the problem words and then discuss the answers.

Reading to and with

There is a tendency for us to think of reading *to* children as something quite distinct from reading *by* children. In the first type of activity the children have no responsibility to decide anything in the text — that is our job. In the second type of activity each child has the responsibility to read every word in the text accurately and independently. Between the two activities lies a neglected territory within which we can develop some of our most powerful learning and teaching procedures. The ideal teaching situation will often be that in which the teacher reads *with* a group of children.[19]

The text chosen may be too difficult for any one child to read independently, but will be of high interest to all the children. After discussing opening pictures the teacher may read into the story until every child has been 'caught' by the developing theme. At this stage she starts to throw over some of the vocabulary difficulties for the children to discuss and solve. Before displaying the text she may have the children discuss possibilities drawn from their mood of active expectation which she had produced by reading into a sentence. Attention to letter detail is then achieved at the moment when the children are expectant of meaning and is reinforced by satisfaction and assurance as the expectation is fulfilled. Furthermore, the children can discuss the grounds in meaning and letter structure for a certain solution, and learn those skills of confirmation upon which their confidence and accuracy depend. Through this sort of procedure the children learn to organize their resources into a powerful method of word attack in an environment which is free from fatigue, distraction and the constant fear of making mistakes.

Make very clear to children that a single skill is inadequate for accurate word solving. Show them how the skills work together and check up on each other. If an unfamiliar word has been properly solved, it should have been checked by a cross reference of skills, and a child, if called upon, should be able to defend his solution in terms of context and letter structure. 'Why do you think this word is x?' Ask children to adopt this critical attitude as the proper counterpart to the creative leap by which they predict words.

Summary

In talking about the integrating processes lying behind the Central Method of Word Attack we have identified three fundamental operations which interact in problem solving.

1. **Demand for meaning or semantic drive.**
   This is the proper centre of the reading process both in terms of purpose and in the moment-by-moment guidance and control of the whole system.
   Supporting this central semantic concern, and arising out of it, are two different modes of conscious activity:

2. **Sampling and predicting.**
   A highly accurate process to be distinguished from guessing. Ease, fluency, and a proper level of automaticity arise from this foraging, predictive process.

3. **Confirming and self-correcting.**This feedback process is the key to self-regulation of the system, to intrinsic reinforcement moment-by-moment, and to the basis of independence at all stages of development.

Any remedial programme will be directed to improve function in these three critical operations. However, because each is a complex human process which cannot be fully analysed, we are inclined to believe that they cannot be accurately measured and monitored. How can we plan precise teaching objectives and evaluate our success in specific behavioural terms? We feel more comfortable with a neatly packaged skills progression.

Psycholinguistic and developmental research have provided us with delicate instruments for this purpose. It is certainly possible to quantify performance and progress in terms more precise than those associated with traditional skills which have broken down into item learning.

Monitoring central processes

1. Demand for meaning

Miscue analysis (or error analysis) provides a precise tool by which to monitor meaning. By calculating the number of semantically acceptable miscues, or errors, as a ratio of all miscues, we have an accurate indicator of central semantic function. We may then set up behavioural objectives to improve this ratio over a period of times towards the ideal of 1:1. (The procedures outlined earlier in the chapter are designed to do this.) We may post-test, or measure improvement on material at the same level after any interval with considerable accuracy. (After six months we may use the pre-test material as post-test material.)

The formula:

Semantically acceptable miscues: All miscues

Semantic coherence in silent reading may be monitored through the cloze procedure i.e. the ability to make semantically appropriate replacements in a text from which words have been deleted at a specified frequency. This procedure, of course, probes also the specifically predictive part of the semantic process. For this reason we will deal with it under 2.

2. Sampling and predicting

Cloze tests of several kinds may be used to quantify predictive activity. By calculating semantically acceptable cloze completions as a ratio of total number of gaps, we arrive at an accurate measure of predictive function. Again, we may set up clearly quantifiable objectives and evaluate progress by giving a *closely* comparable cloze test at a later date. Constructing cloze tests is discussed below.

The formula:

Semantically acceptable completions: Total number of gaps.

The sampling aspect may be monitored by including specific kinds of grapho-phonic, or letter cues in the cloze gaps, requiring completion of letter detail e.g. final consonant/s, medial consonants, regular vowel/s, and finally, irregular letter combinations. Other useful variations to monitor sampling would include:

Word length shown.

Number of letters shown.

Initial letter given.

Response may be individual and oral, or group and written. When evaluating or post-testing, make certain that you have used *exactly* the same deletion pattern in *as nearly comparable material* as possible. The pre-test may be used as a post-test after six months but not under that time. When using a cloze task to probe sampling, i.e. where *some* grapho-phonic information is provided in the gaps, only exact replacements are tallied, of course. And in replicating the situation for post-testing, the same pattern of grapho-phonic cues should be provided in addition to the same rate of deletion and the same level of material.

The formula:

Number of exact replacements: Total number of gaps.

Any material of known difficulty may be used to construct a cloze test. Select a passage of suitable length to provide at least 20 deletions at a rate of every seventh or eighth word. Do not delete from the first paragraph — allow the reader to establish set for the passage. (This would mean a passage of around 200 words for a 1 in 8 deletion.)

3. Confirmation and self-correction.

In this instance we use a self-correction ratio as a measure. Calculate all successful self-corrections as a ratio of the total number of errors or miscues, including those self-corrected. Monitoring may then be achieved at a later date by using material of the same length and difficulty, with the objective of improving the self correction ratio towards 1:1.

A more delicate measure of confirmation is to calculate all successfully self-corrected miscues as a ratio of all semantically *unacceptable* miscues, including, of course, those which were self-corrected. Here we exclude those acceptable miscues which the mature, efficient reader would both make and leave uncorrected.

Formula:

All successfully corrected miscues: All semantically unacceptable miscues.

These suggestions, of course, represent an extreme simplification of miscue and cloze monitoring — they exclude, for instance, the syntactic area. However, in the busy hustle of committed remedial teaching, they represent a valuable index of function — certainly more accurate in specific behavioural terms than the typical phonic checklists or comprehension tests. Their successful use may also induce a closer study of these powerful ways of monitoring process.

In planning remedial activities for children with special needs in reading, it may be profitable to study the progression of Read-along activities described at the end of the chapter *Group Teaching*. The progression will be found suitable for individual tuition if some help can be obtained in creating the tapes. For seriously retarded older readers there is no more powerful technique.

Developing Study Skills

Because it is more difficult to see how the development of word recognition skills may be catered for in an individualized programme, we have dealt with this problem at some length. It is not difficult to see how the study skills may be developed as a natural part of the programme. These skills are put to constant and purposive use through individual and group projects which culminate in shared experiences.

Simply establishing this type of programme, then, provides the opportunity for highly motivated practice of the skills associated with study and performance. However, a great deal of planned teaching and guidance is required to capitalize on these opportunities.

Setting the Environment for Study

The classroom should be provided with a good reference centre. A range of dictionaries catering for children reading at different levels and satisfying different needs is very important. Dictionaries designed for adult use are usually unsatisfactory, as are the small, abbreviated, desk dictionaries often used for purposes quite unsuited to their cryptic style. The Scott, Foresman poster, *What's in a Dictionary*, is a useful classroom adjunct. This publisher also produces an elementary Thesaurus which is extremely useful at the seven to ten year levels. A full Roget should be provided beyond this stage. The Oxford *Advanced Learner's Dictionary* will be found much more useful and intelligible to children aged nine to fifteen years than the erudite *Concise* or *Pocket* dictionaries.

Two or three encyclopedias are desirable, at least one at reading level of seven or eight years. The Golden Book encyclopedias are colourful, readable and reasonably priced. Above the ten or eleven year levels a New Zealand, Australian or Australasian encyclopedia is valuable. A really large Atlas designed for children is essential. A few resource books on central topics such as dinosaurs or whales or inventors help the children to realise that no encyclopedia or single book is adequate for certain purposes.

The physical setting and conditions for study need to be carefully planned. At certain times of the day noise and physical activity should be restricted to the level conducive to serious study. Use of the school library when it is not required for other classes can often be arranged for individuals and small groups.

Planning to teach study skills.

Before beginning the programme, or in the first week, an opportunity should be made for instruction in the use of dictionaries and encyclopedias. Deal with problems of using an alphabetic index to locate information, and the choice of an appropriate and readable reference. Later in the programme attention should be given to the use of a phonetic key for pronunciation. *Appendix D*, Sections 7 and 8 give more detailed guidance.

An early opportunity should be made to visit a library — either the school library or a community library — or to have a librarian visit the class. In this session the major principles of library organization should be introduced: the catalogue, shelving, the Dewey Decimal Classification. Arrangements should be made at this stage for the use of request services. See *Appendix D*, Section 10.

Later in the programme class or group lessons on summarizing and note-taking should be undertaken. Older children should receive some instruction in making a precis or a paraphrase in very simple terms. They should be taught to locate information from picture files, film-strips, records, films and specialized magazines such as *National Geographic* or *Popular Mechanics*.

Guidance and group work in study

During Sharing Time and Conferences many opportunities will arise for offering help in locating, organizing and presenting material. A small group of advanced pupils may undertake to prepare a card file index of all materials in the school and district relating to central topics of study. A few children may take over the operation of a Request Service for the class.

The techniques and procedures for interviewing visitors or people in the community should be discussed with the whole class. Older, or more capable children may be taught how to operate a tape-recorder and select relevant material for presentation to the class. When reports of any kind are presented, the question of relevance should be open to discussion.

The SQ3R Approach to Study

Early in the establishment of the programme some attention could well be given to the use of sound study techniques suited to the particular level of the children. Perhaps the most simple and useful approach is the Survey, Question, Read, Recite, Review technique. *Appendix D*, Section 14, makes suggestion for teaching progressions.

Adapting Rate and Style of Reading to Suit Purpose

Here again the activities into which this programme propels children provide natural learning situations for becoming a versatile reader capable of adjusting rate and style of reading to suit the purpose and the nature of the material. However, at certain points the teacher may draw the attention of the whole class or of special groups to techniques of skimming and rapid reading. Again, *Appendix D*, Section 14, provides suggestions at different levels.

Mastering the Technical Vocabulary of Scholarship

In a programme which is alive with many different study projects it is necessary to ensure that children have mastered an adequate technical vocabulary for the tasks at their level. This is set out in Section 13 of *Appendix D*. The teacher should check early in the programme that technical vocabulary is progressively introduced, discussed and used in Conferences and in Sharing Time.

The modern scholar must be capable of —

Using a library
Locating information
Keeping up to date

Checking sources
Evaluating information
Organizing knowledge
Discussing ideas
Responding creatively
Using references
Keeping records
Communicating clearly
Withholding judgement
Determining what is relevant
Questioning searchingly
Tolerating unanswered questions
Adapting reading to purpose
Reacting objectively
Using committee and team procedures
Interpreting many symbol systems and special media in conjunction.

Audience Reading

By beginning with silent reading the programme itself underlines the need for preparation of any reading to be presented to an audience. The more general questions of rate, clarity, intonation and breathing etc. may be discussed in full class sessions. Some group teaching of children experiencing special problems may be arranged from time to time. Often the Conference will provide an ideal opportunity for individual help following the shared oral reading.

Once the programme is in operation children will be in contact with a great variety of books. They will be following personal interests through a number of different books and using reference and library skills in doing so. Some of the children's independent activities will have stimulated topic studies of many kinds, and the activities of Sharing Time will have provided clear purposes for careful preparation and presentation. The need to practise audience reading skills will be strongly felt by most of the children.

Underconfident children should be encouraged to read their favourite stories or poems. Where a listening post with read-along stories is in use, allow slower children to share part of a very familiar story which they have processed several times. See notes on the read-along technique in the next chapter on *Group Teaching*.

A powerful stimulant to lively oral reading will be the continuing model presented by the teacher as she reads selections from books during the Opening Sessions of Sharing Time. Detailed suggestions for the teaching of audience reading at different levels will be found in Section 17 of *Appendix D*.

The rewards of skill

The entire programme should emphasize the immense storehouse of pleasure which books represent. If children are able to meet their own personally realised needs through reading, the development of skills will receive an impetus which no other technique can provide — regular, immediate, positive reinforcement or reward. The labour of attention and persistence required to develop skill of any kind should be abundantly repaid in joy.

Group Teaching

This programme places a great deal of emphasis on individual learning and instruction. It is true, of course, that a group of children will often display a common need. Furthermore, the feeling of solidarity engendered by working with others makes group instruction the most efficient means of handling certain learning tasks.

Flexible grouping:
It is possible to group children in many different ways in an individualized programme, on such bases as:

Common needs — instruction in specific skills — short sessions of five to ten minutes followed by practice

Common interest — arising from independent activities — group-directed rather than teacher-directed

Instructional level — for guided silent reading lessons

Voluntary grouping
It is within the spirit of the programme to place group instruction on a basis of guided choice. After alerting individual children to special needs during the Conference, the teacher may plan a series of lessons on a particular topic, such as syllabification, and invite those who wish to participate to join the group. Placing group instruction on this voluntary basis greatly increases its impact.

To the obvious question, *What about those who need instruction but do not opt into the group*? There are clear answers: such children are not ready for the instruction if they cannot recognise their need for it, and it is highly unlikely that they would profit from the instruction if it were forced upon them. The fact that some children opt *out* provides important information that the teacher would not otherwise have. He now knows that his task is to induce *readiness* with these children rather than waste his time and that of children who *are* ready for instruction. When the reluctant ones are ready to opt *in*, instruction will prove very much more efficient and rewarding.

Discussion before and after reading
There are two important needs which may be met very efficiently in a sound basic reading programme but are less easily met in the central procedures of individualized reading. On occasion most children need

a carefully controlled oral introduction to a text

the opportunity to discuss a shared experience with others

The ideal technique for meeting these two needs, however, is the directed silent reading lesson with children grouped in terms of instructional reading level and using reading material carefully matched to their ability and interests. There is an important place for this type of lesson within the individualized programme

Objectives of the Directed Silent Reading Lesson

If the special values of the directed or guided silent reading lesson are to be realised, careful planning is required.

1. Select material at correct instructional level — so that all children are able to cope with the problems presented (no more than one difficulty in twenty running words).
2. Achieve a high level of interest in the story.
3. Prepare the children adequately for reading the passage, making sure that they have recent spoken experience of new vocabulary and understand the central concepts of the story.
4. Help children to achieve a high level of comprehension as reading takes place.
5. Clarify understanding of the text where necessary by continuous or subsequent discussion and questioning.
6. Ensure a high degree of satisfaction from the experience for all children.
7. Assist the children to react appropriately to what they have read and to integrate their understanding of the story with their own experience.
8. Provide incidental teaching as necessary of skills required in reading the story.
9. Motivate the children to think critically about what they have read.
10. Determine individual and group needs for teaching and practice in specific skills.
11. Stimulate activities and interests arising out of the story and provide fruitful follow-up activities.

It is within the spirit of the individualized programme to allow the children to participate in choosing the story which the group will read together.

Lowering readability

The point should be made here that the extent of difficulty children experience in reading a particular selection is *to some degree* under the control of the teacher. By more careful introduction of the selection in the preparatory section of the directed silent reading lesson, the teacher may effectively lower the difficulty level. In particular, the teacher may achieve this by:

increasing motivation to read

relating difficult concepts to the children's background of experience

working through particular word recognition problems in a similar context

reading the opening part of the selection to the group and discussing such matters as characters and the developing plot, the children reading on to enjoy outcomes once their interest has been aroused.

Varying activities in directed reading

There are a number of procedures which may be used to break up a longer story into shorter, profitable activities, while at the same time substantially lowering the readability of the material. These procedures are particularly valuable where the teacher wishes to escape the use of insultingly simple material with older retarded readers.

1. Read-in with oral cloze

Here the teacher reads into the story orally, throwing over some of the more difficult but contextually supported words to the group. Pupils do not have a copy of the text. Letter detail, e.g. initial consonant or syllable, may be written on the blackboard. Valuable teaching of the Central Method of Word Attack may be undertaken in this session. At the same time, the difficult process of beginning a story — determining setting, proper names, characters and concepts — may be discussed. This will lower readability of the story by up to one year.

2. Progressive exposure
Make an overhead transparency of *part* of the story. Cover the text on the projector with a cardboard baffle. Use a narrow strip of cardboard cut to the width of the print line to expose each new line of the text word by word. The children read in unison. Sometimes stop and ask for predictions of the next word/s or show just the beginning letters. Ask the children from time to time to tell you what letters they expect in the rest of the word, then check. This is a highly motivating way of inducing prediction and confirmation.

3. Written cloze
Heat copy or type and stencil a page or two from the text. Delete appropriate words at the rate of between 1 in 15 and 1 in 20. (More frequent deletions in the instructional setting as distinct from the test situation interfere unduly with enjoyment and flow of the story.) The children complete the gaps. Discuss completions before moving on with the story. Don't require *exact* replacements — accept intelligent synonyms. The post-cloze discussion can be a very valuable learning experience. You may wish to collect and file the children's responses, or use them diagnostically to determine which children need special assistance.

A valuable variation of this activity is to include *some* grapho-phonic information in the gaps while the children write in the missing letters. The length of the word may be shown. The number of letters may be shown. Or one or more letters, e.g. initial consonant blends, may be given. In the latter case, the nature of the letters chosen for completion should fit into the current phonic learning of the children.

4. Read-on
If the flow of the story has been interrupted noticeably, the teacher may read on rapidly into the story until high interest has been achieved again, or until an exciting part of the text is imminent.

5. Guided silent reading from typescript
If the teacher has only one copy of the text, a portion of the story — ideally the climactic part — may be distributed in typescript without illustrations. The teacher may then use the illustrations either before reading to produce set, or following reading as a reward. Sometimes the teacher should discuss the children's own imagery, or allow them to make their own illustrations, before displaying the illustrations in the original text.

6. Unison Reading
The end of the story, or some other suitable part, may be read in unison from an overhead transparency or a copy of the text. This establishes a feeling of social solidarity and common purpose in the group. It is often a deeply satisfying way to end a story or to recapitulate its special feeling.

These procedures are ideal when the teacher has only one copy of a highly engaging or well-illustrated book. It becomes possible to engage a large group of children in the enjoyment of a special book borrowed from the library, or to get optimum use from an expensive text such as one of the Bill Martin and Peggy Brogan 'Sounds of Language' series. Furthermore, in combination these techniques may lower readability by up to two years.

The Read-along situation

The use of taped stories with tape recorder or listening post while the pupil/s follow in the text provides a most valuable addition to our range of techniques in improving reading. Such a process, for instance, makes it possible to remotivate retarded readers by using mature material at their level of interest and general development. This is one of the ways by which we can escape the crippling cycle caused by insulting more mature children with material beneath their dignity. Read-along is a private activity which some of the children may engage in profitably while the more confident engage in sustained silent reading within the individualized reading framework. These children are then able to take their part in related activities and shared experiences at a level comparable to others in the programme.

Read-along with cloze

The instructional power of the pure read-along situation may be greatly enhanced by including a cloze element. The following progression leads directly towards independent, unsupported reading.

1. Pure read-along. Material at maturity level.
2. Read-along with oral cloze from 1 word in 20 progressively down to 1 word in 10.
    a. after a pause of 2-3 seconds the word is given naturally and the reading proceeds to the next gap.
    b. after the pause, the word is *not* given, and the reading proceeds.
3. Read-along with written cloze.
    The reader has a copy of the text (e.g. heat copy) with deletions identical to those on the tape. In a pause of 3-4 seconds the reader is required:
    a. to complete initial letter/s when no letters are shown.
    b. to complete final or medial letters when other letters shown.
    c. to complete final letter/s when no letters are shown.
    With each activity the deletion rate is gradually increased from 1 in 20 words to 1 in 10 words, and as the pupil moves on to the next activity, the deletion rate returns to 1 word in 20.
4. Read-along sentence cloze.
    On material somewhat easier than maturity level *at first*, the reader independently reads every second sentence. A suitable time slot is allowed between the taped sentences. Begin by *repeating* the omitted sentence on the tape. Later, do not repeat the omitted sentence but simply read every second sentence with suitable time left between each. Progression may be achieved by increasing the difficulty of the material.
5. Read-along with paragraph cloze.
    Tape the first two or three paragraphs (perhaps involving oral cloze as in 2. above) then ask the reader to turn off the recorder and read the next paragraph independently. Begin again by repeating that paragraph for two or three paragraphs, then simply comment on the salient content of each paragraph and read the next.

It is a good idea to complete each sentence or paragraph cloze session by a short written cloze test covering the last part of the story or article and using a deletion rate of about 1 in 15 words. In this way the teacher has an accurate indication of how the pupil coped, and a record of the activity to file.

Records and Evaluation

The experience of independence includes self-evaluation and the children should be encouraged to examine their own progress and to keep simple records. In making his own evaluations, both of individual and of class performance, the teacher should refer back repeatedly to the chapter, *Objectives of Development in Reading*.

Good records should serve both to simplify daily organisation and to support the process of continuous diagnosis and evaluation. They should be no more complex than is required to fulfil these functions.

The Children's Reading Log

An ordinary exercise book is adequate. Some teachers prefer an interleaved book for illustrations, especially at the junior level. The record should include:

Invariably
a. Titles read and dates.
b. Brief note of impact — My Opinion — 'I did not enjoy this book because . . .'
c. Self-evaluation — My Reading Skills — 'I understood this book without difficulty.'

Sometimes
a. Words-to-remember — list, with meaning and context, of words the child would *like* to make his own.
b. Brief synopsis of the book.
c. Brief review — which may be shared.

Alternative Headings for Children's Reading Log

1	Book Title	Author	Dates	Opinion

2	Book and Author	Dates	Opinion	Difficulty

3	First page			Second page	
Dates	**Book and Author**	**Opinion**	**Difficulties**	**Activities**	
9/6 12/6	*First Days of the World* by G. Ames and R. Wyler.	Not as exciting as *They Turned to Stone.* I liked the part about evolution. The illustrations were too dark.	The beginning was difficult to understand.	I made a clay model of a tuatara. It is like a dinosaur	

4. Place the headings on a chart, and have the children make diary entries in their personal *Reading Logs*, following the headings listed.

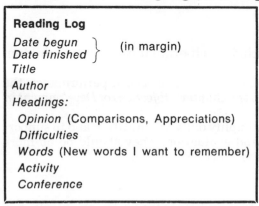

> **Reading Log**
>
> Date begun ⎫ (in margin)
> Date finished ⎭
> Title
> Author
> Headings:
>   Opinion (Comparisons, Appreciations)
>   Difficulties
>   Words (New words I want to remember)
>   Activity
>   Conference

EXAMPLE

17/6 *Little Witch*
19/6 Anna Elizabeth Bennett
    Opinion: This was a really funny witch story. Not as scary as Spook. I liked the part where the witch turned herself into an anteater.
    Difficulties: Just right for me. I had to puzzle at some words.
    Words:
    amiable — friendly; mollified — softened; jovial — jolly
    Activity: I drew a nixie coming out of a big wave.
    Conference: (Teacher's signature and note:) Read in a lively way.

This last format has the advantage of page economy. It also allows children to develop ideas in as much length as they desire.

Teacher's 'Conference Log'

The most convenient form is a simple loose-leaf folder with an opening for each child in alphabetical order and a section at the back for records of group teaching and reports on *Sharing Time* highlights. Notes on individual children will include:

a. **Opening details** — age, reading level, results of recent standardised tests.
b. **Interests** — results of Interest Inventory.
c. **Conference Record** (refer chapter on the *Conference*) The following order of entries will be found convenient:

Date:
Book/s read: (since last Conference)
Time taken: (to read book/s)
Comment: (noteworthy details of attitude, application, comprehension, oral reading, or activities)

Action: (guidance given, practice work set, or teaching plans)

You may find it convenient to use a mimeographed sheet set out with the major headings above and use one for each individual conference, filing later. You may prefer simple column records for each child, e.g.

| Name | Reading Level |
| Age | Interests |

Date	Book	Comments	Action

An essential part of the teacher's individual files on pupils should be dated records of any monitored reading such as Informal Prose Inventory sheets, 'Running Records' (Clay 1972a) or 'Miscue Analyses' (e.g. Johnson, 1979). See also the earlier chapter, *Evaluating Reading*.

Final evaluation

At the end of the period during which the programme is used, make an evaluation of the development of each child. Refer to your *Conference Log* a. 'Opening details' and b. 'Interests' in the light of *Objectives of Development in Reading*. Strengthen your evaluation by the use of standardised test results if this is possible.

Evaluation of the total programme

Whatever length of time you spend on this programme you will wish to make some general assessment of accomplishments and future needs. Here is a possible approach:

A. Summarise final individual evaluations.

B. Administer standardised tests which may be available and desirable at the time.

C. Evaluate *with* the class —

    1. Conduct a general discussion, or better still, have one of the children chair such a session.

    Topic: Advantages and Disadvantages of the Individualized Reading Programme.

    Encourage children to examine each section as outlined in the *Overview*.

    Calculate total number of books read, and average number of books read per child. (For your own information, note highest and lowest number of books read.)

    2. Design a questionnaire.
    (See suggested format below.)

D. Evaluate personally as a teacher:
    Did this programme add or detract from general class objectives?
    Was the programme manageable in day to day operation?
    What would you do differently next time?
    Will there *be* a next time if you have a choice?

E. Discuss the programme with others:
    Headmaster
    Colleagues
    Parents

Suggested questionnaire

Modify to suit younger or older pupils.

My Enjoyment of reading

I enjoyed most of my reading greatly/moderately/not at all.

The book I enjoyed most was ....

My Progress in Reading

I believe I progressed in reading skill greatly/moderately/not at all.

Evidence:

Shared Activities

I enjoyed participating greatly/moderately/not at all.

I felt that the activities helped my reading greatly/moderately/not at all.

Reasons:

I felt that they helped me develop personally a great deal/moderately/not at all.

Reasons:

The Conference

I found the Conferences extremely helpful/helpful/not very helpful.

Reasons:

General

I would like to continue this programme/return to it again/drop it.

My greatest strength in reading is ....

My greatest difficulty in reading is ....

I would like a reading programme that would ....

Personal Development Through Reading

It is characteristic of all developmental tasks that they support general development and meet personal desires as they are being mastered. Standing, walking, and running each bring immense personal rewards with each progressive stage of competence, but they also widen general experience and contribute to general well-being.

The proper use of a developmental task at any stage of development can be said to be *good for you*. This should be as true for reading as it is for climbing, talking, singing, and manipulating. When we think of such tasks together we become aware of the way progress in each contributes something to progress in the others. Reading should fit into this general pattern of interdependent development. Too often, however, the limitations of the instructional setting reduce the returns that reading makes to well-being or even turn reading into a source of mental disease. (Merritt, 1972.)

For many children the process of being taught to read is most harmful to general development, and it can also be said of these children that their failure to learn to read stems to a greater or lesser extent, from the rupture in their healthy general development brought about by failure. Several months of failure may do great harm to general development; the years of unremitting failure without effective intervention experienced by some children in learning to read can find no form of justification. The responsibility lies squarely upon the school system.

It may be safely said that if books do not make a deeply felt and satisfying contribution to the problems of growing up during the ten or more years of schooling imposed on the modern child, we cannot expect a literate or educated community. Literate skills must contribute something of special excellence to the lives of those who struggle with them throughout the long years which are necessary to the mastery of such a complex set of behaviours. If during these years print becomes an instrument of personal assault or subtle torture — as it is for many children in our schools today — we can expect neither literacy nor the valuing of literate goals from our victims. We may be able to develop a driving excellence in an intellectual *elite* by rewarding them competitively for the performance of literate drudgery, but if we want a *literate society*, print itself must bring rewards at every stage of learning and development.

Can print reward application?
As a medium, print is not naturally cold and narrow — traditional schooling has made it so. In proper alliance with the human voice, and focused strongly upon the most relevant human concerns, print has always been a powerfully moving

medium. Restored to its proper alliance with speech, and participating in fellowship with the whole range of modern media, print will continue its powerful and indispensable contribution at the centre of human experience. You can't have a Shakespearean play, a political philosophy, an enriching religion — *or* a television programme of any quality — without a script.

Nothing can replace human language or the written code which fixes the most considered and memorable language. The modern school has a responsibility to restore the power of print, which traditional schooling has systematically destroyed through boredom, abstraction, irrelevance, didacticism, and carping fastidiousness in the lives of so many of its captive subjects.

The possibility of schooling centred upon the rewards of literacy at every stage of development is open to us today in the quality of a new literature for children, created for the most part in the last fifty years. The books are now available if we will only use them in the spirit of adventure and exploration which they embody.

Written words have always had the potential to come alight in men's minds. Taken up by the skilled reader, they may communicate deeply to the whole nervous system and consciousness of man. A book can represent the extension of human consciousness with the same immediacy as electronic media, *provided that the reader has truly mastered the skills of reading*. It is the pedantic, verbal literalness of teaching which turns reading into a limited, linear experience of alienation for a large proportion of the population. The child who learns to think and respond personally as he reads creates all the competencies of electronic media in his own system of behaviour — he outstrips the computer in speed, in range, in subtlety, and in creativeness.

Development through reading

At every stage of development children face common problems which are characteristic of their level of maturity. The finest children's books embody and clarify these crucial experiences of being a person at a certain stage of development. They achieve a remarkable resonance in the consciousness of children attempting to live out the painful conflicts and absurdities of culturing their animal energies towards insight and human control. Children gain a sense of membership in the human community with all the hope and comfort which that can bring.

Problems of personal development will have a different colour and content for different children, but the world of books matches this diversity of need. The same book brings different satisfactions to different children, and the range of books available makes it possible for children with exceptional needs to experience insight and social support in especially appropriate ways. For this reason, children must be provided with a very wide range of books at every stage of growth and *must be taught at the earliest stage to search, select, and enter books* from the literature appropriate to their personal needs.

Some examples

At the six to seven year level, for instance, children may be overwhelmed by anger, fear, or ecstacy. They need to find objective forms for their intense and turbulent emotions which rise up unbidden as incommunicable forces, casting light and shadow over the external world and distorting their perceptions. Stories help them to externalize, examine, and master these formless emotional realities, especially through the experience of identification and fantasy. There are real giants in the experience of the young child.

At seven or eight years of age fear continues to loom as a threat. Each child knows that he experiences fear, and he questions his own bravery. Books help him to see that fear is universal and that to be brave is not to be without fear. He may be able to read Sendak's *Where the Wild Things Are* or *Benny and the Bear* by B. Carleton — or a dozen other simple books which handle the problem in a powerful and sensitive way. He will be lucky if someone has read to him some of *Grimm's Fairy Tales* or the story of David and Goliath.

As he passes through middle childhood, books again may support his continuing development towards a purposeful courage based on the defence of worthy values. He may read *The Boy Who Was Afraid* by Sherry Armstrong or *The Apple and the Arrow* by M. & C. Buff. If she is a girl, she may find *Carolyn and Her Kettle Named Maud* by M. Mason, a deeply satisfying and comforting experience. A teacher with a taste for Tolkien may read from the *Ring* trilogy, and open a whole new world of symbols to embody and bring insight to a range of upwelling emotions.

Adolescence will bring a new and frightening intensity of emotion and the need for self-dependent courage in establishing selfhood. *Anne Frank's Diary* or Hinton's *The Outsider* may be discovered at a crucial period in coming to terms with life, and may contribute a dimension of self-awareness to personhood, extending horizons of personal courage and endeavour. He will find continuing sustenance from books as he faces the frustrating anxieties or the passionate fears of adult experience. All these experiences will be associated with pleasure and satisfaction despite the fact that they deal with some of the problem areas of human experience.

The teacher who allows these matters of central relevance in growing up to be explored through using books in community, and through making a wide range of books available under guidance and with stimulation to read, will feel a powerful force sustaining the reading programme. The major concerns of human development at a particular stage should become major themes of classroom exploration, supported by the diversity and concreteness of children's literature. If the best books for a particular age level are not made available and promoted by the school, children are deprived of a most vital influence in their development which cannot be enjoyed after that stage has passed.

Developmental needs

We have taken the example of fear and courage in personal development. A few more examples may suggest the range of themes which can for a time energize classroom life, supported by children's literature.

Family — understanding parents
Sibling relationships — place in family
Companionship and peer relationships
Becoming independent — being yourself
Freedom and responsibility
Tolerance and prejudice
Objectivity, involvement, and tentativeness
Popularity and values
Male and female roles
Developing a sense of humour

Beyond culture

The preoccupations of an open literature tend to be those deep, universal human concerns which transcend cultural differences. Through translation and international publishing we find these concerns expressed in many cultural or ethnic forms. Techniques which allow us to use an open literature in teaching reading help to overcome cultural barriers — the fundamental needs and joys of all people are the same. Such techniques further allow us to energize the most powerful of human motivations regardless of race or class. Individualized reading offers that sort of possibility.

The Language-arts or Related-arts Approach

When reading and other language skills are taught with proper concern for their human significance, artificial divisions into subject areas become less and less appropriate. If literate attitudes and skills are to be developed, the programme should have wide-ranging implications in the commitment of children to thought, expression, and communication of many kinds — not simply verbal or linguistic concerns. The most effective programme will, therefore, lose its identity as a reading programme and become a learning experience of life relevancy.

Perhaps the most forceful reason for advocating the individualized reading procedures for part of the instructional enterprise lies in the ease with which they relate to other parts of the curriculum. A lively programme, which claims the participation and commitment of children in the adventure of learning and mastering skills, develops naturally from individualized reading techniques. And a day-long programme which draws much of its energy, excitement, and satisfaction from books best meets the needs of children facing the complexities of mastering literate skills as they learn to live.

Appendices

Appendix A
An Informal Prose Inventory

Purpose

The informal prose inventory has established itself as a valuable instrument of classroom diagnosis. It provides information not readily obtained from standardised tests, such as how a child operates in the reading situation, and his specific needs for instruction. The procedure falls very naturally into the conference situation of an individualized programme.

Description

An informal prose inventory is essentially a set of graded prose passages of increasing difficulty for children to read in an individual, diagnostic situation with the teacher. Eight short prose passages from the 6-7 to the 13-14 year level are provided in the test. The test passages for use with the children are labelled alphabetically from B to I. Year levels are provided for the teacher on the relevant pages following in this Handbook. Each passage is divided into a section to be read orally and a section to be read silently.

(**N.B.** This is *not* a test of fluent oral or audience reading — such reading would require the opportunity for careful preparation. You should observe prepared oral reading during a normal Conference or during Sharing Time.)

The procedures of Miscue Analysis developed by Ken and Yetta Goodman (Goodman and Burke 1972) provide a much deeper and more adequate analysis of the reader in action than does the prose inventory. However, the advantages — a full-length story analysis and a detailed miscue taxonomy, among others — also constitute a disadvantage for classroom use. Even in modified form as outlined, for instance, in the fine recent study, *Reading Appraisal Guide* by Barbara Johnson (1979), the procedures can be very time-consuming. Where time is available, however, the procedures provide delicate diagnostic guidelines. All teachers should at least familiarize themselves with the techniques and outcomes of miscue analysis.

The Informal Prose Inventory provides a useful and sensitive compromise. The prose passages are necessarily short and to that extent unreliable, but they do provide an opportunity to monitor, record, and analyze actual reading behaviour within a framework that is economic for the classroom teacher. The record forms, which may be heat-copied from this handbook, provide a simple and ready format for recording. The opportunity is provided to monitor silent as well as oral reading, albeit briefly, and the subtests help to diagnose reading needs rapidly at the lower levels. An attempt has been made to compensate in some measure for the brevity of the passages by readying the reader for the nature of the content by a preparatory statement inducing an appropriate set for the topic.

Nature of the prose passages:

The passages embody a gradual progression of language leading from everyday speech to formal, expository prose. From the seven year level they reflect practical and scientific interests rather than narrative or literary interests. Short, self-contained passages of fiction tend to be unnatural and lacking in interest. There are also some advantages in maintaining an evenness of style from one passage to the next.

Testing understanding:

Questions covering literal and inferential comprehension and recall are provided for each level. An estimate of Independent Reading Level may be obtained by calculating error rate on the oral section and total comprehension score over the whole passage as described below under *Administration*.

Under the heading *Recall* there is first a group of items which should be spontaneously recalled by the pupil after reading the passage silently. Such responses will of course reflect Literal Comprehension. (The questions here are only used if prompting is necessary.) Then follow one or more direct questions: these are to check Inferential Comprehension.

Questions to test emotional reaction, sensory imagery, and creative or critical reading are also included. Responses to such questions cannot, of course, be tallied as right or wrong, but they do give the teacher a valuable guide to the depth of reading and to possible instructional needs which might otherwise be overlooked. These questions should be regarded as essential components of the inventory for they provide information seldom obtained from standardized tests, and are essential to the overall assessment of effectiveness in reading.

Language background

Many children experience difficulty in reading because they have had limited meaningful exposure to the formal language of books. As they face the increasing text-book density of successive years at school, their problems in reading grow ever more imposing. Their difficulty in interpretation cuts them off from the most powerful aids to decoding and they begin to display global difficulties in reading. It is important for teachers to identify such children as early as possible and to provide an appropriate programme of language enrichment rather than an unnecessary programme in basic reading skills.

Recording the tests

Permission is provided by the publisher to heat-copy the record sheets from this handbook. Use the pupil's copy of the test passages in the handbook for the pupil to read. It may be sensible to heat-copy the Administration section of this introduction to have before you if you are unfamiliar with the procedures.

Tests of basic decoding skills

One reason for using an informal prose test is to observe the operation of word recognition skills in genuine reading situations, and the information provided in this way is usually adequate for diagnosing learning needs. However, it is sometimes useful to clarify a diagnosis by a more specific probe and short additional tests have been provided at the five lower levels for this purpose. The copy to be read by the child will be found on the reverse side of the test card at the appropriate level, and instructions are provided on the relevant pages of the Handbook.

These tests allow a sampling of the child's problem-solving strategies in word recognition when further information is required. They are not intended to test the entire inventory of word recognition skills which are set out in later appendices. Rather, they serve to check whether or not the child has developed crucial decoding skills of increasing complexity, and whether or not he is able to call on an adequate set of associations in doing so.

5-6 year level

No test has been provided for the 5-6 year level. Younger children should be monitored on material with which they are in some way familiar (e.g. a supplementary reader from the basic series they are using). The most appropriate procedure for this purpose is keeping a 'running record' (Clay 1979). See also *Appendix C, Literacy Set,* and *Level.*

Older retarded readers are likely to be offended by immature material. For such readers who are at Frustration Level on the Level B (6-7 year) passage, refer to *Appendix C: Literacy Set* and *Level A; Appendix B: Basic Sight Vocabulary in Context*; and the suggestions made in the chapter, *Developing Reading Skills and Strategies*.

Key to abbreviations

IL	Independent Level	(L)	Literal
Q	Question	(I)	Inferential
R	Response	(V)	Vocabulary

Example of completed Record Sheet
See following four pages.
Key to recording symbols
See page 94.

An Informal Prose Inventory

Level E (9-10 years)

Name: Jim Jones   **Age:** 8:10   **Date:** 4/3/80

Set: This report tells about safety provisions on the giant Boeing 747 passenger jet.

A Jumbo Slide

Sliding to/safety is one of the latest ideas

~~jump~~ *jumo*

for getting people off an aeroplane/rapidly.
move

Accidents to aircraft are more likely to
than s.c.

happen on the ground,/especially during

take-off and landing, than in the air. It is not

easy to provide for the safety of all

passengers on the giant jumbo jets of today.

The/Boeing 747 holds up to five hundred

people and towers above the/tarmac like a

(mobile) hotel. The passenger deck is higher
stat s.c.

than a two-storey building. A passenger who
off

leaped from the plane while it was stationary

on the ground would very likely be killed.

Oral — IL: up to 4 errors

Q1 When are accidents to aircraft most likely to happen? (L)
R1 *On the ground, during take-off and landing.*   ☑

Q2 How high is the passenger deck of a Boeing 747? (L) *Than a hotel*   ☒
R2 *Higher than a two-storey building.*

Q3 What do you think the report will go on to tell us? (I) *Getting out in a crash*   ☑
R3 *Something about safety measures.*

Jottings: Persistent and generally successful.

Block 1

Silent:

How could so many passengers get out

quickly in case of emergency? A folded slide,

up to thirty-eight feet long, is carried near

each plane door. When needed, it will

automatically flip out of the plane and

inflate. It takes just ninety seconds for a

plane-load of people to start to slide to

safety.

What fun it would be to practise for an

emergency in this plane.

Recall:

R4	The 747 has a folded slide for rapid emergency exit.
	Q4 What has the 747 to allow passengers to get out quickly in an emergency?
R5	The slide is 38 feet long.
	Q5 How long is the slide?
R6	There is a slide by each door of the aeroplane.
	Q6 Where are the slides on the aeroplane?
R7	The slides automatically flip out and inflate.
	Q7 How do the slides work?
R8	It takes just 90 seconds before passengers can begin to leave.
	Q8 How long does it take before passengers begin to get out?
Q9	Why does the slide need to be so long? (I)
	R9 Such a huge plane is high off the ground. Others may add that the angle of descent should not be too steep.
Q10	Give an alternative title to this report without using any word from the original title. (I)

[boxes: 1 | ✓ | ✓ | 3 | 2 ✗ | ✓ | ✓]

Comprehension — IL: 7 correct responses

N.B. Items recalled in order shown.

SUMMARY

Errors in oral section: (4)

Comprehension score: (8)

Level: Recreational (Independent) Frustration

Further Details:

Self-correction ratio: 2 : 6
(Ratio of total self-corrections to all errors.)

Semantic ratio: 2 : 4 ('jump' & 'prove' not acceptable)
(Ratio of semantically acceptable errors to all errors.)

(Note *outstanding* strengths and weaknesses in Inference, Reaction, Imagery, Critical thinking, Spontaneous recall, Rate, Oral/silent comparison, etc.)

Very fast especially in silent. Good grasp of meaning. Spontaneous recall not sequential. Imagery and reaction good, if a little shallow.

Word recognition: (Results of subtests, Levels B-E, and other relevant comments.)

Does not always use his good intelligence and phonic knowledge to check guesses. Syllabification adequate to this level.

Comment: (Note *significant* characteristics concerning attitudes, anxiety, dependence, and major needs.)

Impetuous. Likes reading but doesn't get as much out of books as he could - needs impact books.
Generally a healthy reader and advanced for his age.

Block 4

Reaction: What do you think it would feel like to use one of these slides?

Scary but firm.

Imagery: What material do you think the slide is made from?

Plastic I think.

Creative thinking: How would the slide need to be shaped to see that people did not fall off as they slide to safety? (Trough-shaped, or with sides).

Would it have rails?

Word recognition skills

Simple syllabification: If difficulty is experienced with two or more of the following words, refer to syllabification in *Appendix C, Level D*:

rapidly accidents aircraft especially passengers mobile hotel two-storey stationery emergency automatically inflate

Central method of word attack: Check that the child is able to use context plus first syllable(s) to work out unknown words: (Subtest)

1. The jet flew at a great alt - - ✓ - -
2. One of the engines suddenly *explored* ✗
3. The passengers were absolutely horr *ible* ✗

Check that the child is able to use final syllables to check his guesses.
Ask:

What syllable would you expect at the end of the word you guessed for Number 1, for Number 2 and for Number 3?

Could use prediction to greater effect.

Block 3

Coins have been used as money for

monkey
th-ŏ-ŭ-sănd
thousands of years but a new way of using

people s.c.
coins is becoming popular today. Many

things can be bought simply by dropping a

coin into a slot in a machine. We often pay

for (parking) our cars or for using a public

going
telephone in ∧ this way.

Machines which work when / money is fed

into them are called vending machines.

?
T.
There are vending machines which play

music, take (photos,) wash clothes, or even
HAT
(shine) shoes.

Key to recording symbols:

Incorrect response: Write child's response above text.

Phonetic attempt: Phonetic script.

Self-correction: Write S.C. beside error.

Repetition: Underline the section repeated.

Double repetition: Double underline.

Omission: Circle the word/s omitted and tally as errors.

Insertion: Use insertion sign and write in the inserted response.

Pause over one second: Diagonal stroke in text.

Punctuation over-ridden: Double parallel bars.

Block or Request for aid: Question mark.

Clues provided, or word/s pronounced by teacher: Encircle in text.

Advice: 'Have a try'. If child fails, circle and tell.

Administration

Use a heat copy of the relevant Record Sheet for administration.
It is advisable to make a tape-recording of the interview and complete the record later.

1. Put the child at ease. Say:

   I would like you to read some short passages to me in just the same way as if you were reading to yourself. Don't worry about mistakes — stop and correct them if you want to. I want to find out the sort of difficulties you have so that I can help you. Try to work out the words you don't know *aloud* **so that I can find out how you do it.**

2. Begin with a passage one or two years below the level you expect the child to be able to handle according to previous records.
3. Set the scene and tune the child in by reading the short introduction following the heading, *Set* on the Record Sheet.
4. Note and tally errors and appeals for aid — which are circled and tallied as errors. Note successful self-corrections but do not tally these as errors. Observe intonation patterns and response to punctuation as they influence meaning. Endeavour to determine what strategies of word solving are being used.Question after reading if necessary to determine this. Keep as full a record as possible — ideally, one which would make it possible for you to reconstruct later how the text was read.
5. Ask the questions from the *Oral* section and discuss where necessary.
6. Ask the child to proceed with the selection silently so that he can tell you about it after he has finished. Say:

   Read the next part to yourself and tell me about it when you have finished. If you are unable to work out a word, show it to me and I'll help you.

7. Note extremes of rate — noticeably slow or fast; noticeably slower or faster than the oral reading. Note observable silent reading habits which may indicate interest, attitude or difficulty. Do not regard pointing as significant below the nine year level or subvocalization below the twelve year level. Both habits are proper strategies at or near frustration level *at any age*.
8. Ask the child to tell you all he can remember about what he has read. Note the correct and the incorrect responses and the *sequence* of responses. The responses listed are in the words of the text. The child, however, should not be required to reproduce the exact words of the text. If the main idea of the item is recalled, it should be scored correct. An accurate response in the child's own words may be superior to an exact recall of the words from the text since this is usually a sign that higher order, integrative skills have been operating.
9. For any response which the child fails to recall spontaneously ask the question printed on the Record Sheet below that response. Score positively any correct response to these questions.
10. Ask the inferential question(s) which follow, and score.
11. Calculate total comprehension score.
12. Note the adequacy of responses to the questions given to determine reaction, sensory imagery, and creative or critical thinking.
13. Use the subtests only when performance suggests that further information is required.
14. Continue with the next test passage until Independent Reading Level has been determined. Do not proceed to Frustration level: if the difficulty rate nears one in ten running words, discontinue the test.

15. You may proceed to determine the level of *listening comprehension* by reading succeeding tests *to* the child until he can no longer answer three quarters of the question material. The level of listening comprehension may be taken as an estimate of expectancy in reading. An approximate measure of retardation is the difference between independent reading level and listening comprehension level.

Scoring

Tally as errors all uncorrected mistakes, including omissions, aid or clues provided (also circled as omissions), and punctuation over-ridden at sentence junctures. Do not tally self-corrections, repetitions or pauses as errors.

Interpretation

1. Independent Reading Level

For the purposes of this inventory, Independent Level is defined as the level of material within his interest which a child may handle independently. This level is approximately equivalent to Instructional Level in a basal programme, although it may be a little lower. (In other words, the passages in this inventory lie at the more difficult extreme of each level as measured by standardized tests.) In an individualized programme children read independently without teacher introduction or guidance. This test may, therefore, place them a year below the level at which they can operate within a guided silent reading structure. If a child meets the criteria for a particular level, he or she will be able to handle graded material at that level *independently*.

2. Independent reading and self-correction

You will have noted successful self-corrections. Now, if over the passages read the child has corrected no more than one or two errors , it is *likely* that:

a. He will have difficulty in independent, as distinct from guided, silent reading.
b. There is a need to *teach* independent habits of self-correction and evaluation. (See *Developing Reading Skills*.)
c. There is a need to place greater emphasis on self-satisfaction and understanding for that child — particularly if the comprehension score falls at or below the level indicated for independent reading of that passage.

3. Word recognition skills

The application of word recognition skills appropriate to each level is briefly noted following the questions for that level. Where the test indicates a possible weakness, follow up by further testing and appropriate instruction. Refer to the chapter *Developing Reading Skills* and to *Appendices B and C*.

4. Comparing accuracy and comprehension

There may be a significant difference between the child's ability to recognize words accurately and his ability to understand what he reads. He may gain a pass score at a particular level for accuracy and a fail score for comprehension, or *vice versa*.

If accuracy is superior to comprehension, it is likely that either:

a. The child is a 'word-caller' who thinks of reading as a performance skill and should be encouraged to read silently for self-satisfaction.
b. The child is reading beyond his intellectual or experiential level and should be encouraged to read material which he understands and enjoys.

If comprehension is superior to accuracy, it is likely that either:

a. The child is not independent in self-correction. See chapter *Developing Reading Skills*.
b. Diagnosis of difficulty in specific word recognition skills and appropriate instruction are required.
   See subtests and *Appendix C*.

5. Organization, reaction and integration of ideas

If the child experiences undue difficulty in the following types of questions, give instruction in that area. For suggestions refer to the section of *Appendix D* indicated.

a.   Sequence — spontaneous recall disordered: 3.3.
b.   Reaction — poor emotional response: 4.2; 4.3; 4.4
c.   Imagery — thin sensory images accompanying reading: 4.1
d.   Creative and critical thinking — limited integration of ideas with own experience and difficulty in thinking through the wider implications of the text: 3.4 to 3.8

6. Rate

Where reading is extremely slow, encourage the choice of easier materials, silent rather than oral reading, and less tension over the need to perform or answer test questions.

Where the reading is very fast and very inaccurate, the problem may be rather more complex and intractable, especially in an individualized programme. Regular Conferences will be necessary. A useful strategy is to have such a child regularly tape-record some of his own reading, and then independently locate and correct his own errors during playback. See also *Developing Reading Skills*.

7. Comparing oral and silent reading

If the child handles the oral section very much better than the silent section, it is likely that he thinks of reading as a performance task to be carried our for someone else's approval rather than as a personally satisfying task. Such a child may be extremely dependent or disturbed at first in an individualized programme. He should be helped to *see* that *he* is the one who must be satisfied at every point with his own reading. Emphasis should be placed on reading for personal satisfaction which may lead to real purposes for sharing. Opportunities for satisfying performance of many kinds can be made *following* a deep personal involvement in independent reading.

If the child handles the silent reading very much better than the oral section, it is likely that he has experienced tension and embarrassment in the audience reading situation, or has been forced to read unseen material orally, making a public display of his hesitations. He should be encouraged to continue his healthy development of silent reading skills, but special help should be given to assist him to achieve confidence and pleasure from genuine audience reading for which he feels adequately prepared. See *Appendix D*, Section 17.

8. Estimating expectancy and retardation

An estimate of reading potential or expectancy may be obtained by testing listening comprehension as described in para. 14 *Administration* above. The difference between Independent Level and the level of listening comprehension provides a measure of retardation. Greater confidence may be given to this estimate if it is confirmed by other criteria such as intelligence and spoken language skills.

Final evaluation

After having administered this reading inventory to a particular child you should have a clear picture of how he is operating or misoperating in the reading situation.

You will have obtained an accurate idea of Independent Reading Level.

You will be able to guide his reading into vigorous, balanced, and healthy ways of operating, providing instruction and practice appropriate to his needs. Where he has displayed needs in common with other children, you will be able to place him in profitable group situations for the detailed or sequential instruction he may require.

B   A Birthday Surprise

One day a little boy said to his father,
"Soon my birthday will come.
Will you give me a big present?"
"Yes," said his father.
"Do you want something fast
or something slow?"
"I want something fast," said the boy.
"A car is fast.
A boat is fast.
But what is slow?"

At last the birthday came.
"Here," said the father. "Happy
Birthday!
Here is your surprise present."
"A puppy," the boy laughed.
"He is fast when he is running
and he is slow when he is sleeping.
Thank you for a good surprise."

Consonant Knowledge Group A:

M S B H T N K W

D F J G C P L R V

Group 1:

ch   sh   th   wh

Group 2:

bl fl pl sl st z qu br cr dr fr gr tr str

Group 3:

sm sn sw pr cl gl tw kn wr sp spr

Elementary Structural Analysis

The boys walked slowly. The girl walks fast. The puppies are running.

Elementary Word Attack

1. The big dog b - - me.

2. My cat likes to eat f - - -.

3. My mother asked me to h - - : her with the dishes.

C

Fun with Paper Bags

Making a mask can be fun. Do it this way. Get a large paper bag and hold it in front of your face. Mark the places for your eyes, nose, and mouth. Lay the bag on a table, and cut holes the right shape. When it is finished the mask will fit right over your head.

What kind of mask will you make? Good ones are Indians, animals, flowers, and clowns. For Indians you will need feathers. For animals you will need fur or hair. Wool makes fine hair and whiskers. For flowers and clowns you will need bright colours. Use crayons or paint. A better way may be to paste on coloured paper or cloth.

Sub-test Level C

Consonant Knowledge

scr   sk   squ   thr   soft c   soft g

Central Method of Word Attack

1. She dropped the cup on the fl - - -.

2. Our baby can cr - - - a long way.

3. The sleepy cat str - - - - - in the sun.

D

Money and Machines

Coins have been used as money for thousands of years but a new way of using coins is becoming popular today. Many things can be bought simply by dropping a coin into a slot in a machine. We often pay for parking our cars or for using a public telephone in this way.

Machines which work when money is fed into them are called vending machines. There are vending machines which play music, take photos, wash clothes, or even shine shoes.

Vending machines do the job of a shopkeeper. Many things can be bought from machines when shops are closed. The time may come when machines take the place of many shops.

Vending machines could not be used if coins were not perfectly made. Each coin must be exactly the right size to pass through the slot. Some machines even weigh each coin to make sure that the right price has been paid. It is not easy to cheat a vending machine.

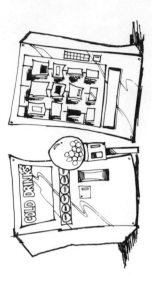

Sub-test Level D

Use of Vowel Mastery in the Central Method of Word Attack

1. Mike was afraid to go to the dent - - -.

   Paul said that the dentist's new turbine drill was quite painl - - -.

2. Virginia would not sh - - - her chocolates. Rebecca told

   her not to be so sel - - - - and sp - - - the fun.

E

A Jumbo Slide

Sliding to safety is one of the latest ideas for getting people off an aeroplane rapidly. Accidents to aircraft are more likely to happen on the ground, especially during take-off and landing, than in the air. It is not easy to provide for the safety of all passengers on the giant jumbo jets of today. The Boeing 747 holds up to five hundred people and towers above the tarmac like a mobile hotel. The passenger deck is higher than a two-storey building. A passenger who leaped from the plane while it was stationary on the ground would very likely be killed.

How could so many passengers get out quickly in case of emergency? A folded slide, up to thirty-eight feet long, is carried near each plane door. When needed, it will automatically flip out of the plane and inflate. It takes just ninety seconds for a plane-load of people to start to slide to safety.

What fun it would be to practise for an emergency in this plane.

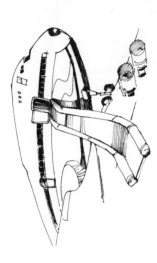

Sub-test Level E

Central Method of Word Attack

1. The jet flew at a great alt - - - - -.

2. One of the engines suddenly expl - - - -.

3. The passengers were absolutely horr - - - - -.

F

Experiment in Living

On the first day of September two men went down into a cave in France. They finally came out five months later. They had volunteered to live in the cave as part of an experiment. Scientists wanted to see how men would behave without clocks, calendars or the sun to tell them what time or what day it was.

Plastic tents were put one hundred feet apart in the cave. Each man had lights, hundreds of books, furniture and food — but no clocks or calendars. They each read about five hundred books.

How did the men react? Very soon they lost track of time. They began living on a forty-eight hour schedule. They stayed awake for thirty six hours and slept for twelve. When they came out of the cave at the end of January they thought it was November.

"The certainty that the experiment will be useful to man helped me to go through with it," said one of the volunteers. Information about men's natural habits may help scientists prepare astronauts for space travel.

G

Bent Sunlight

We see rainbows in many places: in the sky after showers, in a droplet of water bathed in sunshine, or in the angle at the edge of a mirror. In each case rays of sunlight have been refracted, or bent, as they passed through a transparent object. When the objects have a polished surface, refraction causes the colourless rays of sunlight to be broken up in to seven visible colours — red, orange, yellow, green, blue, indigo, and violet. A rainbow is formed in the sky when tiny droplets of rain bend the sunshine as it passes through them.

The brightness of our sky during daylight is also caused by refraction. Particles of air in the atmosphere bend sunlight in every possible direction. We are surrounded by daylight coming from all angles, whether or not we are in direct sunshine. We can even see the underside of a table in a room illuminated by daylight coming from the sky. This is why it is quite light well before sunrise and well after sunset. If sunlight were not refracted by our atmosphere, the sky would be deep black and star-filled even during the day — as it is from any point in space.

H

Underwater Habitat

"It was a nice place to visit, but I wouldn't want to live there", reported John Van Derwalker, one of four marine scientists who "splashed-up" after a record-breaking sixty days of living under the sea.

Of the four men taking part in Project Tektite I, two were oceanographers, one was a geologist, the other a fishery biologist. Their habitat, which was based about forty seven feet underwater off St. John, Virgin Islands, was made up of two vertical cylinders, each eighteen feet tall and twelve and a half feet in diameter.

As the scientists ventured outside of their habitat each day to map the ocean floor and study marine life, they were objects of study to Project Tektite sponsors: the U.S. Navy, the National Aeronautics and Space Administration (NASA), and the General Electric Company.

NASA was especially interested in learning what physical and mental problems might crop up while scientists work in isolated conditions. The men could not easily return to the surface. Underwater they breathed pressurized nitrogen and oxygen to counter-balance sea pressure on the bottom. They had to spend twenty hours in a special decompression chamber to help them rid their systems of nitrogen before they could re-enter sea-level atmosphere.

I

Rebuilding War-Torn Europe

At the end of World War II in 1945, the nations of Europe — both victors and vanquished — found themselves near economic collapse. To rescue these nations and revive their economies, the United States devised its first large-scale foreign aid plan, called the Marshall Plan. By establishing this programme, the U.S. not only hoped to rebuild these war-torn nations but also to stem the spread of communism in Western Europe.

The war had left in its wake a heavy toll of destruction. After the last bomb had fallen and the final bullet had been fired, many nations lay in ruins. These conditions of unprecedented destruction threatened the political stability of many nations, and America feared that traditional forms of democracy may give way to communism. This fear was heightened by the emergence of Russia as a world power second only to the United States, and as the dominating influence in restructuring the patterns of government in Eastern European nations.

With U.S. aid supporting the tremendous energy and determination of the people, the factories and the farms of Western Europe began producing again. By 1951, industrial production was forty per cent higher than before the war.

The newly reconstructed nations were soon operating as strong parliamentary democracies, resistant to communist influences, and a powerful counter-balance to the Russian satellite countries of Eastern Europe. The Marshall Plan proved an extraordinary success in this post-war European context.

The fact that it placed more emphasis on economic recovery than on military aid may account in some measure for this phenomenal success, especially when compared with foreign aid programmes applied later in other parts of the world, such as Israel or Vietnam. However, the long history of vigorous civilization and representational government among the people of Europe was undoubtedly the most important contributing factor in the success of the Marshall Plan.

An Informal Prose Inventory

Name: **Age:**   **Date:**   **Level B (6-7 years)**

Set: This is a story about a boy who gets a very pleasant surprise.

A Birthday Surprise

One day a little boy said to his father,

"I want something fast," said the boy.

"Soon my birthday will come.

"A car is fast.

Will you give me a big present?"

A boat is fast.

"Yes," said his father.

But what is slow?"

"Do you want something fast

or something slow?"

Oral — IL: up to 3 errors

☐

Q1 Why did the boy think his father would give
him a present? (L)
R1 It would soon be his birthday.

☐

Q2 What did the boy want for his birthday? (L)
R2 Nothing in particular. Something fast.

Q3 What puzzled the boy when his father asked
him if he wanted something fast or something
slow? (L)
R3 What present might be slow?

☐

Jottings: *Block 1*

Silent:

At last the birthday came.

"Here," said the father. "Happy Birthday!

Here is your surprise present."

"A puppy," the boy laughed.

"He is fast when he is running

and he is slow when he is sleeping.

Thank you for a good surprise."

Recall:

R4 When his birthday came . . . .
    Q4 When did he get the surprise?

R5 Father said "Happy Birthday!"
    Q5 What did the boy's father say as he gave him the present?

R6 The boy was given a puppy.
    Q6 What present was the boy given?

R7 The boy said the puppy would be fast when it was running and slow when it was sleeping.
    Q7 How did the boy think the present was both fast and slow?

R8 The boy laughed.
    Q8 What did the boy do when he saw the puppy?

R9 The boy thanked his father for the good surprise.
    Q9 What was the last thing the boy said to his father?

Q10 Why did the boy laugh? (I)
R10 Because he thought it was funny that the puppy could be both fast and slow.

Comprehension — IL: 7 correct responses

Reaction: How did the boy feel about his present?

Imagery: What kind of puppy did you see in your mind?

SUMMARY

Errors in oral section: ◯

Self-correction ratio:
(Ratio of total self-corrections to all errors.)

Comprehension score: ◯

Semantic ratio:
(Ratio of semantically acceptable errors to all errors.)

Level: Recreational Independent Frustration

Further Details:

(Note *outstanding* strengths and weaknesses in Inference, Reaction, Imagery, Critical thinking, Spontaneous recall, Rate, Oral/silent comparison, etc.)

Word recognition: (Results of subtests, Levels B-E, and other relevant comments.)

Comment: (Note *significant* characteristics concerning attitudes, anxiety, dependence, and major needs.)

Block 4

Group A: **m s b h t n k w**
　　　　　d f j g c p l r v

1. Name letters at random and ask the child to point to each.
2. Point to letters in order and ask 'What do we call this letter?'
3. Point to the letters in order and ask 'Can you tell me a word beginning with this letter?'

Tell me a word which begins with:

Group 1: **ch   sh   th   wh**

Group 2:

bl fl pl sl st z qu br cr dr fr gr tr str

Group 3:

sm sn sw pr cl gl tw kn wr sp spr

Elementary word attack: Check whether the child is able to use context plus initial consonant to determine unknown words:

1. The big dog b - - me.
2. My cat likes to eat f - - -.
3. My mother asked me to h - - -　her with the dishes.

Check whether the child is able to use consonant endings to check accuracy. Ask:
What would the last letter be in the word you guessed for Number 1, for Number 2, and the last two letters for Number 3?

Block 3

Creative thinking: The present I'm thinking of is not fast and not slow — it's just right. What could it be? (Observe acceptance and rejection of possibilities, such as a *clock, bike, pony,* etc.)

Word recognition skills

Basic sight vocabulary: If two or more of the following words are misread, check sight vocabulary more thoroughly. See *Appendix B.*

one little give big yes do want fast slow what

Elementary structural analysis: Indicated by difficulty with *running* and *laughed.* Check -ed, -ing, -s, -ly. (See also subtest)

The boys walked slowly. The girl walks fast.
The puppies are running.

Initial consonant or blend: If difficulty is experienced with the consonant beginning of the following words refer to *Appendix C, Level B:*

boy give fast puppy running laughed slow present

An Informal Prose Inventory

Level C (7-8 years)

Name: **Age:**   **Date:**

Set: Do you like making things? This story will give you some ideas.

Fun with Paper Bags

Making a mask can be fun. Do it this way.

Get a large paper bag and hold it in front

of your face. Mark the places for your eyes,

nose, and mouth. Lay the bag on a table,

and cut holes the right shape. When it

is finished the mask will fit right over

your head.

Oral — IL: up to 4 errors.

Q1 What does the story suggest you use to make a mask? (L)   ☐
  R1   A large paper bag.

Q2 How can you be sure that the eyes will be in the right place? (L)   ☐
  R2   Hold the bag in front of the face and mark the place for eyes, etc.

Q3 Would people be able to see your ears? (I)   ☐
  R3   No. Paper bag right over head and no hole for ears.

Silent:

What kind of mask will you make? Good

ones are Indians, animals, flowers, and

Jottings: *Block 1*

clowns. For Indians you will need feathers.

For animals you will need fur or hair. Wool

makes fine hair and whiskers. For flowers

and clowns you will need bright colours.

Use crayons or paint. A better way may be

to paste on coloured paper or cloth.

Recall:

R4 Good masks are Indians, animals, flowers and clowns.
Q4 What would be good masks to make?

R5 For an Indian mask you will need feathers.
Q5 What would you need for the Indian mask?

R6 For animals you will need fur or hair.
Q6 What would you need for making animal masks?

R7 Wool makes fine hair and whiskers.
Q7 What could you use to make the hair?
What else could you make from wool?

R8 You need bright colours for flowers and clowns.
Q8 What kind of colours are best for flowers and clowns?

R9 Make bright colours with crayon, or paste on coloured paper.
Q9 How would you make these bright colours?

Q10 Suggest a completely new title. (I)
R10 Open-ended. No words from original title.

Comprehension — IL: 7 correct responses

Reaction: Which mask would you most like to make?

Imagery: What animal mask did you see in your mind as you were reading?

Creative thinking: What other mask would be suitable to make from a paper bag?

116

SUMMARY

Errors in oral section:

Self-correction ratio:
(Ratio of total self-corrections to all errors.)

Comprehension score:

Semantic ratio:
(Ratio of semantically acceptable errors to all errors.)

◯ ◯

Level: Recreational Independent Frustration

Further Details:

(Note *outstanding* strengths and weaknesses in Inference, Reaction, Imagery, Critical thinking, Spontaneous recall, Rate, Oral/silent comparison, etc.)

Word recognition: (Results of subtests, Levels B-E, and other relevant comments.)

Comment: (Note *significant* characteristics concerning attitudes, anxiety, dependence, and major needs.)

Block 4

Word recognition skills

Basic sight vocabulary: Should be mastered at this stage, but difficulty with one or more of the following words should be followed by covering the last four pages of the test in *Appendix B*:

large front face eyes mouth table right

Consonant mastery: Especially initial consonant blends and digraphs. If there was difficulty in one or more of the following, refer *Appendix C, Level B*:

front flowers clown shape crayons feathers

(See also subtest below)

Consonant knowledge: Say and point —
Tell me a word which begins with:

scr sk squ thr soft c soft g

Common vowel combinations: Indicated by difficulty with one or more of the following:

fun paper bag face mark hole shape flowers wool

Central method of word attack: Check whether the child is able to work out unknown words by use of context plus initial consonant blend:

1. She dropped the cup on the fl - - -.

2. Our baby can cr - - - a long way.

3. The sleepy cat st - - - - - in the sun.

Check whether the child is able to use consonant endings to check guesses.
Ask:

What would the last letter be in the word you guessed for Number 1, and for Number 2? What common ending was added to the root word in Number 3? What two letters would you expect to see at the end of the root word?

Block 3

An Informal Prose Inventory

Level D (8-9 years)

Name: Age: Date:

Set: Here is a story about the increasing use being made of coins.

Money and Machines

Coins have been used as money for thousands of years but a new way of using coins is becoming popular today. Many things can be bought simply by dropping a coin into a slot in a machine. We often pay for parking our cars or for using a public telephone in this way.

Machines which work when money is fed into them are called vending machines.

There are vending machines which play music, take photos, wash clothes, or even shine shoes.

Oral — IL: up to 4 errors

Q1 What new use is being made of coins today? (L)
R1 *Slot or vending machines.*

Q2 What are coin machines called? (V)
R2 *Vending machines.*

Q3 What did the writer think was the most strange vending machine? (I)
R3 *The machine to shine shoes.*

☐
☐
☐

Jottings:

Block 1

Silent:

Vending machines do the job of a

shopkeeper. Many things can be bought

from machines when shops are closed. The

time may come when machines take the

place of many shops.

Vending machines could not be used if

coins were not perfectly made. Each coin

must be exactly the right size to pass

through the slot. Some machines even

weigh each coin to make sure that the right

price has been paid. It is not easy to cheat a

vending machine.

Recall:

☐ **R4** Vending machines do the job of a shopkeeper.
Q4 *What job do vending machines do?*

☐ **R5** Many things can be bought from machines when shops are closed.
Q5 *When are vending machines most useful?*

☐ **R6** The time may come when vending machines take the place of many shops.
Q6 *What did the story say may happen in the future?*

☐ **R7** Vending machines could not be used if coins were not perfectly made.
Q7 *What makes it possible for vending machines to work with ordinary money?*

☐ **R8** Some machines even weigh each coin.
Q8 *How do some machines check that the right money has been paid?*

☐ **Q9** Why is it hard to cheat a vending machine? (I)
R9 *They measure and sometimes weigh coins.*

☐ **Q10** Give this story another title using the word *shops* or *shopping.*

Comprehension — IL: 7 correct responses

SUMMARY

Errors in oral section: ◯

Self-correction ratio:
(Ratio of total self-corrections to all errors.)

Comprehension score: ◯

Semantic ratio:
(Ratio of semantically acceptable errors to all errors.)

Level: Recreational Independent Frustration

Further Details:

(Note *outstanding* strengths and weaknesses in Inference, Reaction, Imagery, Critical thinking, Spontaneous recall, Rate, Oral/silent comparison, etc.)

Word recognition: (Results of subtests, Levels B-E, and other relevant comments.)

Comment: (Note *significant* characteristics concerning attitudes, anxiety, dependence, and major needs.)

Structural analysis: If there is any difficulty with the structure of one or more of the following words, refer *Appendix C, Level C:*

becoming   dropping   using   shopkeeper   perfectly

Vowel combinations: If there is difficulty with one or more of the following words, refer to *Appendix C, Levels C and D:*

coin   thousands   slot   public   vending   photos

Central Method of Word Attack: Check whether the child can use knowledge of vowel combinations to work out strange words: (Subtest)

Use of Vowel Mastery in the Central Method of Word Attack

1. Mike was afraid to go to the dent - - -.
   Paul said that the dentist's new turbine drill was quite painl - - -.

2. Virginia would not sh - - - her chocolates. Rebecca told her not to be so sel - - - - and sp - - - the fun.

Reaction: What do you think of vending machines?

Imagery: What do you think the machine for shining shoes looked like?

Creative thinking: How do you think a machine could detect a coin that was too small?

Word recognition skills

Basic sight vocabulary: Should be complete for all heavy-duty words. If there was difficulty with one or more of the following words, check the last three pages of the test in *Appendix B:*

money   machines   bought   often   through   weigh

An Informal Prose Inventory

Level E (9-10 years)

Name: Age: Date:

Set: This report tells about safety provisions on the giant Boeing 747 passenger jet.

A Jumbo Slide

Sliding to safety is one of the latest ideas

for getting people off an aeroplane rapidly.

Accidents to aircraft are more likely to

happen on the ground, especially during

take-off and landing, than in the air. It is not

easy to provide for the safety of all

passengers on the giant jumbo jets of today.

The Boeing 747 holds up to five hundred

people and towers above the tarmac like a

mobile hotel. The passenger deck is higher

than a two-storey building. A passenger who

leaped from the plane while it was stationary

on the ground would very likely be killed.

Oral — IL: up to 4 errors

Q1 When are accidents to aircraft most likely to happen? (L)
    R1 *On the ground, during take-off and landing.*

☐

Q2 How high is the passenger deck of a Boeing 747? (L)
    R2 *Higher than a two-storey building.*

☐

Q3 What do you think the report will go on to tell us? (I)
    R3 *Something about safety measures.*

☐

Jottings:

Block 1

Silent:

How could so many passengers get out

quickly in case of emergency? A folded slide,

up to thirty-eight feet long, is carried near

each plane door. When needed, it will

automatically flip out of the plane and

inflate. It takes just ninety seconds for a

plane-load of people to start to slide to

safety.

What fun it would be to practise for an

emergency in this plane.

Recall:

☐ ☐ ☐ ☐ ☐ ☐ ☐

R4 The 747 has a folded slide for rapid emergency exit.
Q4 What has the 747 to allow passengers to get out quickly in an emergency?

R5 The slide is 38 feet long.
Q5 How long is the slide?

R6 There is a slide by each door of the aeroplane.
Q6 Where are the slides on the aeroplane?

R7 The slides automatically flip out and inflate.
Q7 How do the slides work?

R8 It takes just 90 seconds before passengers can begin to leave.
Q8 How long does it take before passengers begin to get out?

Q9 Why does the slide need to be so long? (I)
R9 Such a huge plane is high off the ground. Others may add that the angle of descent should not be too steep.

Q10 Give an alternative title to this report without using any word from the original title. (I)

Comprehension — IL: 7 correct responses

SUMMARY

Errors in oral section: ◯

Self-correction ratio:
(Ratio of total self-corrections to all errors.)

Comprehension score: ◯

Semantic ratio:
(Ratio of semantically acceptable errors to all errors.)

Level: Recreational Independent Frustration

Further Details:

(Note *outstanding* strengths and weaknesses in Inference, Reaction, Imagery, Critical thinking, Spontaneous recall, Rate, Oral/silent comparison, etc.)

Word recognition: (Results of subtests, Levels B-E, and other relevant comments.)

Comment: (Note *significant* characteristics concerning attitudes, anxiety, dependence, and major needs.)

Block 4

Reaction: What do you think it would feel like to use one of these slides?

Imagery: What material do you think the slide is made from?

Creative thinking: How would the slide need to be shaped to see that people did not fall off as they slide to safety? (Trough-shaped, or with sides).

Word recognition skills

Simple syllabification: If difficulty is experienced with two or more of the following words, refer to syllabification in *Appendix C, Level D*:

rapidly accidents aircraft especially passengers mobile hotel two-storey stationery emergency automatically inflate

Central method of word attack: Check that the child is able to use context plus first syllable(s) to work out unknown words: (Subtest)

1. **The jet flew at a great alt - - - - -**
2. **One of the engines suddenly expl - - - -**
3. **The passengers were absolutely horr - - - - -**

Check that the child is able to use final syllables to check his guesses.
Ask:

What syllable would you expect at the end of the word you guessed for Number 1, for Number 2 and for Number 3?

Block 3

An Informal Prose Inventory

Level F (10-11 years)

Name: **Age:** **Date:**

Set: What do you think it would be like to be shut away from the daylight, for weeks on end? This report tells us what happened to some men who tried.

Experiment in Living

On the first day of September two men went down into a cave in France. They finally came out five months later. They had volunteered to live in the cave as part of an experiment. Scientists wanted to see how men would behave without clocks, calendars or the sun to tell them what time or what day it was.

Plastic tents were put one hundred feet apart in the cave. Each man had lights, hundreds of books, furniture and food — but no clocks or calendars. They each read about five hundred books.

Oral — IL: up to 4 errors

Q1 How long were the men in the cave? (L)
R1 *Five months.*

Q2 What were the men not allowed to have in the cave? (L)
R2 *Clocks and calendars.*

Q3 Could the men communicate with each other? (I)
R3 *Probably yes. Their tents were only 100 feet apart and there is no mention of isolation.*

☐

☐

☐

Jottings: *Block 1*

127

Silent:

How did the men react? Very soon they lost track of time. They began living on a forty-eight hour schedule. They stayed awake for thirty six hours and slept for twelve. When they came out of the cave at the end of January they thought it was November. "The certainty that the experiment will be useful to man helped me to go through with it," said one of the volunteers. Information about men's natural habits may help scientists prepare astronauts for space travel.

Recall:

R4 The men lost track of time.
Q4 *How did the men react?*

R5 They began living on a 48 hour schedule.
Q5 *How long was the day-and-night schedule that the men began living to?*

R6 They stayed awake for 36 hours and slept for 12.
Q6 *How long did the men stay awake and asleep?*

R7 When they came out of the cave in January they thought it was November.
Q7 *How did the men miscalculate the months?*

R8 The certainty of the usefulness of the experiment helped one of the volunteers to go through with it.
Q8 *What helped one of the volunteers go through the experiment?*

R9 Information from the experiment may help scientists prepare astronauts for space travel.
Q9 *How may information from the experiment help scientists?*

Q10 Why did the men think they had been down for only three months? (I)
R10 *Since their days were longer, there were less days to count.*

Comprehension: IL: 7 correct responses

Block 2

SUMMARY

Errors in oral section: ◯

Self-correction ratio:
(Ratio of total self-corrections to all errors.)

Comprehension score: ◯

Semantic ratio:
(Ratio of semantically acceptable
errors to all errors.)

Level: Recreational Independent Frustration

Further Details:

(Note *outstanding* strengths and weaknesses in Inference, Reaction, Imagery, Critical thinking, Spontaneous recall, Rate,
Oral/silent comparison, etc.)

Word recognition: (Results of subtests, Levels B-E, and other relevant comments.)

Comment: (Note *significant* characteristics concerning attitudes, anxiety, dependence, and major needs.)

Reaction: What do you think would be hardest about living so long in a cave?

Imagery: What sort of beds did you see in your mind? Were there any special sounds or smells that you thought of?

Critical thinking: How would this experiment help scientists to understand how men might behave in space?
(Space travel also involves confinement, isolation, limited things to do, no natural way of measuring the passage of time, and being surrounded by an environment of darkness.)

An Informal Prose Inventory

Level G (11-12 years)

Name:

Age: **Date:**

Set: The way light behaves when it passes through transparent substances is fascinating. Let's read something about it.

Bent Sunlight

We see rainbows in many places: in the sky after

showers, in a droplet of water bathed in sunshine, or

in the angle at the edge of a mirror. In each case rays

of sunlight have been refracted, or bent, as they

passed through a transparent object. When the

objects have a polished surface, refraction causes the

colourless rays of sunlight to be broken up in to

seven visible colours — red, orange, yellow, green,

blue, indigo, and violet. A rainbow is formed in the

sky when tiny droplets of rain bend the sunshine as it

passes through them.

Oral — IL: up to 4 errors

Q1 What does the word *refraction* mean? (V)
  R1 *The bending of light rays.*

☐

Q2 When is colourless sunlight broken into seven colours? (L)
  R2 *When it is refracted by objects with a polished surface.*

☐

Q3 What weather conditions are required to form a rainbow in the sky? (I)
  R3 *Showery conditions with patches of sunshine.*

☐

Jottings:

Silent:

The brightness of our sky during daylight is also

caused by refraction. Particles of air in the

atmosphere bend sunlight in every possible direction.

We are surrounded by daylight coming from all

angles, whether or not we are in direct sunshine. We

can even see the underside of a table in a room

illuminated by daylight coming from the sky. This is

why it is quite light well before sunrise and well after

sunset. If sunlight were not refracted by our

atmosphere, the sky would be deep black and

star-filled even during the day — as it is from any

point in space.

Recall:

R4 The brightness of the sky during daylight is
also caused by refraction.
*Q4 What does refraction cause during
daylight?*

R5 Particles of air bend sunlight in every possible
direction.
Q5 How does the air affect sunlight?

R6 We can see the underside of a table in a room
illuminated by daylight.
*Q6 What can we see in a room illuminated
by daylight?*

R7 This is why it is light before sunrise and after
sunset.
*Q7 Why is it light before the sun rises and
after it sets:*

R8 If sunlight were not refracted by the
atmosphere, the sky would be deep black and
star-filled even during the day.
*Q8 How would the sky appear during
daytime if it were not for the
atmosphere?*

R9 The sky is black and star-filled from any point
in space.
Q9 How does the sky appear from space?

Q10 Why are we unable to see stars in our sky
during daytime? (l)
*R10 A satisfactory answer should include the
idea of sunlight being refracted by the
atmosphere. The idea of sunlight alone is
inadequate.*

Block 2

SUMMARY

Errors in oral section: ◯

Self-correction ratio:
(Ratio of total self-corrections to all errors.)

Comprehension score: ◯

Semantic ratio:
(Ratio of semantically acceptable errors to all errors.)

Level: Recreational Independent Frustration

Further Details:

(Note *outstanding* strengths and weaknesses in Inference, Reaction, Imagery, Critical thinking, Spontaneous recall, Rate, Oral/silent comparison, etc.)

Word recognition: (Results of subtests, Levels B-E, and other relevant comments.)

Comment: (Note *significant* characteristics concerning attitudes, anxiety, dependence, and major needs.)

Block 4

Q11 Why are you able to see the underside of an aeroplane flying overhead?

R11 Because sunlight is refracted or bent in all directions by the atmosphere (or a similar account of the basic principle).

Comprehension — IL: 7 correct responses

Reaction: What would you miss most about our world if you were in space?

Critical thinking: The report leaves out something very important when it states that the polished surface of transparent objects breaks sunlight up into seven colours. We know that the flat surface of a sheet of glass or a mirror does not produce a rainbow when sunlight passes through it.
What else do you think should have been said about the surface?
(From the instances given of raindrops and the bevelled edge of a mirror it may be inferred that the surface must be curved or angular as in a prism.)

Imagery: What did you see in your mind when it said, '... from any point in space'?

Block 3

Word recognition skills

Syllabification: Full syllabification should present no problem at this level. Indicated by difficulty with:

transparent   polished   refracted   refraction   visible indigo

An Informal Prose Inventory

Level H (12-13 years)

Name: **Age:**   **Date:**

Set: This article is about a strange place to live.

Underwater Habitat

"It was a nice place to visit, but I wouldn't want to

live there", reported John Van Derwalker, one of four

marine scientists who "splashed-up" after a

record-breaking sixty days of living under the sea.

Of the four men taking part in Project Tektite I, two

were oceanographers, one was a geologist, the other

a fishery biologist. Their habitat, which was based

about forty seven feet underwater off St. John, Virgin

Islands, was made up of two vertical cylinders, each

eighteen feet tall and twelve and a half feet in

diameter.

Oral — IL: up to 4 errors

Q1 How many months did the scientists spend
underwater? (L)
R1 Two months (60 days). ☐

Q2 How far underwater did the scientists live? (L)
R2 About 47 feet. ☐

Q3 Why was the term *splashed-up* placed in
quotation marks? (I)
*R3 It is not a normal word — it is made on
the model of splash-down.* ☐

Silent:

As the scientists ventured outside of their habitat each day to map the ocean floor and study marine life, they were objects of study to Project Tektite sponsors: the U.S. Navy, the National Aeronautics and Space Administration (NASA), and the General Electric Company.

NASA was especially interested in learning what physical and mental problems might crop up while scientists work in isolated conditions. The men could not easily return to the surface. Underwater they breathed pressurized nitrogen and oxygen to counter-balance sea pressure on the bottom. They had to spend twenty hours in a special decompression chamber to help them rid their systems of nitrogen before they could re-enter sea-level atmosphere.

Recall:

R4 The scientists left their habitat each day to map the ocean floor and study marine life.
Q4 *What did the scientists do each day?*

R5 They were studied in turn by the sponsors of the project.
Q5 *Who studied the scientists?*

R6 The sponsors were the U.S. Navy, NASA, and the General Electric Company.
Q6 *Who were the sponsors?*

R7 NASA was interested in the physical and mental problems of working in isolated conditions.
Q7 *What was NASA interested in finding out?*

R8 Underwater the men breathed pressurized oxygen and nitrogen to counterbalance sea pressure.
Q8 *What did the men breathe underwater?*

SUMMARY

Errors in oral section: ◯ ◯

Self-correction ratio:
(Ratio of total self-corrections to all errors.)

Comprehension score:

Semantic ratio:
(Ratio of semantically acceptable errors to all errors.)

Level: Recreational Independent Frustration

Further Details:

(Note *outstanding* strengths and weaknesses in Inference, Reaction, Imagery, Critical thinking, Spontaneous recall, Rate, Oral/silent comparison, etc.)

Word recognition: (Results of subtests, Levels B-E, and other relevant comments.)

Comment: (Note *significant* characteristics concerning attitudes, anxiety, dependence, and major needs.)

Block 4

R9 They had to spend 20 hours in a decompression chamber to help rid their systems of nitrogen before they could re-enter sea-level atmosphere.
Q9 What did they have to do before they could re-enter sea-level atmosphere?

Q10 What does the term *habitat* mean in this context? (V)
R10 It means special living unit like a house under water.

Comprehension — IL: 7 correct responses

Reaction: What did the scientist mean by saying, 'It was a nice place to *visit*'?

Imagery: What do you think the interior of the habitat looked like? Did you have any special feeling about it — smell, etc?

Critical and creative thinking: Why do you think the US Navy and the General Electric Company were sponsors?
(Navy interested in underwater work — rescue, repair ships, sabotage. General Electric interested in special problems of electric power underwater — batteries?)

□

□

Advanced structural analysis and syllabification:
Indicated by difficulty with:

oceanographers biologist habitat vertical cylinders diameter ventured Aeronautics Administration pressurized counterbalance decompression

Block 3

An Informal Prose Inventory

Level I (13-14 years)

Name: **Age:**   **Date:**

Set: Nations can help each other and help themselves.

Rebuilding War-Torn Europe

At the end of World War II in 1945, the nations of Europe — both victors and vanquished — found themselves near economic collapse. To rescue these nations and revive their economies, the United States devised its first large-scale foreign aid plan, called the Marshall Plan. By establishing this programme, the U.S. not only hoped to rebuild these war-torn nations but also to stem the spread of communism in Western Europe.

The war had left in its wake a heavy toll of destruction. After the last bomb had fallen and the final bullet had been fired, many nations lay in ruins. These conditions of unprecedented destruction threatened the political stability of many nations, and America feared that traditional forms of democracy may give way to communism. This fear was heightened by the emergence of Russia as a world power second only to the United States, and as the dominating influence in restructuring the patterns of government in Eastern European nations.

Oral: Up to 5 errors.

Q1 What was the condition of most European countries in 1945? (L)
R1 Near economic collapse. ☐

Q2 Why did the US devise the Marshall Plan? (L)
R2 To help rebuild the war-torn nations of Western Europe and prevent the spread of Communism. ☐

Q3 From the evidence given here, why did the Marshall Plan not apply to all European nations? (I)
   R3   Eastern European nations were under the influence of Russia.

Silent:

With U.S. aid supporting the tremendous energy and determination of the people, the factories and the farms of Western Europe began producing again. By 1951, industrial production was forty per cent higher than before the war.

The newly reconstructed nations were soon operating as strong parliamentary democracies, resistant to communist influences, and a powerful counter-balance to the Russian satellite countries of Eastern Europe. The Marshall Plan proved an extraordinary success in this post-war European context.

The fact that it placed more emphasis on economic recovery than on military aid may account in some measure for this phenomenal success, especially when compared with foreign aid programmes applied later in other parts of the world, such as Israel or Vietnam. However, the long history of vigorous civilization and representational government among the people of Europe was undoubtedly the most important contributing factor in the success of the Marshall Plan.

Recall:

R4 Contents of first paragraph.
   Q4   Question omissions in recall.

R5 Contents of second paragraph.
   Q5   Question omissions in recall.

R6 Contents of third paragraph.
   Q6   Question omissions in recall.

Q7 What does the word *context* mean as used in the phrase, 'in this post-war European context'? (V)
   R7   Situation or set of conditions.

SUMMARY

Errors in oral section:

Self-correction ratio:
(Ratio of total self-corrections to all errors.)

Comprehension score:

Semantic ratio:
(Ratio of semantically acceptable errors to all errors.)

Level: Recreational Independent Frustration

Further Details:

(Note *outstanding* strengths and weaknesses in Inference, Reaction, Imagery, Critical thinking, Spontaneous recall, Rate, Oral/silent comparison, etc.)

Word recognition: (Results of subtests, Levels B-E, and other relevant comments.)

Comment: (Note *significant* characteristics concerning attitudes, anxiety, dependence, and major needs.)

Block 4

Block 3

Q8 The author implies that the comparative failure of foreign aid programmes in other parts of the world at a later date may have been caused by a change of emphasis from economic to military aid. What other cause could be implied from what he says about the reasons for success of the Marshall Plan? (I)

  R8   Other countries may have lacked a long history of responsible representative government.

Q9 What political bias does the author display, if any? (I)

  R9   He writes fairly objectively but displays some favour for parliamentary democracy. In particular, he links 'vigorous civilization' with 'representational government' in the last sentence, and he speaks of 'rebuilding' Western European nations in contrast to Russian influence in 'restructuring the patterns of government' in Eastern Europe.

Comprehension — IL: 7 correct responses

Reaction: How did the author make you feel about the people of Western Europe?

Imagery: What did you associate in your mind with the political stability of many nations being threatened?

Critical thinking: From the evidence in this short passage, how responsible do you think this writer is in giving his account of events? What evidence can you point to in the text to bear out your judgement?

(The author is generally careful to qualify what he says as in, 'in this post-war European context' and 'America feared that', and he uses appropriately tentative phrases such as, 'may account in some measure for'. The evidence he states or implies is generally adequate for his conclusions such as, the 'extraordinary success' of the Marshall Plan. However, he is surprisingly dogmatic in the statement of his favoured interpretation without presenting adequate evidence in the last sentence — note the 'undoubtely the most important').

Appendix B
Basic Sight Words in Context

The List

A list of heavy-duty words arranged roughly in order of utility in reading, with learning contexts which display them at their centre of usage in children's speech. The list includes:
a.   280 high-frequency relational words including the Dolch List of 220 words.
b.   70 high-frequency nouns of some phonetic difficulty.
c.   56 middle-frequency relational words which are likely to occur as head words in English constructions (and therefore often need to be recognised at sight before contextual possibilities become apparent.)

Using the List

1. This list may be used not only to test basic sight vocabulary but also to discover a suitable learning context at the moment of testing. Cover the contexts and allow the child to proceed down the list until he fails to recognise a word, misreads a word, hesitates or wavers between two possibilities.
2. Slip down the cover sheet exposing the contexts for that word. Allow the child to study them or ask him to read them. Almost without exception he will work out the word with complete assurance.
3. Praise his success, note the context which assisted him, and proceed. From the moment of testing, that particular context becomes a certain means of discrimination which can be relied on by both teacher and child.
4. If the contexts listed fail to provide unaided identification of the word, note the word and proceed through the test. Return to that word after a few weeks.
5. Continue through the test only far enough to collect the few words required for learning in the next week or ten days.
6. Prepare learning cards (approximately 3 ins. by 1 in.) printing the isolated word on one side and the successful context on the other. In many cases the child will be able to use the list after testing to make out his own learning cards.

Using the Learning Cards

The child checks *himself* with these cards two or three times daily. At each learning he places in one heap all the cards he knew at sight, and in a second heap all those for which he required help from the context. He then proceeds *immediately* through the second pack again, dividing in the same way. This means that he may see the words causing persistent difficulty three or four times at each learning session. Similar cards for other learning tasks such as phonetic clue words, or substitution lists (see *Appendix C*) may also be included

in the pack. With a current learning pack of fifteen to twenty cards, each learning session takes no longer than two to three minutes. **Check this list every week or ten days.**

1. Extract the cards known by sight — immediate, automatic, assured response.
2. Have the child file these in alphabetical order in a personal Reference File — they are too valuable to lose.
3. Keep a master card on which the accumulating total is recorded.
4. Give praise for success.
5. Proceed through test to collect learnings for next period.
6. Check the Reference File for words requiring revision once or twice a term.

For older retarded readers, use an individual heat-copy of the list. The student learns by using a cover card. Do not overload the learner.

Advantages of a contextual approach

This testing and learning procedure has important advantages over isolated word study:

a. The results of testing are put to immediate use in learning.
b. The test builds confidence instead of further destroying it.
    The child comes out of the test situation with assurance that he can use these contexts to solve his word problems without depending on outside aid.
c. Independence in word solving is encouraged from the beginning.
d. The skill he uses in ascertaining the words for himself is the most important skill which he needs in normal reading — his confidence and ability in using context clues is reinforced.
e. He learns to see words as part of a larger language pattern which he has already mastered in speaking and listening, instead of seeing them as a series of isolated problems with visually confusing traps.
f. The teacher is given the opportunity during testing to offer sincere praise for genuine success *following each initial failure*. This is a necessity for remedial teaching which is seldom possible in classroom work.

Persistent confusions

When a child experiences persistent confusion over a particular word in his learning file for two or three weeks, use one of the tracing procedures based on the work of Grace Fernald. You will find instructions in many professional texts. However, classroom teachers are able to work most effectively with the contextual materials provided here, and this other powerful but time-consuming procedure should be kept fresh for use with persistent confusions only. Since you will wish to obtain the maximum impact when you *do* use a tracing procedure, a sand tray with finely sifted sand covering a brightly coloured base will prove a useful aid.

The bed-rock sight vocabulary.

The following words of extremely high frequency have been used freely in the learning contexts, and may be taken as a 'bed-rock' sight vocabulary. If any of them is unknown, try one or more simple personal contexts until one is found which brings the word to the child's mind without aid. Use words which have already been recognised. For instance, if the child knows all except **big** and **said** you could try something like:

We have a **big** car.	*or*	Dad is a **big** man.
"Come in the car," **said** Dad.	*or*	Mother **said** I can go.

It is not necessary for all words in a context to be known sight words — the one important thing is that the child is able to identify the unknown word **without any form of aid** from the teacher. The test of this is to write or display the context **without comment**.

(1-20)

---

a	in	he	am	the	big	will	said	come	Mother
it	I	is	go	me	car	and	Dad	look	home

Before beginning the next section enter the following personal names on the child's individual record as indicated for use in personal contexts where required:

brother:

sister:

friend:

uncle:

aunt:

cousin:

---

like	I like my mother. I like ice-cream. I like	21
get	Get in the car. Go and get me an apple.	22
have	Can I have one please? Have a good time! I have	23
can	I can do that. I can run fast.	24
do	I can do that. I saw him do it.	25
boy	I am a boy. .... is a boy.	26
to	Come to me. I like to help Dad.	27
see	I can see you. Can you see me?	28
good	Good boy. Good girl. That was a good book.	29
you	I like you. You are mad.	30
no	No you don't. "Yes or no."	31
here	Here we go. Come here	32
girl	I am a girl. .... is a girl. You are a pretty girl.	33
all	Can we all go? Is that all you can do?	34
up	Get up. Go up to the top.	35

at	Look at me. Look at that.	36
that	I can do that. Don't do that.	37
one	I want that one. Can I have that one please?	38
this	Look at this. Did you do this?	39
she	See that girl — she is pretty. (She is my sister/is mad.)	40
of	I like him best of all. Can I have one of those please?	41
was	That was a big one. It was good fun.	42
we	We can go in the car. Can we all go?	43
jump	See me jump. That made you jump.	44
are	We are going in the car. Are you coming home?	45
play	Come and play over here.	46
down	Up and down. Get down from there.	47
my	I like my Mother. That is my book.	48
live	I live at	49
thing	Look at that thing. Don't get into my things.	50
when	You say when. When can I come?	51
new	We have a new car. That's a new one on me.	52
did	I did it. Did you do this?	53
name	My name is	54
yes	Yes I can. Yes I will.	55
run	I can run fast. Run home.	56
with	Come with me. I went with my mother.	57
don't	I don't like him. No you don't.	58
what	See what I can do. What is your name?	59
little	She is a little girl. A little bit.	60
take	Take one. Take me with you. Take a look at that.	61
put	Put that book down. Where did you put it?	62
him	I will go with him. .... is my friend. I like him.	63
on	On we go. Get on the horse.	64
some	Can I have some of that? That is some car.	65
his	He likes his mother. That's not mine — it's his.	66
went	I went home. The children went mad.	67
into	Get into the car. Don't get into my things.	68

not	I did not. That is not mine.	69
has	He has my book. Has the postman been yet?	70
two	I saw two of them. Two big eyes.	71
know	I know I can do it. I don't know him.	72
can't	I can't do it. I can't come today.	73
her	Her name is .... is my friend — I like her.	74
brother	.... is my brother. I have no brother.	75
over	Up and over. I can't get over it.	76
three	One, two, three, go!	77
sister	.... is my sister. I have no sister.	78
them	See them go. I want one of them.	79
make	Did you make it up? Make a cake.	80
away	Run away. Get away from me.	81
for	One for me. What did you do that for?	82
walk	I walk to school. I walk home.	83
they	Mr. and Mrs. .... They are my father and mother.	84
way	Do you know the way home? That is the way to do it.	85
going	I'm going home. I am going with you.	86
where	Where are you going? Where did you put it?	87
give	Give me a go. Give it to me.	88
very	I like him very much. She is a very good girl.	89
got	Look what I've got. I got in the car.	90
bring	Bring it to me. Did you bring your book?	91
fall	Look out — don't fall. I will fall down.	92
too	It is too hot in the sun. I like Jim and he likes me too.	93
by	Can I sit by you? I can do it by myself.	94
let	Let me do it. Don't let go. A house to let.	95
be	Be a good boy. I want to be a	96
fast	The car went fast. I can run fast.	97
want	I want that one. Do you want it?	98
only	I only want one. That is my only one.	99
made	You made me do it. What is is made of?	100
been	Where have you been. We have been out.	101

read	I can read now. Read a book.	102
off	Get off the garden. I fell off the wall.	103
(*Check colours*: **red, blue, green, black, white, yellow, brown**).		104-110
now	What will he do now? I can read now.	111
tell	Tell me a story. Don't tell lies. I won't tell you.	112
under	Hide under the bed. Dad got under the car.	113
four	There were four of us in the car. One, two, three, four.	114
ask	Don't ask me. Did you ask him for it?	115
its	The cat likes its milk. Give the dog its bone.	116
saw	I saw you do it. I saw him go.	117
water	Water is wet. Give me a drink of water.	118
top	Up on top. Run up to the top of the hill.	119
think	I think I can do it. What do you think?	120
head	I can stand on my head. Use your head.	121
about	What is this all about? Tell me about it.	122
does	Where does this go? He does what he likes.	123
five	One, two, three, four five, I caught a fish alive.	124
from	Where did you come from? It is not far from here.	125
who	Who do you think you are? Who is that?	126
had	Mum said I had to go home.	127
eat	Can I have something to eat please?	128
long	Wait for me — I won't be long.	129
old	Dad is an old man. As old as the hills.	130
an	Can I have an apple? He is an old man.	131
our	That is our car. Come in our car.	132
those	What are those things over there?	133
could	You could if you tried. Do you think he could?	134
right	That's right. This is the right way to do it.	135
soon	Dad will soon be home. I will come soon.	136
I'll	That's what I'll do. I'll come when I can.	137
six	I get up at six o'clock. Five, six, pick up sticks.	138
try	Have a try. Try, try, try, again.	139
then	What will we do then? I'll go, then you come too.	140

but	Yes I'll come, but not now. No-one went but me.	141
won't	The car won't go. No I won't.	142
as	I'll come as fast as I can. As big as a house.	143
light	Put on the light. Light the fire.	144
if	Come if you can. I'll come if I can.	145
more	Can I have some more please?	146
any	Do you want any more? Are there any over?	147
before	Girls before boys.	148
stop	Can't you stop that? Stop or I fire!	149
out	Get out of my way. Run out to play.	150
children	Children go to school. I like little children.	151
us	Come with us. That belongs to us.	152
were	You were there — I saw you. What were you doing?	153
please	Can I have one please? May I go now please?	154
next	It's my turn — I'm next. What will you do next?	155
just	I'll just be a minute or two. Just a little for me.	156
your	What is your name? Is this your car?	157
ride	Ride him cowboy. Go for a ride in the car.	158
help	Help, murder, Police. I can't help it.	159
call	Did you call me? What do you call that?	160
there	There she goes. Put it down there.	161
sleep	I want to go to sleep. We sleep at night.	162
cold	As cold as ice. The water is cold.	163
pretty	I like pretty girls. That girl is pretty.	164
cried	He fell over and cried. He cried to go home.	165
round	A ball is round.	166
funny	Don't try to be funny. You think you're funny.	167
came	Dad came home from work. The postman came.	168
other	Not that one — the other one.	169
ran	He ran fast. I hit him and he ran away.	170
work	Get on with your work. Dad is at work.	171
first	I came first in the race. I was first to get here.	172
high	Go up high. I like going high on a swing.	173

myself	I'll do it myself. I fell over and hurt myself.	174
after	Don't run after me all the time. I can do it after all.	175
cut	Stop that! Cut it out will you! I cut my foot.	176
lady	We have a lady teacher. .... is a lady.	177
thank	Thank you very much.	178
I'm	I'm going — are you? See what I'm doing.	179
colour	What colour is your hair? .... is my favourite colour.	180
again	Here we are again. Don't do it again.	181
well	I don't feel well.	182
how	How did that happen? Let me show you how to do it.	183
farm	Cows on the farm. Pigs on the farm.	184
keep	Keep off the grass. Can I keep it for myself?	185
sit	Sit down.	186
people	What will people say? Too many people.	187
these	What are these things here?	188
left	I left my coat at school.	189
finish	Did you finish your work? I'll finish that job tomorrow.	190
seven	There are seven days in the week.	191
gone	Where has he gone?	192
why	Tell my why you did it. I know why you came.	193
tomorrow	I'll see you tomorrow.	194
ate	I ate all my dinner. He ate all the apples.	195
it's	Give it to me. It's mine. It's a big one.	196
many	How many do you want? I have many friends.	197
warm	It is warm in bed. As warm as toast.	198
done	I've done all my work. What have you done with it?	199
would	Would you like to come? He said he would come.	200
hot	The sun is hot. My dinner is too hot.	201
open	Open the door. I can't get it open.	202
talk	He won't talk to me. Don't talk all the time.	203
their	They came in their new car. I like their house.	204
pull	Don't pull my hair. Pull your socks up.	205
fire	Light the fire. Put out that fire.	206

may	May I go? You may go now.	207
goes	Off she goes. There she goes.	208
small	I lost my small ball. He is a small boy.	209
find	Help me find my ball. I can't find where it is.	210
draw	I can draw a good picture. Draw it on paper.	211
fly	The aeroplane can fly. Kill that fly.	212
pick	Pick that up. Pick one for me.	213
gave	I gave him a hiding. Who gave you that?	214
every	Every now and then. School every day.	215
which	Which one of you did this? Tell me which one you want.	216
knock	Knock on the door. I'll knock your head off.	217
foot	Get off my foot. You stood on my foot.	218
hard	I like hard work. That is too hard.	219
might	She might let me go. I might come if Mum lets me.	220
different	I do it a different way. That one looks different to me.	221
each	You can have one each.	222
took	Who took my pencil? It took a long time to get there.	223
lost	I lost my way home. What have you lost?	224
dark	It is getting dark outside. It is dark at night.	225
friend	Who is your best friend? .... is my best friend.	226
same	They are all just the same. We go home at the same time.	227
far	Don't go too far away. That's not far to go.	228
found	Look what I found. What's that you've found?	229
piece	Can I have a piece of cake please?	230
ever	Have you ever been in an aeroplane? The best I ever saw.	231
front	Don't come in the front door.	232
party	Mum gave me a birthday party. I'm coming to your party.	233
break	Don't break that cup. That will break my back.	234
push	Help me push the car. I'll push you over.	235
or	You stop that or look out. Is that for you or me?	236
buy	Go to the shop and buy one. What did you buy?	237
so	I told you so. So it was **you**.	238
kind	I like him — he is a kind man. That's a funny kind of hat.	239

wish	I wish I could go too. I wish we had a car like that.	240
carry	Help me carry these things home. You carry the little one.	241
today	Get it done today. I'll do it today.	242
eye	Hit him in the eye. I've got my eye on you.	243
ready	Ready, set, go! All ready to go.	244
thought	I thought I could do it. I thought so.	245
heard	I heard you the first time. I heard all about that.	246
around	Stop running around. Don't run around the room.	247
meet	I'll meet you there. Meet me at the shops.	248
box	Put it in a box. I'll box your ears.	249
must	You must come again. You **must** have done it.	250
chair	Sit in this chair.	251
sing	Sing a song of sixpence. Sing baby to sleep.	252
naughty	Don't be a naughty boy.	253
mouth	Take that out of your mouth. Shut your mouth.	254
bridge	The road goes over the bridge.	255
upon	Once upon a time	256
road	Run down the road. Get out of my road.	257
once	Once upon a time - - - - - I was a baby once.	258
together	All pull together. Let's all do it together.	259
behind	Look behind you. He came at me from behind.	260
begin	Where do you begin? I will have to begin again.	261
laugh	Don't laugh at me. It was so funny I had to laugh.	262
show	Show me the way home. Show me how to do it.	263
face	She has a pretty face. Don't pull a face at me.	264
always	I always do it like that. He is always the same.	265
much	I don't like him much. That is much too big.	266
bought	I bought it at the shop with my own money.	267
build	Let's build a hut. I can built a bigger one.	268
best	I like him best. .... is my best friend.	269
because	I did it because I had to. I like you because you are nice.	270
grow	Grow up. How does your garden grow?	271
better	You had better go home now. I feel better now.	272

clean	Are your hands clean?	273
through	He ran through the door.	274
write	Write your name here.	275
never	I will never do that again.	276
both	Come here both of you.	277
shall	What **shall** I do?	278
own	I did it all on my own. I own a bike.	279
hurt	I fell over and hurt my leg. You can't hurt me.	280
eight	Breakfast at eight o'clock.	281
wash	Wash your face and hands before dinner.	282
full	Three bags full. No more thank you — I'm full.	283
use	Use your head. I know what to use that for.	284
wasn't	It wasn't me. I wasn't there.	285
care	I don't care. What do you care?	286
still	Are you still here? Stand still.	287
early	Get up early in the morning. I get to school early.	288
last	This is the last one left. Can I be last?	289
most	I like him the most. I like that one most of all.	290
above	The blue sky above. Put one above the other.	291
quiet	Sit still and be quiet. Keep quiet.	292
sure	I am sure I can do that.	293
bottle	A bottle of pills. Take out the milk bottle.	294
knife	Cut it with a knife.	295
start	When do we start? The car won't start.	296
such	Don't make such a row. We had such a good time.	297
answered	I answered you the first time. I answered the telephone.	298
back	Danger — stand back! Get off my back.	299
nearly	We are nearly there. I nearly did it.	300
hour	It took an hour to get home.	301
engine	Did you see the fire engine? The car engine stopped.	302
belong	Does that belong to you?	303
also	He was there also. I want one of those also.	304
cupboard	The cups are in the cupboard.	305

guess	Guess who came today. Guess what I've got.	306
pencil	Can someone lend me a pencil please?	307
breakfast	I got up too late for breakfast.	308
cousin	.... is my cousin.	309
wrong	That is the wrong way. What's wrong with you?	310
below	Down below. His head was below the water.	311
mean	What do you mean by that? I didn't mean to do it.	312
kept	I just kept on going. I kept one for you.	313
even	One for you — now we are even. Even you can do that.	314
whose	Whose bag is this? Do you know whose it is?	315
heavy	That's too heavy to carry.	316
knew	I knew I could do it. He said he knew you.	317
rough	This is a rough road. Don't be rough with the baby.	318
notice	I didn't notice you there. What does it say on the notice?	319
listen	You won't listen to what I say. Listen to the birds.	320
wear	What will I wear to go out? Don't wear yourself out.	321
lose	Did you lose your coat? Don't lose your head.	322
touch	I didn't touch it. I can just touch the bottom.	323
money	You get lots of money for working.	324
drink	Have a drink of tea. Coca Cola is a good drink.	325
shoe	My shoe won't fit you. Put on your shoes.	326
class	Our class is the best at school.	327
enough	Have you had enough to eat yet? Stop. That's enough.	328
used	I'm not used to riding a horse. The paper is all used up.	329
either	I don't like him, and he doesn't like me either. You can have either this one or that one.	330
clothes	Keep your clothes clean. Hang the clothes on the line.	331
handle	I broke the handle of the cup.	332
half	Give me half your apple. I'm only half awake.	333
watch	Watch out — that dog might go for you.	334
key	The back door key is lost. Where is the car key?	335
queen	God save the Queen.	336
uncle	My favourite uncle is Uncle	337
aunt	My favourite aunty is Aunty	338

fell	I fell over and hurt myself.	339
quite	It cost quite a lot. I can't quite reach it.	340
young	You are too young to stay out late.	341
lovely	What a lovely day!	342
close	Close the door. Don't come too close.	343
city	This bus goes to the city.	344
busy	I can't come now — I'm too busy.	345
glad	I'm glad you came.	346
twelve	. . . ten, eleven, twelve.	347
comb	Did you comb your hair?	348
already	Are you back already? I've done that already.	349
between	Stand between the two of us.	350
except	Everyone except me got a cake.	351
often	I often get home late. I hope you will come often.	352
weigh	How much do you weigh?	353
dare	Don't you dare take my bike. I dare you to do it.	354
real	We had real fun. What is his real name?	355
scissors	Cut it with the scissors.	356
biscuit	Can I have a biscuit to eat, please Mum?	357
police	I'll call the police. The police are after him.	358
sugar	Sugar is sweet. I take sugar in my tea.	359
word	That's a hard word. I give you my word I won't tell.	360
parcel	What's in the parcel? The postman brought a parcel.	361
usual	Rain again as usual. That's the usual way to do it.	362
saucer	Cup and saucer.	363
minute	Wait a minute. I won't be a minute.	364
dance	The clowns did a silly dance. I like to dance.	365
caught	I got wet and caught a cold.	366
soldier	He got shot when he was a soldier.	367
dead	They shot him dead.	368
wolf	Little Red Riding Hood and the big bad wolf.	369
circus	There are lots of elephants at the circus.	370
giant	Jack the giant-killer. Jack killed the giant.	371
shovel	You need a pick and shovel for this job.	372

country	Farmers live in the country. N.Z. is a small country.	373
fruit	Don't pick the fruit. I like sweet fruit.	374
square	I like to play four square. A square peg in a round hole.	375
straight	Come straight home.	376
though	I'd like to go. It's a long way though.	377
able	I'm not able to come.	378
month	What month were you born? I'll come next month.	379
island	Tasmania is an island. The North Island of New Zealand.	380
river	The boat sailed up the river.	381
oven	Put the cakes in the oven.	382
double	If the paper is too big, double it over.	383
favourite	That's my favourite colour. .... are my favourite	384
tongue	Hold your tongue. Put out your tongue.	385
chimney	The smoke went up the chimney.	386
salt	Pass me the salt please. Salt and pepper please.	387
earn	I earn some money. How much do you earn at work?	388
shirt	Put on a clean shirt.	389
machine	Put them in the washing machine. It is made by machine.	390
sauce	I like sauce on my meat. Pass the tomato sauce.	391
large	We have a large car. They have a large house.	392
roll	Roll the ball to me. Rock and roll.	393
whether	I don't know whether I can come or not.	394
garage	Put the car in the garage.	395
voice	Yell at the top of your voice.	396
world	All over the world. A trip around the world.	397
climb	Can you climb up that tree?	398
neither	Mum said neither of us could go.	399
whole	The best in the whole wide world. I ate the whole lot.	400
angry	Don't make me angry. I'll get angry with you.	401
beautiful	It is a beautiful day. She is a beautiful girl.	402
believe	I don't believe you. I can't believe that.	403
cover	Don't draw on the cover of the book.	404
fierce	A fierce lion. A fierce Indian chief.	405
forward	Pull your chair forward. Put your best foot forward.	406

Appendix C

A Simplified Progression of Word Recognition Skills

The following checklist summarizes the important print-related learnings of the pre-reading or emergent literacy stage. For further details see Holdaway (1979) pp. 38-80. See also Butler and Clay (1980) pp. 5-28, and Clay (1980) *Concepts About Print*.

Literacy Set

A. MOTIVATIONAL FACTORS (High expectations of print)
Enjoys books and stories — appreciates the special rewards of print.
Has had extensive, repetitive experience of a wide range of favourite books.
Seeks book experiences — asks for stories, goes to books independently.
Is curious about all aspects of print, e.g. signs, labels, advertisements.
Experiments with producing written language.

B. LINGUISTIC FACTORS (Familiarity with written dialect in oral form)
Has built extensive models for the special features of written dialect.
Syntax – grammatical structures learned through meaningful use. e.g. full forms of contractions such as 'I'm' or 'What's', structures which imply consequence, e.g. 'If . . . then . . .'
Vocabulary – words not normally used in conversation e.g. 'however', 'dine'.
Intonation Patterns – appropriate intonations for literary or non-conversational English e.g. 'Fat, indeed! The very idea of it!'
Idioms – Special usage contrary to normal grammatical or semantic rules e.g. same example as for intonation.

C. OPERATIONAL FACTORS (Strategies for handling written language)
Self-monitoring operations: Self-correction and confirmation.
Predictive operations: Ability to 'use the context' to fill language slots.
Structural operations: Ability to follow plot, temporal and causal sequences, logical arrangements, etc.
Non-situational operations: Ability to understand language without the help of immediate sensory context.
Imaginative operations: Ability to create images which have not been experienced or represented in sensory reality, and apply metaphorical meanings.

D. ORTHOGRAPHIC FACTORS (Knowledge of the conventions of print)
Story comes from print, not from pictures.
Directional conventions — a complex progression:
    Front of book has spine on left; Story begins where print begins
    Left hand page comes before right; Move from top to bottom of page
    Begin left along line to right; Return to next line on left margin
Print components — clear concept of 'words', 'spaces', 'letters'
Letter-form generalizations — same letter may be written in upper and lower
    case, and in different print styles
Punctuation conventions
Phonetic principle — letters have some relationship to speech sounds
Consistency principle — same word always has same spelling

Level A 5-6 years   Emergent to Early Reading

1. Establish what reading is about

a. It always makes sense — its end is not saying words but understanding.

This is the central theme which should run through all reading instruction — an emphasis never lost, even in the apparently automatic or analytical skills.
An insistent demand for meaning is fundamental to the operation of reading skill.

b. It is based on the familiar forms of spoken language.

The children should see reading as a reflection of the language they speak.
Experience-reading techniques are important in achieving this perspective.

c. It involves visual conventions of print representing the sounds of language.

The conventions of print should be seen as symbols for the sounds of speech.
An interest in print detail and a heightened interest in speech sounds are necessary to economic learning of reading skills.

2. Establish a reading set

a. Apply good listening habits to reading.

Read to the children with all the skill in choice of material and in presentation you have at your disposal. Achieve skilled listening to book language.

b. Induce an active tone of expectation from stories:
— predict outcomes
— predict vocabulary

Induce the children to predict actively and with growing precision. Seek to produce an attitude of optimistic problem-solving. Ask 'What will happen now?' 'What do you think he will say?' etc. Pause in reading and allow the children to complete sentences, predict vocabulary, fill gaps.

c. Induce a desire to read.

Make books a joyful part of the children's daily lives.

3. Establish directional habits

a. Begin left top.

Children should handle books and see you handle books in such a way as to learn directional conventions as automatic reflexes.

b. Proceed left to right, back and down.

Pointing is an aid at this stage. Any attempt to use phonetic associations before the directional habits have been achieved must cause confusion.

c. Double meaning of terms *beginning* and *end* for print and for speech.

Phonetic analysis is a directional skill. When attending to print, the term *beginning* means *left*. When attending to sounds, the term *beginning* means *first in time*.

d. Active and accurate matching.

Children need to make an eye-ear-voice link with words, and later with letters and sounds.

4. Identify print forms

a. Sentence line.

b. Words — identified by spaces — related to spoken words in a one-to-one relationship

By reading *with* the teacher, following the line and contributing to word-solving, children may learn to recognize the sentence form, the word form and the letter form. Words are the smallest movable units in speech and they are clearly demarcated in print: children should habitually match the spoken word and the printed word set off by spaces in the sentence line.

c. Letters.

5. Build a stock of sight words

   a. Names and items of high interest

Names, with their highly personal meaning and their highly distinctive shape, are often the first words recognized at sight.

   b. Basic sight vocabulary

See *Appendix B* for the teaching of basic sight vocabulary — which is a major task of this stage.

   c. Personal sight vocabulary.

Encourage children to learn also words of high personal interest to them.

6. Prepare for later analysis and association

   a. A rich extension of spoken language experience.

Many stories and poems read to the children, read in unison, talked about, and written about.

   b. Critical listening to beginning sounds and rhymes.

Use material such as McKee *Getting Ready* or Scott, Foresman *Open Highways* 'Starter Concept' material. Children's names. Verse and jingles.

   c. Auditory discrimination of major consonant sounds.

As for above. Begin with highly contrastive sounds, e.g. /m/ /s/ /k/ /t/. Avoid teaching confusables together, e.g. /m/ and /n/ /p/ and /b/. (The enclosing of the letter within oblique strokes indicates that it is the *sound* being discussed, not the letter itself.)

   d. Learning the letter names.

Best associated with learning to write the letters. Use children's names.

7. Teach letter-sound associations for the major consonants

See 6b and c above. Again begin with high contrasts and avoid confusables. Exclude x, z, q. Include ch, sh, th, wh.

8. Introduce a central method of word attack

CONTEXT plus INITIAL CONSONANT checked by SENSE (and final consonant)

See the chapter, *Developing Reading Skills*, for a thorough treatment. Note that checking is done by the child and not by the teacher:
Induce and encourage self-corrective habits. See Note 15.

Note 1:
The progression is intended as a guide in diagnosis and planning. Ages should be interpreted as Reading Levels — related, in particular, to the skills required for handling standard graded materials.

Note 2:
It may be salutory to point out before considering the representation of vowel sounds that English is a highly irregular language in this respect. Any rule must be qualified by 'normally' or 'usually' or 'probably' — it can never do more than point to a *possibility*. Children should be fully aware of this. Phonics is one cue which may in fact mislead — hence context must be given priority Accuracy and ease stem from the cross-reference of semantic, syntactic, and grapho-phonic cues. 'Context' is a combination of semantic and syntactic cues.

Level B Reading Level 6-7 years   Early Reading

1. Consolidate Level A

In particular, as consonant-letter sounds are studied, ensure that the habit of prior attention to initial letters is formed.

2. Establish knowledge of simple structural analysis

i.e. knowledge of common endings, prefixes, and compound words as the key to using structure to solve appropriate words, only.

Inflexions **-s -ed -ing -es -er**
Simple compound words
Prefixes: Initial **a** (as in *away*)
be-
Contractions: **-n't -'ll**
Apostrophe **s**
See *Developing Reading Skills*.

3. Establish a central method of attack

CONTEXT focused upon INITIAL CONSONANT or BLEND
CHECKED by sense and final letters.

This is the most important task at this level, all other skills fitting into their proper place as they are used to support the central method. Other skills are studied in association with solving real problems of word recognition by use of this method. See *Developing Reading Skills*.

4. Establish consonant-sound associations

both for single consonants (*b* in *bat*) and blends (*bl* in blue).
Establish clue words from sight vocabulary where necessary.

Group 1
Knowledge of letter-sound associations for all consonants except x z qu soft c and g.
Also speech consonants th wh sh ch. (If not complete in Level A).

Group 2
bl fl pl sl st
br cr dr fr gr tr str
x z qu

Group 3
sm sn sw pr cl gl tw kn wr sp spr
(Optional: scr sk squ thr)
Recognition of final consonants for checking purposes.
b d p ck st t g n m k nt nd sh ng ss l ll ch
Understanding that final e is silent.
(Note that the major purpose of substitution techniques, 5 below, is to consolidate initial consonant learnings.)

5. Teach substitution techniques.

i.e. substitution of initial consonants or blends forming new words which rhyme with the original.

a. Use only simple common words familiar to the children in spoken language — **not** e.g. *ban, tan, nan*, in studying *an*. (See Level A paragraph 1)
b. Use in context wherever possible.
c. At this stage substitution with rhyming groups based on the following words:
at an and make day ball get then tell it will thing night not down fun my

6. Provide auditory experience in the recognition of vowel-sounds

See manual or workbooks to any Basic Reader at this level. Substitition techniques provide a natural introduction, as do the techniques of checking.

7. Establish Knowledge of the letter-names

Much of this reference to letters by name will be associated with proving an intelligent guess. See Notes 10 and 15.

in distinction from letter-sounds so that the multiple sound associations of any given letter can be discussed without ambiguity (for instance, *t* in *ten, this, think,* and *listen.*)

Level C Reading Level 7-8 Early to Fluent Reading

1 **Consolidate Levels A and B**	In particular, consolidate the Central Method of Attack until it becomes second nature to approach words in this way.
2. **Establish proficiency in substitution.**	Groups built on the following words will prove adequate: **had, came, date, fast, dark, catch, race, rain, bang, car, cart, farm, walk, back, care, tail, tell, went, bread, hear, led, eat, nest, new, in, fine, hide, ice, kick, mile, find, old, hook, hop, song, fool, out, round, hose, mother,** and **jump.**
3. **Complete consonant knowledge**	Initial blends **scr sk squ thr** final consonants g le ce nk f sk Silent b, soft c and g

4. **Study in detail short and long sounds of the vowels**

Establish clue words for each major configuration. Bring out the typical isolation of the short vowel from the following vowels.

Short a
at can hand scratch
happen chapter candle

Long a
age make rain day
hating crazy table
For the other vowels, see below.
Begin by stating the nature of the problem, using known sight words. Certain other common vowel associations may be taught at this stage:

oo	school good	**ow**	cow blow		
ar	car	**or**	storm	**er**	*her*

5. **Begin teaching use of simple phonetic key.**	First, simple respelling, e.g. tough — tuff. Then the use of a simple key such as the Thorndike — any basic reading scheme provides progressions.
6. **Continue work in structural analysis**	Endings **-ly -y -er** (comparative) **-est -y** to **-ies -ied** Dropped silent e (restoration of the true root, e.g. *make* from *making*) Doubled consonant (ditto e.g. *sit* from *sitting*) Endings **-en -n -ful -less -self** Prefix **un-** Compound words Contractions.
7. **Recognition of the first syllable**	Work in syllabification can be commenced by inviting children to read up to the first middle consonant in words like *mid/dle* and *dif/ferent*, and later, *sand/wich* and *scamp/er*.

8. **Refine Central Method of Attack**

CONTEXT focused upon
FIRST SYLLABLE
CHECKED by sense and
subsequent syllables

See Chapter, *Developing Reading Skills*.

SHORT VOWELS		LONG VOWELS	
e egg	leg best stretch better bending	eat	need meat Pete be Peter
i in	sit kick spring kitten chicken fiddle	ice	ride pie right by silent
o on	hot song strong shopping pocket	open	hope coat go blow grocer
u up	fun shut sprung supper jumping	use	tube blue rude stupid truly
y		by	(long i)
		twenty	(long e in N.Z. speech)

Level D   Reading Level 8-9   Fluent Reading

1. Consolidate Levels A, B, and C.

In particular, use of growing vowel knowledge to determine the first syllable of multisyllabic words.

---

2. Complete vowel study including work with the phonetic key of a Thorndike type dictionary. Establish clue words for each major configuration.

Modified by r

ar	car		-are	care
			-air	hair
er	her		-ear	hear
ir	girl			
or	separate storm		-oar	roar
ur	hurt			

Modified by u and w

au	autumn		aw	draw
			ew	new blew
ou	out		ow	down blow

Modified by l

al	all		el	bell **ul** bull

Long and short oo: school   good

oi and oy

oi	boil		oy	boy

---

3. Continue structural analysis

Suffixes	-tion	-less	-ty
	-(b)le	-(d)le	-(c)le
	-ish	-ment	-able
Prefixes	dis-	mis-	re-
	com-	con-	
	pre-	pro-	

Abbreviations
Contractions

---

4. Teach syllabification taking care to keep the work functional by use in the central method of attack.

Establish the distinction between vowel-letters and vowel-sounds.
It can then be taught that a syllable has one and only one vowel-sound.
Some helpful points to make:
a. When two consonants separate adjacent vowels, divide between the consonants, e.g. car/rot, win/dow.
   In this case the first vowel will normally be short.
b. When only one consonant separates adjacent vowels, divide after the first vowel, e.g. fa/tal gro/cer.
   In this case the first vowel will normally be long.
c. When a word ends in -le, the last syllable normally includes the consonant preceding the l, e.g. can/dle ta/ble

---

5. Ensure that children can attack words independently by:

a. use of structural analysis where appropriate

At this stage work in structural analysis should tie in very closely with the phonetic work done in association with syllabification. For instance, children should readily recognize the common syllables involved in prefixes and suffixes. Further work centred on syllabification should include:

b. a refinement of the central method of attack: **CONTEXT** plus **FIRST SYLLABLE(S)** plus **CHECK**

1. Accent — stressed and unstressed syllables.
2. The indefinite vowel in unstressed syllables, symbolized by the inverted e, or schwa.
3. The use of a simple phonetic key, such as that used by Thorndike.

c. full syllabification where necessary.

d. use of the phonetic key in Thorndike-type dictionary.

APPENDIX D

Sequential Development of Reading Skills

A comprehensive survey of reading skills other than Word Recognition Skills covered in *Appendices B & C*. The conventions of written language associated with each skill are listed where relevant. Sequential development of each sub-skill at three broad stages is shown with suggestions for teaching. See *Objectives of Development in Reading* for rationale of the major classification.

Summary of Contents

A UNDERSTANDING THE TEXT

1. Word Meaning
1.1 Listening for and using new words and meanings
1.2 Adapting spoken vocabulary to written meanings — predicting vocabulary
1.3 Using context clues to determine meaning
1.4 Structural analysis and meaning — roots and affixes — simple derivation.
1.5 Naming
1.6 Specialized vocabulary — foreign terms

2. Sentence and Word-Group Meanings
2.1 Becoming familiar with increasingly complex sentences
2.2 The code of intonation

3 Drawing inferences with the Help of Organization
3.1 Main ideas
3.2 Supporting detail — relevance
3.3 Sequence — temporal and spatial order
3.4 Logical order and relationship — classification
3.5 Symbolic or metaphorical meanings
3.6 Building characters from textual clues
3.7 Determining the author's tone — mood
3.8 Determining theme and point of view
3.9 Analysing plot
3.10 Questioning the text to produce appropriate expectations

4. Responding Appropriately
4.1 Creating sensory imagery
4.2 Relating text to personal experience
4.3 Identifying with characters
4.4 Devloping emotional sensitivity
4.5 Following directions

5.   Judging and Evaluating
5.1   Judging truth — fact and opinion, etc.
5.2   Making value judgements
5.3   Analysing the techniques of persuasion and propaganda
5.4   Comparing and contrasting texts
5.5   Devising criteria for literary criticism

6.   Supportive Symbol Systems
6.1   Pictures and diagrams
6.2   Graphs, tablets, etc.
6.3   Maps, globes, etc.

B   STUDY SKILLS

7.   Locating Information
7.1   Use of alphabetical order
7.2   Using special parts of books
7.3   Interpreting abbreviations

8.   Using Dictionaries
8.1   Selecting the appropriate dictionary
8.2   Distinguishing between multiple meanings
8.3   Using pronunciation keys

9.   Using Other Reference Materials

10. Library Skills
10.1 Organization of the Library
10.2 Card Catalogue and Request Service

11. Using Magazines, Journals, etc.

12. Using Supportive Media — Film, Filmstrip, Records, Radio, TV.

13. Vocabulary of Criticism — Talking About Books
13.1 Qualities of writing
13.2 Elements of writing

14. Surveying and Adjusting Reading Rate

15. Organizing Information for Presentation or Recall — Note-taking

16. Carrying Out a Topic Study
16.1 Combining skills towards a specific study purpose
16.2 Working in a team
16.3 Keeping up to date
16.4 Presenting a study

C   AUDIENCE READING

17. Oral Reading to Share Understanding and Pleasure
17.1 Preparation
17.2 Presentation

D   USING READING TO MEET LIFE PURPOSES

18. Developing Satisfying Reading Habits
18.1 Reading for pleasure
18.2 Using books — adapting rate and style

Developmental levels

Approximate reading levels are shown marginally as follows:
J Junior — Reading levels 6-8 years
M Middle — Reading levels 9-11
S Senior — Reading levels 12-15

UNDERSTANDING THE TEXT

1. Word Meaning

1.1 Listening for and using new words and meanings

J Read to children daily — especially books that will extend their vocabulary beyond current reading level. Mix conversation and reading — this is the ideal way to deal with new words, rather than in an isolated lesson. Develop a fascination for the sounds of words, and where appropriate the simple 'relatives' of the word, and simple multiple meanings, e.g. **dress:** (as verb) *cover, clothe, prepare; dress the table, dressed poultry; dresser* (cupboard for things used in dressing the table); *dressing* (salad), *top-dressing; dress up, dress down;* etc. Enjoy unison work, especially with verse which introduces lively words. Ponder on words of songs. Children are fascinated with topical technical words, e.g. *incubator, articulator, fly-over.*

M Continue as above. Introduce derivations where these are simple and concrete. e.g.
litter: *bed, stretcher, animal bed* — hence *straw in a mess* — hence rubbish, animals born on the same bed.
Extend vocabulary of precision — synonyms and antonyms — let children use a *Junior Thesaurus.*

bad:	*evil*	*wicked*	*cruel*	*sinful*	*vicious*
	good	*noble*	*kind*	*righteous*	*virtuous*

S Prior to this level books have reflected children's vocabulary fairly closely. The words now entering their vocabulary will stem increasingly from the literary language and specialist fields, rather than from ordinary conversation. If this vocabulary is to be accepted and used with confidence by the ordinary child, it must be familiar to his ear and come readily to his tongue. Opportunities to hear and to use the vocabulary of formal English must be provided. Continuing to read to children regularly is one such opportunity. Discussion, debate and dramatization arising from books will return dividends in the growth of functional vocabulary.

1.2 Adapting spoken vocabulary to written meanings — predicting vocabulary

Conventions:
Contractions, greater formality of written vocabulary, appropriate levels of language.

J Children note differences between speech and writing — such as less general use of contractions. They can predict vocabulary to fill a space left in speech or writing provided context clues are strong and the language is familiar. Provide many opportunities to practise this skill which is the basis of word-attack and vocabulary extension.

M The children become conscious of different levels of language and are able to change level appropriately for different purposes: polite, informal, colloquial, slang, and vulgar vocabulary. Selection of the appropriate word for context or occasion.

₀ **S**   Children begin to accept the formal vocabulary of written English as natural and proper in explanatory or expository prose. They continue to develop awareness of registers and the ability to shift register when appropriate. The vocabulary of the written dialect begins to be used naturally in appropriate oral situations such as formal discussion, debate, and committee procedure. There should be continuing discussion of the criteria for determining the right word for the context and the occasion.

1.3 Using context clues to determine meaning — including new and multiple meanings

a. syntactical clues — word order and grammatical form (see 2.1)

b. semantic clues — unfolding sentence meaning

c. definition within the context

Conventions:
Verbal signs of synonyms and antonyms; punctuation; double comma and dash, parentheses, footnote, asterisk, verbal signs of definition.

d. total meaning development (see 3.5 and 4.1)

e. picture clues

J   Children are able to derive new and variant meanings from using simple forms of the clues a-e above, e.g.

a. *Show me your* pass. *(n.) I saw him* pass *out (v.)*

b. Walter told his sister not to pester *him all the time.*

c. For breakfast she ate mash, *which is a kind of porridge.* (comma followed by 'which is') *The men wore coloured* hose, *or stockings.* (comma followed by 'or')
   To the Littles even a mouse was enormous. (contrast)
   The farmer was a good man but his wife was wicked. (formal contrast with 'but')

d. *And so the prince and princess were* wed.

e. Intelligent study of illustrations is important to vocabulary extension, especially at this stage.

M   Steady development and refinement in the use of clues above. Extend especially to

c. *Many war-captives, the* thralls, *carried heavy loads.* (double comma)
   He carried lager — *his favourite drink* — *to quench etc.* (double dash)
   The patriots *(men who loved their country) banded etc.* (parentheses)
   Introduction to use of footnotes and use of asterisk.

S   Further development in each area. Extend especially in

d. Interpretation of more subtle context clues including metaphor.
   A heavy silence fell. Looks darkened or dropped. It was ominous.

1.4 Structural analysis and meaning — roots and affixes — simple derivation

(see also 8.3)

J   Children readily recognize the modification to the meaning of roots by the addition of common suffixes such as *-est*, the prefixing of *un-*, and by compounding such as in *marketplace* or *overjoyed.* (See details under Structural Analysis in Appendix C.) They are capable of intense interest in the derivation of words like *wireless* or *holiday* where the meanings are obscured by the familiarity of the whole word form in common speech. These relationships need to be pointed out at this stage.

M   Uses the meanings of common suffixes such as *-ness, -less, -ish;* common prefixes such as *pre-, dis-, in-, super-, inter-.* May begin to take an interest in derivations listed simply in a good school dictionary. A lively word-attention set may be produced by teaching at the growing point of derivation — current, recent vocabulary additions: e.g. *automobile, capsule, jumbo-jet, articulator, tranquilizer.*

S Adds meaning cues to common affixes and roots very rapidly, e.g. *circum-, sub-, -dom, aqua-, -vapour-.*

1.5 Naming

Conventions: Capital letters, italics.

J Capitalizing for names is one of the earliest conventions of print learned. However, the distinction between special names and common nouns is not clarified until the next stage.

M Classification of the full range of special names requiring initial capitals should be mastered. Capitals in titles for important words, and the use of italics to show the title of the book.

1.6 Specialized vocabulary — foreign terms

Convention: Glossary.

J A beginning should be made in noticing words which have special meanings in certain contexts. Take care to see that these contexts are familiar to the children. Examples: *picture tube, spine* of a book, *character* of a play, *strike* for higher wages or in softball.

M Children become familiar with the use of a **glossary** in books on specialized topics.

S Children are able to determine that a word is being used in its specialized sense without any clues other than context. Foreign terms are usually italicized.

2. Sentence and Word-Group Meanings

2.1 Becoming familiar with increasingly complex sentences

a. through listening

b. through reading — especially the interpretation of the structures and conventions of literary language

Conventions: Direct and indirect speech; structures natural to writing but not to speech; punctuation — colon, semi-colon, dash.

J By reading to children daily at a level slightly above their own instructional reading level, the teacher is able to familiarize them with the structures, idioms and conventions of the written dialect. Children should be encouraged to read many different kinds of books so that they are steadily introduced to the more precise language of writing. It is essential at this stage to provide for discussion and questioning by the children so that the new forms of print receive immediate illumination from speech. Much enjoyment of verse and song in unison helps children to claim the new language as their own — familiar to the tongue and loved.

M During these years the books that the children read will approximate much more closely to the standard conventions of written language. The children are being introduced to the complex structures of expository prose in a very gradual progression over the course of four or five years. It is very necessary to keep the conventions within the comprehension of the ordinary child through continued oral reading and discussion by the teacher.

The conventions of **direct speech** (quotation marks, punctuation, new speaker on a new line) and the structures of **indirect speech** (the shift from present to past tense, and from first and second persons of the pronoun to the third) should become familiar to children — by intuition and use rather than by analysis. However the type of analysis shown in the example below is intelligible to most children.

Direct Speech	Indirect Speech
Jean called to Tom, 'We're going on by ourselves'.	Jean called to Tom that they were going on by themselves.
'No! Come with me,' shouted Tom.	Tom protested and shouted for Jean to go with him.
'You can get lost!' retorted Jean.	Jean retorted that he could get lost.

An example of the increasing complexity and formality of written language may help to pinpoint the sort of learnings that the nine to twelve year old must accomplish:

Gigantic, long-vanished, strangely built, it is not surprising that the dinosaurs evoke our wonder and stir our imaginations. Though their mounted skeletons in the museums give us some idea of their body proportions, we need reconstructions of their original appearance to be able to think of them as more than collections of lifeless bones.

Going along with the increasing complexity of sentence structure are the conventions of punctuation which help to give visual shape to these complex forms. Children need to become familiar with the function of the colon, semi-colon and dash as exemplified in prose that is full of interest and meaning to them. This implies studying examples from longer stories in which wider meanings are plain, rather than analysing snippets which have no other function than to exemplify the punctuation. (Too often punctuation points are taught as pointers to the pointless.)

S   At this stage the language of the school and of books may become so abstract and formal that it threatens the ordinary child's sense of purpose and relevance. (It may drive the disadvantaged child into open revolt.) Opportunities to clarify and enlighten reading through many forms of oral presentation are as vital as ever. Children should feel comfortable with the different forms of written language,and especially with expository prose which is the most complex and also the most vital for understanding the modern world. The example from the expository prose of C. C. Fries given at the bottom of the page may help to point up some of the types of complexity accepted as normal and natural by an educated person, but never occurring in normal speech.

Some implications will be immediately clear:

1. Children should learn the written dialect by a gradual process of increasing exposure to and use of these forms in thoroughly meaningful contexts. If they are ever faced with a text which is so unintelligible to them that it must be translated, as has been done with the case below, you will not be able to escape or answer the question, 'Well, if that's what he meant, why didn't he say it?'

2. The children should learn to understand and accept elaborated structures because they see their justification in a context of absorbing interest to them. There should be no working with inane snippets, no pointless analysis, no dull and meaningless exercises. It is better for a child to be able to use standard English without being able to analyse it than to analyse and reject it.

Example of expository prose:

A sentence from C. C. Fries on 'Standard English' in typical written dialect . (Printed bold.)
The equivalent of this sentence in normal speech is given below the comment.
Note the shrinkage in the length of the sentence in normal speech.

Enough has been said to enforce the point that it is "standard" not because it is any more

has been said	*the point that*	*"standard"*	*not because*
Impersonalizing effect of passive verb form.	Device to signal expected structure.	Special use of quotation marks.	Heralds a complex logical contrast.

I've said enough to show you that we don't call it "standard"   because it's more

---

correct or more beautiful or more capable than other varieties of English; it is "standard"

	capable	*varieties*
	More precise use of vocabulary.	

correct or more beautiful or more useful than other kinds of English.   It's "standard"

---

solely because it is the particular type of English which is used in the conduct of

solely	*particular*	*in the conduct of*
More precise use of vocabulary again.		Precise linkage.

only because it's the kind of English used

---

the important affairs of our people.

important affairs of our people
Formal declamatory tone.

for important purposes.

2.2 The code of intonation — stress, pitch and juncture as clues to meaning

Conventions:

Punctuation clues to major intonation patterns; italics, capitalization and bold-face as signals of stress.

J Children must be aware from the beginnings of reading that intonation carries meaning. Certain meanings are carried by intonation *alone*, that is, the passage cannot be read or interpreted without recreating the appropriate pattern. The difficulty for reading is that there are few visual clues to stress and pitch — although juncture is fairly fully and clearly represented. Each sentence or clause may, of course, be spoken in a neutral intonation. But we often vary this neutral intonation in order to modify meaning in highly significant ways. When we take a sentence out of context there is seldom call to read it in any but the neutral manner, e.g.

He was a little boy.

But when we place this sentence in a wider context, we find that it is almost impossible to read in the neutral manner:

Poor Herman. He wasn't a bear. He was a little boy.

These sentences have not been *read* until the appropriate intonation patterns have been perceived. In certain cases the neutral intonation cannot be used and we are faced with a clear choice between one significant pattern and another:

Oh no! That would *happen.*
Oh no? Who does he think he is?
I think it was blue. Oh no — now I remember — it was pale green.

Punctuation *may* give a clear guide in many cases — provided the complex conventions have been mastered, and that the particular pattern of idiom has been heard in speech. The important thing is that the reader, from his knowledge of what is going on, and from his experience of the spoken language, must *supply* the missing intonation. Thus a child must have three items of knowledge before he can read such sentences as are given in the examples above:

a. he must know what he is reading about
b. he must know what the punctuation means
c. he must have heard the utterance spoken

If he lacks any of these, or fails to relate them, he must fail to interpret or read the passage. Only children of middle class English background, can be expected to read for instance:

Little beast indeed! The idea of calling me little!

The practical implications of all this are fortunately much more simple than the rather complex analysis that has been necessary to introduce the matter. In the first place, we must not confuse the matter with 'nice reading' in the oral situation: it applies equally to silent reading, and is concerned with the intonation patterns that are *essential to meaning* rather than to those we associate with fluency and expression in the oral reading situation. A child may perceive these intonations without being a good oral reader — although sound instruction in audience reading will certainly assist him to carry out this decoding of intonation.

A high demand for meaning is essential (implied by a). Sound teaching of punctuation clues to intonation is required (implied by b). A wide experience of spoken language forms and good models are necessary (implied by c). Reading to the children comes forward again as a vital part of the learning-to-read programme. Unison response to verse and song and lilting language help to provide the right models. Dramatization and soundly prepared audience reading reinforce attention to patterns of intonation. The natural intonations of normal speech are what must be encouraged — avoid both over-emphasis or flatness of tone. Encourage children to 'hear' the intonations in their silent reading. Attention should be drawn to the conventions of bold-face, capitals and italics as they arise in normal reading.

Children at this stage may experiment with manipulating **stress** and **pitch** as suggested in 17.2.   **Juncture** — the significant pauses or breaks in the flow of speech — will be taught in relationship to sentence form and the use of the period, comma and dash.

M Children should become aware of the importance of stress in syllables, as for instance in distinguishing between the noun and verb forms of *conflict*. At this stage, growing competence in audience reading should make increasing returns to silent reading. The children should be developing greater awareness of the more subtle intonations which characterize mood, atmosphere, pace and tension. They should be familiar with the level tone of objectivity appropriate to informational reading and expository prose. Experiment and adventure should still be the ruling principle rather than analysis for its own sake. Provide a wide tonal experience of language through the ear and across the tongue.

S Many experts believe that there is a conflict between emphasizing the sounds of the language in reading and the needs of speed and comprehension, and they would probably disagree with my suggestions above. I have seen no research which establishes a conflict. We know surprisingly little about the actual processes involved in rapid reading, despite the attention it has received in the literature. We do know that the process involves cue reduction rather than physically faster movements, i.e. more and more is interpreted from seeing less and less. It may very well be that in these processes of cue reduction the smaller units — words — become less important, while the wide sweeping rhythms of intonation become more important as representing larger thought units.

Let us be clear that much of the significance of reading is lost to the child who does not learn to transform the deadness of print into the lively rhythms of our language.

3. Drawing Inferences with the Help of Organization

3.1 Main ideas

Conventions:

Paragraph; chapter, chapter title; title; table of contents; headings; numeration; boldface and italics as signs of structure.

J   Children at this stage are able to give the main idea of a story or chapter and suggest or select alternative titles. Their attention should be drawn to the table of contents and to headings of all kinds. Simple numeration should be introduced, especially as an index to time sequence. In making experience charts, sometimes number the events that the children engaged in, or the functions of whatever was studied, etc.

M   Through experience with chapter headings and titles, the children will come to understand the principle of **paragraphing** and be able to identify the **topic sentence**. The children should also begin to discuss **major concepts, principles and themes** in stories and books. Note-taking skills will give practice in identifying main ideas. (See 15.)

S   Understanding the structure of the paragraph is a major task of this stage. Identification of the main idea, subordinate ideas and supporting detail. (See 3.3., 3.4.)

Topic sentence —normally first sentence — sometimes last sentence — occasionally the second sentence.

The children should be able to generalize on the basis of information gathered from several sources, and weigh one generalization against another. They should perceive the author's intention and contrast this with his achievement. They may compare major concepts as presented by one author with those presented by another. (See also 3.8.)

3.2 Supporting detail — relevance — humour

J   Given a main idea at this stage, children should be able to give supporting detail from the text in answer to the question, *'Why?'* or *'How do we know?'* They should be given simple problems of relevance to solve — *'What does not belong?' 'Which sentence is silly?'* Developing a sense of humour and a sense of the ridiculous is excellent training in the perception of relevance.

M   Can now begin to discuss the function of detail in supporting a main idea: substantiating, extending, clarifying, stating exceptions, giving examples, etc.

Sees the relationship between supportive details: sequence in time, premises to a conclusion, a certain order of classification, etc. (See also 3.4.) Responsive to simple **signal words:** *but; not only . . . but also; firstly; finally; therefore; however; etc.* Can give a simple reason for rejecting a detail as irrelevant. A lively sense of humour is a great help here.

S   Organizes detail under a major heading — stated or unstated — in order to assist understanding and recall. Responsive to an increasing range of signal words: *moreover; nevertheless; implies; subsequently;* etc. Actively sorts relevant from irrelevant material in carrying out a topic study using multiple sources. The jokes he tells reflect a growing delight in the humour of irrelevant detail.

3.3 Sequence — temporal order — spatial order — other systems of order

J   Young children find it difficult to subordinate principles of **prominence** to any principle of order — what catches attention for any reason becomes number one. Temporal sequence is both the most simple and the most vital system of order to establish — it is the basis for understanding more advanced principles of order, especially causal and logical relationships. A primary scientific meaning of **cause** is **invariable antecedent.** Retelling a story, ordering sequence pictures or sentences, and building experience stories are simple ways or practising sequence thinking. Children may construct a time-line of their own lives.

Spatial order presents difficulties to some children, especially in forming adequate imagery or understanding the changing relationships within a story. Meanings of the major spatial prepositions should be mastered early: *below; within; throughout;* etc. Also positional and dimensional hierarchies, such as: *enormous, huge, big . . . small, tiny, minute, microscopic.*

M Temporal sequence should present no difficulties of understanding at this stage, although the children are still struggling with the principle in their own writing. Biographies begin to fascinate. The historical dimension becomes important. Experience with time-lines will assist children to develop adequate concepts of historical order and related events and movements. The idea of **process** will begin to develop from the simple idea of time.

Visual and tactile imagery will dominate the sensory response to reading: given a situation, the children should be able to discuss relationships within it in response to questions requiring clear spatial orientation. As they read more widely the children will learn that many different systems of order are used, especially in exposition. The geography of their country may be dealt with spatially, temporally (creation of landforms, weathering, influence of man), climatically, in reference to altitude, etc.

S Active historical sequencing and relating. Major gaps in the sequence begin to be filled, resulting in a vaguely continuous sense of history. The lives of major historical figures may be perceived with greater sensitivity to the problems of the time and age.

3.4 Logical order and relationship — classification

a. **cause and effect — predicting outcomes**

b. **hypothetical relationship — (if . . . then)**

c. **disjunctive relationship (either . . . or)**

d. **parallel relationships — contrast**

e. **classification and definition**

f. **premises and conclusion**

J. Predicting outcomes from an experience of temporal sequence is the most important way in which children of this age learn to think logically. Prediction calls upon an awareness of causal relationships and also encourages hypothetical thinking. One of the earliest questions children are expected to answer is, 'Why did you do that?' Personal causation through will, desire, or impulse may be understood much earlier than material causation, and forms a pattern for later causal thinking. *Intention* is often attributed to animals or even to things before the idea of unwilled events arising out of physical causes becomes firmly established. The notion of *accidental* happenings links the subjective and objective approach to causation.

c. Young children readily fall into the disjunctive trap — everything is either black or white. They must begin to learn that disjunctions are seldom exclusive — there are all the greys in between.

d. Logical implications of *and* and *but* in parallel structures, e.g. *The giant was fierce* but *his wife was gentle.* Parallel relations such as *shorter than . . . taller than.*

e.   Children are active in classification from the moment they begin to use language and form concepts: now they need to widen the range of criteria they use, clarify classes and concepts, and learn to use definitions.

M   Able to 'read between the lines' — realize implications. Should be taught to seek and develop these inferences, and to expand literal meanings automatically during reading. Becomes interested in generalizations about behaviour — maxims, proverbs, morals — and can discuss problems rationally.

a.   Manipulates longer and more complex causal chains.

Thinks of possibilities beyond the actual or stated. Often interprets these moralistically — 'He should've. Then ...' Teacher should encourage hypothetical thinking by such questions as, 'What would have happened if ...? Children may rewrite or retell a story or incident changing one important item — 'Suppose Bill had been such-and-such a kind of person rather than what he was: how would the story have been different?'

c.   The classification of experience into opposites or contrasts provides the simplest — and the most dangerous — way of making judgements. Most values fall into three broad categories — a positive quality, a negative quality, and a large in-between class. Disjunctive reasoning falls into forms such as: *Either x is the case or y is the case* (to be valid y must mean everything other than x); *x is not the case; therefore y is the case*. Disjunctive reasoning is only sound if there is no hidden third class — neither white nor black but some shade of grey. Children should be helped to move out of the black and white, 'goodies' versus 'baddies' stage of thinking. **Stereotypes** are often the result of false disjunctive thinking also. The disjunctive is used very commonly because it promises the simplest, most clear-cut answer to a problem, but it usually does so by masking the true state of affairs.

d.   Parallel structures and the relationships they express become increasingly important, e.g. conjunctions *but, although;* conjunctive adverbs *however, nevertheless;* structures such as: *The (longer) ... the (more).* Contrasts should be drawn increasingly between characters, styles, forms, etc. There needs to be a rapid increase in the range of adverbs understood and used.

e.   Classification of more formal terms becomes more important. This will include ability to state criteria in the form of a definition. In discussing characterization, more and more subtle distinctions are made. This implies an increase in the understanding and use of appropriate adjectives. See Section 13.

f.   It is still too early for children to understand the formal principles of logic. However ordinary syntax embodies these principles. The fact that logical relationships are being appealed to is often signalled by such words as *must, it follows* and *surely*. Notice the **formal structure** lying behind each of the categories listed here:

a. *x causes y; x* (has occurred, will happen); *therefore y* (has occurred, will happen).

b. *If x, then y; yes x; therefore y.*

c. *Either x or y; yes x; therefore not y.*

d. *x faster than y; z faster than x; therefore z faster than y.*

S   Much more capable of abstract reasoning. Many principles of logic are used to read creatively and critically.

a. Children should learn that antecedence alone is not sufficient to establish cause: Is the cause invariably sufficient to establish the effect? e.g. 'I caught a cold from Amy.' But were there other possible sources of infection, and what other conditions were necessary before the infection could be successfully transmitted, etc? Is the apparent cause really the effect? e.g. 'Jimmy can't learn to read because he's so lazy.'

b. Checking hypotheticals — finding exceptions — using experimental method. Application to advertising and criticism of mass media: 'If you use this deodorant, everybody will love you.' (Implication: If you don't . . .?)

c. Further analysis of dangers of black and white thinking. Advertising: 'You don't want to be a wallflower, do you?' (The implication is a false disjunction — 'Either you come to our Charm School or you are doomed to the wall.')

d. Clarifying contrasts. Many prejudices and stereotypes are built on falsely associated parallels: 'Black, therefore dirty, dishonest, inferior, etc.' Cleansing concepts of irrelevant associations is a major task of this stage.

e. Children should become proficient in formal definition — **genus and differentia** (the class within which the group falls, and the characteristic which distinguishes this group from other groups within the class).

f. Children should be sensitive to the precise meaning of linguistic structures which embody logical thinking: The universal — *all, no, every, everyone, no-one, never,* etc. The **false universal or generalization** — when there are exceptions of any kind to the *all* or *no* which is asserted. Gifted children of this age make a study of **fallacies** and report to the class. Space does not permit an analysis here. For a delightful clear and hilarious introduction see the story, *Love is a Fallacy*, by Max Shulman, reprinted in *Challenges, The New Basic Readers Grade 8*, Scott, Foresman and Company, 1967.

3.5 Interpreting symbolic or metaphorical meanings

A symbol or a metaphor is different from a name or a sign in that it is *like* what it refers to in some vital way. In figurative language the **image** or **symbol** takes its meanings across to an entirely new context — it acts as a **vehicle**. This goes for all the so-called **figures of speech**. They allow secure, everyday knowledge and concrete experience to be used in exploring more complex and abstract notions. When the speaker is in a strange or new situation and under the need to refer to parts of the situation for which there are no ordinary words, he is likely to use a metaphor.

We are often insensitive to the fact that our entire abstract vocabulary originated in this way — behind every abstract word is a metaphor (*abstract* — to draw out of with effort; *metaphor* — to carry across, to transfer; *symbol* — a mark, token or ticket; *emblem* — a thing put on). If we wish to speak about something for which there is no common name — a feeling, an experience, an insight — we use familiar language and familiar meanings to carry across the new idea. Thus, metaphorical language is always more simple, concrete, familiar and homely than the **literal** language which would be required to say the same thing or carry the same meaning. The difficulty of metaphor lies in the fact that something new and more complex is being communicated. This always implies tuning in to the wider context within which the unique or special experience being pointed to may be perceived. For this reason, metaphors should not be studied in isolation from the wider situations in which they occur. Children must learn to tune in to the total situation sensitively, and exercises which isolate figurative language from the total structure of meaning are likely to be pointless or harmful.

It is in communicating emotion or unique, personal experience that metaphor is indispensable. We need an outside picture of the feeling we wish to communicate — Eliot's *objective correlative*. Often this will be a whole situation or story — a system of metaphors. **Symbolic meanings** are usually of this kind. Falling leaves may carry a special meaning of sadness in a special way for a special situation. A drifting river voyage — such as Huck Finn's — may carry a system of meanings concerned with the search for autonomy in a culture of decaying and inconsistent values which must be constantly rediscovered or remade.

Special aspects of metaphor:

	Examples
slang:	turned on
half-dead metaphor:	chew the fat
assimilated metaphor:	knowledge
jargon:	feedback

J Simple metaphors and similes should be enjoyed at this stage without any form of analysis. The half-dead metaphors of the language — including many of its **cliches** — will often strike the children of this age with something of their original freshness: *busy as a bee, tan your hide, she's an angel*, etc. The children may study simple symbols such as **emblems, badges, coats of arms,** road signs, etc. Draw attention to the human animals of infant books — anthropomorphism is always symbolic in some way. Sometimes the meaning is falsifying in that it makes it harder to understand the animal — *dirty pig, stupid goat*. A good symbol implies that the reader already has a more clear and accurate knowledge of the vehicle (in this case an animal) than of the meaning being carried by the metaphor. Children often know more about their own experience than about animals, such as pigs or goats, and they are therefore likely to make false judgements about animals if anthropomorphic stories are not balanced by many realistic stories.

M As the children begin to develop an abstract vocabulary they should be helped to see that there is often a concrete image behind abstract concepts — they will not misuse *chronic*, for instance, if they realize the image of time and clocks lying behind the use of this word to describe an illness or a state of being. When we *understand* something we say we see the *point* — the image of *seeing* enters into the abstract notions of *reflection* and *revision* and *speculate*. The idea of a *sharp point* has dozens of metaphorical uses in abstract language — *appoint, pointless, pungent, punctual, punctuate* (cf. *puncture*), *poignant, expunge, pugnacious, repugnant, counterpoint, disappoint*. The principles of metaphor and symbolic meaning soon become clear by a study of the dead metaphors in abstract language in the way suggested above.

The children find such an approach helpful — because it goes back to sensory experience and concrete images — immensely enjoyable — because it has a riddling interest and it takes the pomposity out of the big words (cuts them down to size). An introduction to metaphor through a study of current slang will also prove very effective.

S Children may begin to study the way in which metaphor operates — see the introductory comment above. No complex meanings can be communicated without the use of metaphor in one form or another. Extended metaphor, or **analogy**, is used frequently in explanatory prose. False analogy is one of the chief fallacies of thinking — if not in fact *the* chief falacy. The question must always be asked: *What analogy or* **model** *is being used*? *What are the limits of the* **model**? *What irrelevant meanings may be brought across by the analogy*? For instance, your understanding of an educational problem will be modified according to the model being used: Is education writing on a clean sheet, filling an empty tank (that stock of sight words), handing on a gift of culture (casting pearls before swine), fostering a growing process, or inducing self-realization? Keep the study of metaphor close to the discussion of whole books or stories so that the richness of meaning implied by the context is taken into account.

3.6 Building characters from textual clues

J Discussion and dramatization involving the building out of full characters from textual clues should be a continuing preoccupation. **Identification** aids the creation of personal meaning, the integration of meanings into a larger total pattern, and the heightening of interest and concern. The earliest attempts to build characters are based upon self-knowledge. Although identification will play a necessarily dominant part in early reading, children should be increasingly introduced to contrastive characters with whom it may be more difficult to identify. They should be encouraged to perceive and tolerate differences — especially cultural differences — while seeing behind these contrasts to the fundamental human realities.

M At this stage the characters of children's books are usually drawn in a simple and direct way. Additional clues are given in dialogue, in action and in consequence. These should be discussed. Reading to children remains the most effective way of helping them to build characters — they see the deadness of print come alive with the warmth of the human voice. The children are moving away from intense identification towards an interest in diversity, peculiarity and even extravagence in character. They use book situations to explore new experience vicariously, and develop identification to the point where they virtually try themselves out in new roles through the characters of books. It is at this stage that approaches centred around the basic sentence form, *Imagine you are x in such and such circumstances* become very important both as an aid to building characters from textual clues and also as a stimulus to personal exploration through reading.

S More mature fiction relies on the reader to respond creatively to increasingly indirect cues to character. Many children need the help of discussion in learning to respond creatively to oblique methods of character building in books. Nothing can kill a character quite so rapidly as a thoroughly formal and cold analysis — both intellectual and affective responses must have equal weight in these discussions. Comparisons are usually helpful, and here is where the concurrent reading and discussion of a number of books is important.

3.7 Determining the author's tone — establishing mood and atmosphere

J Take advantage of a few well-produced records and tapes to gain that heightened sense of atmosphere which expert story-telling, musical background, or sound-effects may produce. The impact of the human voice is of the first importance in establishing a sense of tone or mood. Dramatization is clearly helpful. Ask very simple questions such as, *How does this story make you feel*? or *How do you think the author felt about such and such a character*? etc. The impact of illustrations should be discussed. Filmstrips will often help to build atmosphere for infant stories.

M Children of nine or ten begin to classify authors according to their normal tone, but they have difficulty in finding words to express their intuitive generalizations. There is not a ready-made technical vocabulary to cover author's tone. Develop a simple scale with the children: *serious; sympathetic; mysterious; good-natured; jolly; gay; only half serious; humorous;* etc. A deeper analysis of illustration will help to direct attention to mood. Reflection of tone and mood in audience reading should be attempted by more competent readers.

S A much more refined analysis of tone, with a consequent filling out of the scale to include such terms as: *earnest; patronizing; pompous; concerned; urgent; unruffled; cool; objective; ironic; satirical; light; amused; hilarious; optimistic; gay; exuberant;* etc. Discuss the author's attitude towards both his material and his audience. A similar scale may be worked up to explore atmosphere.

3.8 Determining author's theme, 'message' or point of view

J Stories with a moral, such as fables, soon produce the awareness that most authors have a wider message to convey than simply the working out of the plot. Ask such questions as, 'What was the author trying to say to us in this story?' However, be careful not to moralize everything — the children should realize that the fundamental purpose of a story is to give pleasure.

M The fact that the author is an ordinary person with a **point of view** comes as a surprise to some children. Discuss the way in which point of view may **bias** an author. Comparing texts on the same topic is an excellent way of demonstrating the subtle influence of personal perspective or purpose. What he has left out is just as important as what he had included: books always involve **selection** of a few items from a vast number of possible items. How has the author handled selection? What is important and unimportant to him? History and biography are always biased to some extent no matter how factal they are, for it is the selection of facts which establishes impressions and generalizations. Opposite conclusions may be drawn from two different sets of true facts selected from the total available on a given event or person.

Children should discuss **major concepts and themes** from a story. Many such discussions will begin at the point where the children relate their own experiences to those of the book rather than as a direct attempt to establish a 'lesson' or 'moral' in the story.

S Refinement of earlier insights. Many children will be able to understand that the total work is an **extended metaphor** (see 3.5) carrying a symbolic meaning above the level of action. Fiction is usually a comment on or criticism of life. Books in the subject fields usually display a total structure which exemplified the author's idea of how the subject should be properly perceived or organized. How does the author convey these larger meanings? To what extent may he convey unintended meanings, as for instance in patronizing writing for children?

3.9 Analysing plot

J Keep plot analysis very simple at this stage. Retelling a story in three or four sentences provides a satisfactory starting point. Have children identify the 'most exciting part' of the 'big surprise', etc.

M Continue to avoid an abstract approach. Simple analysis is helpful to understand and to the needs of summarizing and note-taking (section 15). A sound plot has a beginning (setting the scene, introducing the characters, stating the problem), a middle (developing the action; producing tension), and an ending (often a climax or a resolution). Children should be able to identify the **climax** of a story.

S   Children will begin to see the relationship between plot and theme: the driving force behind the action springs from a clear and strong theme. Action is interesting as it becomes significant — and this involves the author's values. Tension, excitement and urgency all spring from values. Plot should be analysed in these terms rather than in a cold dissecting of action from which all worth has been excluded — it should be learning the steps in a new dance rather than the performing of an autopsy.

3.10 Questioning the text to produce appropriate expectations

J   This will have been a standard procedure used by the teacher since the beginnings of reading — *'See if you can find out . . .?'* However, the children must learn to do this for themselves as soon as possible. Ask the children, *'What do we want to find out now?'* The directed silent reading lesson is valuable in teaching this skill. Divide a story into three or four units, discussing the significance of each as it is completed. Have the children formulate the questions which are relevant to ask before proceeding to the next section.

M   This will be discussed in studying the SQ3R approach (section 14).

S   Develop an aggressive, probing, critical drive to questioning during reading. *Why did he say that? What is he driving at? Why did he say it that way and not another? What is the significance of the detail? Is this padding or does it have some function not yet clear? He is raising strong expectations about what will happen – he had better fulfil them. Am I having my arm twisted? Is he telling me the facts, or is he exaggerating so as to make me feel strongly about the situation?*

4. Responding Appropriately

4.1 Creating sensory imagery from textual clues

J   Sensory imagery must be clear, detailed, sharp and colourful if reading is to develop soundly. This is particularly important while children are still at the 'concrete stage' of thinking. Visual imagery predominates, but auditory, tactile and other sensory images should be created where appropriate. Ask many questions requiring sensory impressions which are not given in the text: *'As you saw him in your mind, how was the man at the station dressed? Did he wear a uniform? What colour was it? What noises could you hear? Was there any special smell?'* Answers to such questions will, of course, vary from individual to individual.

M   Imagery concerned with facial expression, gesture, and response are important. Dramatization and illustration assist this process of creating images.

S   Extend questioning to include bodily sensations and emotions: *'Did you feel Sally's embarrassment? What sensations did you experience — hot flush, blushing, weakness?'* Total scenes including internal relationships between objects and people should be discussed.

4.2 Relating text to personal experience — integrating (See also 3.2)

J   Most young children are only too willing to see personal meanings and associations in their reading. Relevance is an important question here: children are helped to repress irrelevant associations and to amplify relevant ones through the natural filtering of open discussion.

M   Flying off at tangents, so characteristic of the very young, should be well under control by now. The children should be encouraged to weigh everything in the book against evidence of their own experience, and to incorporate the new experiences of the book into their own personal background. Frame simple questions to induce this response. Provide activities which encourage the children to apply themes from books to their own experience, to the local environment, to modern and topical concerns.

S   Reading should provide a constant review of experience — reorganizing ideas, regrouping and extending concepts, questioning assumptions, probing prejudices, awakening forgotten feelings, refreshing stale habits of thinking or of observing.

4.3 Identifying with characters (See also 3.6)

J   Young children's diet of books should be balanced to provide many stories in which helpful identification may take place — not too much hero worship, or the magical simplification of life. Discussion should lead children to identify with characters who are facing the real problems of growing up at this stage.

M   Identification begins to transport children outside their range of common experience at this state — pirates, space-men, knights, and heroes of many kinds lead the children to explore new points of view vicariously. They learn to get into someone else's skin — often crudely, through stereotypes, at first. Drama and role-playing assist this process. Without the vicarious experience of stories it is difficult for the developing person to learn what it feels like to be someone else. Real tolerance and compassion are dependent on this identifying process.

S   Identification should become increasingly realistic and humane during later childhood. There is always a proper place for escape into a day-dream world through books, but this should not be allowed to obsess the children. Introduction to better books, discussion, and critical thinking should bring the imagination back to earth. (See 4.4 and Section 5). In our culture there is a tendency for books to support sentimental simplifications of experience which arouse false expectations about life and people. These sentimental influences should be kept under constant, good-natured criticism — gently laughed into critical attention and rethinking.

4.4 Developing emotional sensitivity

J   Encourage young children to respond to the characters and situations of literature as matters of real importance and then to test and examine their reactions in the free play of discussion.

M   Give the children ample opportunity to express their feelings in many media. The glow of satisfaction left after reading a book will often be an appropriate feeling to express in **verse**. Have the children express their feelings about characters in simple similes: e.g. in the book *M for Mischief*, Peg was like a little old lady, Milly was like an excited puppy, and Jamie was like a mosquito that worries you in bed at night.

S   As emotional experience matures, children will begin to relate towards characters in a similar way as to real people. This is a refinement of identification rather than an abandonment of it, since sympathetic relationships with real people demand a large measure of identification. Feelings of attachment which allow for the difference between the 'me' and 'you' enter reading at this stage. The children may 'fall in love with' a character or despise and resist another character. This marks the development of a strong self-concept in the child.

The characters of books and the situations in which they are presented now become an extension of real experience and provide for the enrichment of personal relationships and the exploration of new dimensions of feeling. The characters of books are often strong and exceptional people, or people with larger than ordinary problems to solve. Through entering into a relationship of concern with these exceptional people the children widen their own range of sensitivity. They learn how to deal with countless situations which they have not faced in real life but which they have worked through to the point where their own natures have been subtly modified and their area of competence in personal relationships has been extended.

It is always necessary to keep these responses under a questioning, critical scrutiny which demands points of ratification in personal experience and in the real world. When the imaginative becomes too distant from the real, emotional health is lost. The children then become prone to the emotional diseases of **sentimentality** and **wishful thinking**. Emotion must always be paid for, even when it springs from reading a book. Emotion must fit the facts, and sensitivity entails a subtle measuring of appropriateness.

4.5 Following directions

J Teach the children to follow directions from print using tabulation guides at one level (See Section 14). They should read the entire task first and then follow the instructions item by item.

M Apply the SQ3R approach to following directions — survey to understand total task; Questions to predict how aspects of the task should be undertaken; Read and follow directions closely, item by item; Recite and Review by going over the finished task to check that it has been fully and accurately accomplished. Teach simple form filling procedures such as telegrams, bank slips, etc.

S Should be capable of following complex written instructions and organizing instructions which have not been clearly or fully set out. (See Section 16.) Teach how to adapt a set of instructions to a slightly different purpose — e.g. a recipe for a smaller serving. Provide experience in interpreting abstract instructions or principles and applying them to concrete situations — e.g. principles of caring for animals to a particular animal.

Introduce a range of form-filling problems and application procedures. Ensure that children can recognize when accuracy is required and operate with precision. Study a range of **manuals** and **handbooks** to determine principles of organization and special conventions.

5. Judging and Evaluating

5.1 Judging truth — distinguishing between

a. true and false

b. fact and opinion

c. objective and subjective

d. emotive and referential

e. reason and prejudice

Books open a marvellous world of makebelieve for the young child. The sense of wonder and the abandonment of imagination should not be killed by the pettiness of fact. It is the *real shortcomings* of particular books that children should be taught to recognize rather than the formal ones of fact and fiction — with fact being somehow superior. The most truthful comment on life is often fictional because imagination, metaphor, image, and symbol are capable of that accurate complexity which abstract concepts lose in the process of generalization. (See 3.5 above.)

Reality judgements are often very crudely made at this level — 'It didn't happen, therefore it's not true.' 'It's only in a book, it's not real.' Children need to be able to make this crude type of distinction between real and imagery before they can learn to distinguish the *true* aspect of an imaginary situation. In learning to make these distinctions, however, the children should be encouraged to avoid dismissing a story because it couldn't have happened. Many boys go off the rails at this point — they turn their backs on print as having no real meaning for them. Bring them back with realistic stories, local if possible, and clearly relevant to their interests and needs.

From the very beginning children should be led to expect high standards of accuracy in non-fiction. They should learn that books *may* be wrong in fact. The fact that something is stated in an encyclopedia is no guarantee of accuracy.

M Have the children distinguish clearly in their own experience between 'I think' and 'I know', and then apply the same rigour in discussing books. In this way establish the distinction between **knowledge** or **fact** and **opinion** or **belief**. There are many things in human experience which are too complex to be verified: these are matters concerning which it is proper to hold an opinion or a belief. However, a *sound opinion* can always be substantiated in part and an author should give **reasons** for his beliefs. These reasons are usually of two kinds: the author refers to concrete **instances** which support his belief or he shows the **consistency** of his belief with wider areas of knowledge. The first method of substantiation requires *many* instances — arguing from a single instance is always unjustified. The second method requires a good grasp of logical principles. (See Section 3.)

That part of our opinions which cannot be substantiated should be *tentative* and open to constant revaluation. However, it is a common human trait to cling to and assert the unjustified elements of belief most dogmatically and arrogantly. Such beliefs are often fathered by fear and accompanied by a refusal to look at the real facts or approach the problem closely enough to achieve first-hand experience. An understanding of this tendency leads to insights in accounting for **prejudice.**

The difference between subjective and objective is rather more subtle. Children at this stage lay the foundations in experience for making the distinction later. They should be guided to explore the *criteria for evidence of different kinds*. A mock court is a valuable dramatic situation in which to explore evidence. Through discussion of **motive** an important area of literary criticism is opened up. Writing is a highly conscious and deliberate

activity: children should begin to discuss the **author's intention**. (See 5.3)
A mock court also helps children to see the distinction between **emotive
and referential use of language**.

Children of this age are only just becoming capable of thinking logically,
and until they develop clear standards for what is reasonable, they cannot
understand their own **prejudices**. They may learn at this stage that
prejudice and pig-headedness tend to go together — that is, prejudice is more
than ignorance: it is the refusal to become informed. Prejudice is actively
resistant to knowledge — it entails a vested interest in ignorance on account
of some ulterior motive — fear, pride, self-assertion. It is usually associated
with a belief in personal superiority.

The perception of what is *true* in fiction should be developed during this
stage. **Fiction** is a reflection of experience. It often uses devices of emphasis
to highlight some aspect of experience which is normally overlooked —
these may amount to exaggeration or distortion which is justified by the
clarity with which a given point is made. **Humour** often operates in this
way.

Discussion of the author's 'message' helps children to see that fiction has
some serious comment to make on life. However, this need not be *moral*
comment — the imaginative artist is often more 'objective' than the
statistician: he shows us new ways of looking at familiar things.

S   Children should be aware that false information may be given in books.
Where any piece of information is of importance for a particular purpose, it
is advisable to check facts. How is this done?

Note the **verbal conventions** used to indicate that an author is giving
an opinion rather than stating an attesting fact. Subjective terms used in
conjunction with a personal pronoun normally indicate such a warning: *I
regard . . . It is my belief . . . In my view . . .* etc. Children should be able to
recognize what is opinion in their own system of ideas and learn to mark any
statement of belief by an '**opinion convention**'.

Most children of this age will distinguish between **objective** and
subjective statements quite readily. A subjective statement may, of course,
be as true as an objective one, but it cannot be verified because it refers to a
unique experience of an individual. Any judgement of **value** is subjective —
a value cannot be observed or sensed. We may discuss values and agree or
disagree about criteria. It may then be possible to construct some sort of
scale to measure what we have agreed to be a sign of value. But the value
itself can never be measured. An **objective statement** is one which refers to
things which can be observed in sensory experience, and therefore may be
verified. Children should learn to take up an **objective point of view** in
appropriate situations, seeking facts and avoiding judgements. This is not
an easy task — many people never learn how to be objective.

Recognizing **prejudice** and avoiding it is a special case of this difficult
task. Discuss the marks of prejudice : judgement before looking at the facts;
judgement regardless of the facts; refusal to find or attend to the facts;
sweeping generalization; stubbornness and dogmatism; personal pride,
smugness and superiority; ulterior motive.

The **point of view** of an author is subjective yet it influences his
selection of facts, the emphasis he places on different aspects of his topic, and
his willingness to support his generalizations with detailed observation. It
is statements which lie *close* to the author's point of view which must be
checked and scrutinized with care, for it is in this area that he is most likely
to replace fact and reason by emotion and prejudice. Furthermore, things
look different from different points of view, without any departure from fact.

Children should discuss the many ways in which fiction and fantasy may be true. The **imagination** is constantly concerned with giving concrete shape to intangible things — to feelings, personal sensations, states of mind. One need only glance at the objective headlines of a daily newspaper to see that giants, dragons and monsters have a place in the real world. Fantasy should not be lightly dismissed.

Brighter children may be able to see the tension which exists between the **abstract concept** and the **concrete image** or symbol. The generalization process involved in abstraction loses in detail and complexity what it gains in clarity: to have everything categorized and pigeon-holed is to miss the organic vitality and uniqueness of living processes. On the other hand the metaphor or symbol has an inbuilt danger of misrepresentation. (See 3.5). What it gains in vitality and truth to the complexity of life, it loses in scientific accuracy. A metaphor should never be pushed too far — this is why it is so necessary to discuss metaphors in their wider context and ascertain exactly what aspects of the vehicle are meant to apply, and what aspects are irrelevant. If a voyage is used as a symbol of life, for instance, the fact that voyages occur on a medium which is changeable — both benign and dangerous — is appropriate, but the fact that the medium contains an abundance of fish is probably not.

The great dilemma of language is that an approach to truth or accuracy by either process — analysis or metaphor — is ultimately distorting. As soon as something has been defined and classified, certain of its qualities have been dismissed as irrelevant; as soon as something has been metaphorically identified with something else, it gains irrelevant qualities. Both modes need to be understood and their dangers realized. There is a place for both **scientific realism** and for **imaginative realism** in children's literature. Both bring us closer to the whole truth.

5.2 Making value judgements

J Young children make ready judgement of characters and books — often in the simplest terms of good and bad. Encourage them to give reasons for these judgements. Ask for positive as well as negative judgements about the same character or book, and *vice versa*. By this type of questioning, encourage the children to become discriminating and tentative. Help the children to become tolerant of difference and strangeness.

M Valuing a book as good or bad should often go further than the quite permissable, *'I liked it'* type of judgement. Discuss such things as truth to life, relevance to personal experience, excitement and pace, characterization, surprise, etc. Develop the insight that people of different cultures, or those living under different conditions or in different times, are likely to have different customs and values. What is peculiar is not necessarily bad.

S Books introduce children to the richness and variety of human values and purposes more than any other medium. The result should be a growth towards **tolerance** and **open-mindedness** on the one hand and the crystalizing of **personal values** on the other. The taste of many children will still be very immature. To sneer at or deride the things they like, however, is to undermine the development of tolerance and tentativeness quite directly. It would be better to abandon teaching literature altogether. Encourage the children to discuss, argue, debate and think about the books they read. Introduce them to as wide a range of intelligible literature as possible, but don't be dismayed at their dismissal of some of your personal favourites. Keep discussion relevant and topical by asking such questions as, 'What would you have done under these circumstances? How would we deal with this sort of problem today? How do we manage this sort of situation in our culture?'

5.3 Analysing the techniques of persuasion and propaganda

J Young children should be able to recognize **sales talk** and the extravagent element in advertising. They should begin to be automatically suspicious of any print which sets out to sell or to persuade. The children can see clearly in this context that that print is not necessarily true.

M Have children collect favourite advertising words and jargon, such as *magic, enchanting, new,* etc. Discuss why each of these words has emotive power. Apply the insights of 5.1 to an analysis of **advertising** and **propaganda**. Discuss why it is important to establish the author's motive — has he any special reason for deceiving you?

S Study **promotion techniques** of many kinds — advertising, proselytizing, political campaigning, etc. Note the tendency towards stating opinion as fact, subjective as objective, prejudice as reason. Compare **slanted** or **biased** accounts of the same event, or product, or idea. Study a consumer magazine alongside typical advertising of a product. Compare letters to the editor noting how the same type of emotive argument and exaggeration is likely to be used by both sides to support contrary ideas. Identify some **common abuses**: quotation out of context, name-calling, unsupported generalization, biased selection of items, appeal to authority (now usually a sports king or a beauty queen), misleading headlines, etc. Discover common fallacies in persuasive writing. Establish the distinction between **emotive** and **referential** writing.

5.4 Comparing and contrasting texts.

J Even very young children should learn that everything that appears in a book is not reliable or sacrosanct:
a. In fiction, let them experience two or more versions of the same tale.
b. In non-fiction, let them see that a single text seldom gives all the important answers about a particular topic — let alone accurately.

M Have the children analyse the differences between two simple texts in biography, in history and science. At this stage concentrate on accuracy, misrepresentation, and omissions. Have the children list facts about which the two books disagree. Discuss criteria for determining which text is most accurate: within the text — sources stated, date of publication, author's comment on the accuracy of his material; beyond the text — reference books, encyclopedias, more authoritative sources, first-hand accounts, manuscripts, etc. In fiction, have the children compare two versions of the same story and give reasons for their preferences of one text above the other.

S Carry comparisons much further in biography, history and science. What was the purpose of each book? How has this affected selection of items? What is historical fiction, and how much license has the author? What are textual indications that the author is going beyond reliable sources — terms such as: *perhaps, it may be, beyond doubt,* etc. In fiction, compare two versions closely in terms of readability — was it simplified for a younger age group, what effects have come off best, what different messages were the authors trying to convey by retelling the story, what effect have illustrations, etc. In collecting folk stories, what advantage is there in knowing the earliest recorded form of the story? How has the author developed the material? Was he justified in doing so?

Begin an interest in **typography** and **layout**. Compare different type faces, sizes, and line spaces. How does page layout affect readability?

5.5. Devising criteria for literary criticism

J   Many of the activities in Section 3, 4 and 5 involve early forms of literary criticism. In comparing texts with personal experience, and with each other, the children begin to form a simple vocabulary and concepts leading towards the forms of criticism. They say a book has a lot of boring detail (relevance); that they could really imagine that it was happening (truth to life); that they found a particular section exciting (suspense or pace); that the book was easy to understand (clarity and simplicity); etc.

M Continue to draw on the natural responses of children to build up criteria for criticism: exciting words (diction, imagery); word pictures (imagery); good story (plot); etc. Look at a few classics like *Charlotte's Web* or *The Blue Dolphin,* and try to determine what makes them superlative. Don't force the use of **technical vocabulary** — the ability to explain judgements in simple, ordinary language is an advantage in literary criticism — and a skill all too quickly lost in the rush to write *onomatopoeia* in the correct examination slot. Section 13 may be useful in determining the sort of vocabulary appropriate to the level.

    The major headings of Section 13.1 are suggestive of important emphases in talking about books. The first consideration for most children is truth to life, and relevance to situations and problems which appear real to them at their particular stage of development. This is why Column 1 lists words in the **Reality** mode, and a full section is also given to **Relevance to life**. This is often a good starting point for talking about a particular book. **Truthfulness** and reliability are dealt with at length in Section 5.1.

    At this age children may be directed to another fundamental quality of style — **Clarity**. The drive to extend children's vocabulary should not be allowed to mislead children into thinking that the big, fancy word is always the best: they should learn that simple words and structures are more effective, provided that they are as precise and economical as more abstruse words in the same context. The **organization of a piece of writing** is likely to influence clarity more than any other single factor. Point to instances of clear organization in both fiction and non-fiction: simple sequence or order; clear topic sentences; headings, etc. Relate to Sections 3, 14, 15, and 16.4, *the form of the written report*. When children have difficulty in understanding a passage or a book, take the opportunity to discuss those qualities in writing which produce obscurity.

S   Children should be familiar with a wide range of **forms** in literature and a range of common **styles**. (See Section 13.) Earlier discussion will have made the children familiar with the idea that the author has a **purpose** and a **point of view**. Does the author achieve his purpose? How does he achieve it? Does he do so in an interesting way — in an economic way — in an honest way? What **technical devices** have been used: first or third person — God's-eye-view; sequence — flashback; figurative language and symbolism; use of dialogue; creation of tension or suspense; etc. What is the **tone** of the book and how is this affected by the author's attitudes — to his material — to his audience? What **audience** was the book intended for? Is the writing completely candid and **sincere** or has the author some ulterior motive? By questions of this kind have the children devise criteria covering **plot**, **characterization** and **theme**.

    Regardless of the author's message, **clarity** is always an advantage — and nothing is worse than an unnecessary show of erudition. If the message is complex, the writing may also need to be complex — but it can still be clear, at least to the audience for which it was written. To *over-simplify* is to distort, but clarity is all the more necessary when complex meanings must be communicated.

6. Interpreting Supportive Symbol Systems.

6.1 Pictures and diagrams

J Young children are very familiar with pictorial aids to print. They need to learn to interpret simple diagrams by a gradual progression from picture material. Ask the children to prepare a diagram to support a given text or *vice versa*. Diagrams normally have **captions** or a **key**. Discuss the various purposes of pictures — to add interest, to arouse curiosity, to convey mood. Discuss the appropriateness of a picture or a diagram to illustrate a particular passage. The **diagram** is a stylized picture showing essential items more clearly than would be the case with a picture. A diagram has no background or context to identify size and other relational features as is the case with a good picture. These must be imagined by interpreting a **scale** — if this is given: half actual size; enlarged three times; etc. At this stage the distinction between a picture and a diagram is not always clear — many illustrations fall somewhere between. It is helpful if children make or use simple charts about their familiar environment — weather; seasons; etc.

M Learning in this area should not be taken for granted or regarded as inessential. The interpretation of pictures, diagrams and other symbols becomes increasingly important as techniques of printing improve and as life problems become more technical. Books are increasingly becoming vehicles for **mixed symbol presentation** — they are no longer the domain of pure print. Other symbol systems should be used where they convey a message more accurately or economically than print. However some print in the form of **captions** or explanations is usually necessary. Children must learn to interpret pictures and diagrams in association with print as an essential part of modern literacy. Have children extract as much information as possible from illustrations and discuss the results critically. Children should use and make increasingly complex charts. Point out the way in which the left to right, top to bottom, **directional conventions** of print apply to many charts, diagrams, and picture sequences (and below, to certain graphs and to tables).

S Study the relationship between story and illustration in fiction and in non-fiction. In fiction the illustration should produce expectation but not tell story. It should aid in establishing atmosphere and provide satisfying patterns of expression. In non-fiction the illustration should give information which may be conveyed more directly, accurately, and efficiently than could be done by print. The diagram is particularly valuable where spatial or functional relationships require clarification. Pictures and diagrams are seldom as efficient as print in displaying **process** — they are too static. A series of pictures or diagrams in combination with print often form the most suitable medium for conveying process. The motion picture and the graph, *in different ways*, display process and change efficiently. Children should discuss the composition of good pictures giving special attention to their values in directing attention, showing relationships, magnifying, changing perspective, etc.

The impact of **cartoons** as criticism of life will begin to be felt at this stage. Much useful work in critical thinking and creative expression may be based on cartoons. Ask children to give verbal interpretations of cartoon meanings, and express their own observations of life in the cartoon medium.

6.2 Graphs, Tables and other mathematical schema

J Rarely used at this level but children should understand simple picture and bar graphs.

M Picture, bar, circle, and line graphs will often be used in association with non-fiction. Simple tables begin to appear in books at this level. Children should come to understand a **time line** in simple form and be able to interpret a simple scale in association with diagrams and maps.

S An understanding of **mathematical schema** becomes increasingly important as children read into subjects of interest to them. The dense and economic nature of mathematical representation in contrast to the redundancy often involved in ordinary language should be discussed. Every symbol is vital in understanding a mathematical statement.

6.3 Maps, globes and other topographical devices

J Any good Social Studies scheme will provide details of a sound progression in learning to interpret maps. **Topographical models** are important to understand at this stage.

M Aerial photographs studied in relationship to simple topographical maps are a useful step in the interpretation of maps. Note that a map is a special type of diagram. As many books open up the excitements of exploration, a thorough grounding in the use of a **globe** and global projections prepares children for a better understanding of these fascinating phases of our historical background. At this stage children's interest in imaginary maps reaches a height and should be used and developed. The introduction of mathematical schema in the form of **scale** and **grid location** should be mastered.

S Children should be capable of making reference outside a text to suitable topographical information when necessary. They should understand that most authors take it for granted that the reader will make independent use of an atlas whenever necessary. (See also 9.2).

Children should learn to interpret **map legends** of many kinds.

7. Locating Information and Interpreting Abbreviations

7.1 Confident use of alphabetical order

J A major skills task at this stage. It is not sufficient for children to know the mnemonic alphabet — especially if they have to go back to the beginning of the series every time they wish to locate something listed alphabetically. Give adequate practice in locating by beginning, middle, and end of the alphabet. Use of order to the first letter place.

M Order to second and third places in alphabetically listed items. Use of **guide words**. Rapid location of any letter without use of serial memory.

S Absolute mastery of alphabetic order to the last place.

7.2 Using special parts of books

J Use of **table of contents** and a simple **index** and **glossary**, **Spine**.

M Information from **title page** and back of title page: author, editor, illustrator; date of publication, edition, publisher, country in which printed, acknowledgements.

S **Bibliography**. Meaning of common conventions in a bibliography. Appendices.
See Section 13.2 List g.

7.3 Interpreting abbreviations — especially in reference materials

J The children should become familiar with the most common abbreviations as units: their own initials; N.Z., Aust., and other abbrevs. used in addressing mail to their own address; St, Ave, Rd, Cres.; Mr, Mrs, Dr, (American usage still favours use of the period); etc. From such instances the children should be assisted to generalize important conventions:
a. Initial capital(s) plus period.
b. First part of word plus period.
c. First and last letters.
Note that suitable reference books for children of this age should *not* be heavily abbreviated.

M The more important literary abbreviations and those most commonly used in dictionaries should be noted.
e.g. *exempli gratia* — for example
cf. *confer* — compare (*see* may be used)
etc. *et cetera* — and so forth
i.e. *id est* — that is
n. noun, **v.** verb, etc.
pl. plural, **fut.** future, etc.
p. page, **pp.** pages.
ch. chapter, **chs.** chapters.
Refer children to the list of abbreviations in particular dictionaries.

S **ibid.** *ibidem* — the same (used in footnotes and bibliographies)
ca. or **c.** *circa* — around a given date
ed. edited by; edition
f. following page
tr. or **trans.** translated by
ff. following pages

8. Using Dictionaries (except locational skills Section 7)

8.1 Selecting the appropriate dictionary

J This will depend greatly on the range of dictionaries available. Children should have available a range of picture dictionaries — preferably one set of a multi-volume picture dictionary. At least one beginning dictionary proper should be available in the classroom in addition to the *Thorndike Junior Dictionary*, which should become the major reference for a number of years. A simple *Junior Thesaurus* has recently become available and this is likely to be followed by examples from other publishers.

M Avoid the small, highly-abbreviated desk dictionary. Word meanings should be fully exemplified in simple contexts using children's language. The *Thorndike Junior* and its variants should continue to be used as a basic reference. A further range may include the Oxford *Advanced Learner's Dictionary*, and *Illustrated Dictionary*, but **not** the *Concise* or the *Pocket* which are directed at the fully literate adult user. Many multi-volume pictorial dictionaries are available and a set should be included in each primary room. A few brighter children may use the full *Roget's Thesaurus of English Words and Phrases*. A good dictionary of **English idioms** and a **dictionary of quotations** begin to be of use. One or two simple books on interesting English words should be available to encourage independent interest in words.

S All the dictionaries listed at the previous level should continue to be available. Brighter children should be introduced to a range of adult dictionaries, of both the Webster and the Oxford type. In the reference section of a library children should meet such full English dictionaries as the *Oxford Shorter* and *Oxford English Dictionary*, as well as such special dictionaries as a **dictionary of biography**.

8.2 Selecting appropriate word meanings — distinguishing between multiple meanings

J One of the earliest insights about words provided for children should be that most words have several or many meanings depending on the way in which they are used and the context in which they are used. Display simple examples such as *run* or *pass*. Draw attention to the multiple listings of meanings in dictionaries at the children's level. Have the children select appropriate meanings from two, three and four possibilities. (Refer to relevant items in Section 1.)

M Dictionaries children use at this level should list multiple meanings in order of frequency of usage, *not* in historical order. The distinction between parts of speech becomes important in selecting meanings listed under different parts of speech — in the first instance, of course, nouns and verbs. Locations of variant forms of a word listed under the root should be undertaken as a natural part of structural analysis.

Use of dictionaries should be made a fascinating and rewarding process. Any teacher who forces children to copy out pages of a dictionary as a penal exercise so misunderstands the principles of language teaching that he would be better engaged in teaching children aversion to some other less vital subject.

S By this stage children should realize that words do not have fixed meanings — that they have a range of common usages which may be listed in a dictionary, but that their precise meanings must be gauged from the actual contexts in which they are used. Words may be given infinite shades of meaning by the contextual influences they are placed under in a given text, paragraph, sentence, or phrase. The commonest groups of meanings are listed in a dictionary — and the number of these meaning groups for each word will depend rather on the fullness of the dictionary than on any objective, countable number of meanings for a given word. Work on word meanings should, therefore, be associated with actual usages in a running context. Isolated dictionary exercises are of questionable value.

8.3 Phonetic respelling and the use of pronunciation keys

J Children should become familiar with the use of **simple respelling** to reflect actual pronunciation. In fact, they are so often punished for their use of phonetic insights in early spelling that this becomes a highly confused area. Follow a simple progression through to the use of a Thorndike-Barnhart **pronunciation key** as outlined in any good basic reading programme. Ideally, this should be closely associated with early work in phonetic analysis. Considering the very confused range of pronunciation keys (or absence of pronunciation keys), in dictionaries traditionally supplied in Australasian schools, it is not surprising that this work is often poorly taught.

M Mastery of the Thorndike-Barnhart respelling with diacritical marks should be a major task of this stage. It is then possible to move on to other systems which are more complex in their conventions — such as the International Phonetic Script and the system used in the Oxford dictionaries. These latter are certain to remain in a frightening no-man's land for all but gifted children, if sound progressions have not been covered in previous years.

S **Stressed and unstressed syllables** constitute a major learning area at this level. Having mastered a simple pronunciation key using diacritical marks, as suggested above, the children may now move into systems which use new characters for phonemes not distinguished in normal spelling such as those symbolized by *sh* and *ir* in *shirt*, and by *s* in *measure*.

9. Using Other Reference Materials

J Elementary encyclopedias are used without difficulty and provide a natural progression towards use of more complex encyclopedias. Children should be actively engaged in the preparatory progressions in map work, but few will be capable of using an atlas independently before the next stage.

M Extensive use is made of **encyclopedias** provided the range available is within the reading competence of the children. Nothing is worse than providing adult versions at this stage. Use of the **atlas** is a major task of these years. It is surprising how much needs to be learned in this area. Progressions should be very carefully worked out — it is dangerous to force such highly stylized and symbolic material before children without taking them through an adequate transition from real topography to its conventional diagrammed form. A field trip with topographical maps to some local vantage point is very helpful, as is the extensive use of aerial photographs. The conventions of **grid location**, **scale** and **colour keys** should be carefully introduced.

    Catalogues of many kinds should be introduced for use by the children. These will include film, film-strip, and record catalogues.

S Children should be quite independent in their use of encyclopedias and atlases. **Yearbooks**, **almanacs**, and **handbooks** of various kinds should be brought to the children's notice. The *Reader's Guide to Periodical Literature* is available in many libraries, but children would need some guidance in the use of its highly condensed and abbreviated entries.

10. Library Skills

10.1 Organization of a library

J   At this level most children will become familiar with the Children's Section of the library. This will include:

a. Fiction — shelved alphabetically by author

b. Non-fiction — shelved on a simplified Dewey Decimal System

c. Reference Section — for use within the library only

d. Magazine Section — filed in appropriate racks.

It may include a separate catalogue, but few children of this age will be ready for using a catalogue.

M   Children should be introduced to the main library as well as the Children's Section. The **Dewey Decimal System** should be clearly explained. Space does not permit a full treatment here. Major divisions are:

000 General Works
100 Philosophy and Psychology
200 Religion
300 Social Sciences
400 Language
500 Science
600 Applied Science
700 Fine Arts
800 Literature
900 History, Travel, Biography

Define the contents of each section in children's terms.

Libraries vary in the conventions used to shelve biography — find out what system is used in your local library. Introduce the children to useful material in the Magazine and Periodical Section.

S   Children should feel completely at home in a library, familiar with all its sections, and capable of locating any material available.

10.2 Using the Library Card Catalogue and Request Service

J   Most inquiries will pass through the Librarian, who is likely to offer sound tuition in these early years.

M   Use of a **Card Catalogue** is a major task of this stage. The Catalogue is to be found in a cabinet of small drawers conveniently placed near the entry to the library. There are four types of card and examples of each should be discussed clearly with the children:

1. Author card filed in alphabetical order of surname

2. Title card filed alphabetically — first word of title excluding articles

3. Subject card — filed alphabetically

4. Cross reference card — filed in the subject card system.

Children should learn to operate the **Request Service** through which virtually any book may be obtained after a time.

Regular class visits to the library should be planned during this period if possible. Close liaison with the local librarians is often helpul to both parties.

S   By this stage, use of a library to meet current needs should be an accepted pattern for most children, and becoming fixed as a life habit. More advanced children should be developing their own card index files for topic study, and may be given the task of preparing a card catalogue of all materials available for a forthcoming topic to be undertaken by the whole class.

11. Using Magazines, Journals, Newspapers and Brochures

J   Vagrant materials should be welcomed in the classroom, particularly if they are relevant in any way to work in progress: they are often vibrant with the daily life and concerns of the community. They also provide an ideal critical foil against which to display the qualities of more permanent literature. The various children's periodical journals and magazines covering science and hobby topics abound in material which is of questionable value in isolation but of considerable value in association with other study materials. This is particularly so in familiarizing children with mixed symbol systems outlined in Section 6 above.

M   Magazines such as *Popular Mechanics* and *National Geographic* begin to come within reading competence of many children, forming ideal study materials along with more ephemeral publications. Children will be active producing newspapers and magazines of their own, and learning some of the skills which lie behind print. They should be able to search for materials relevant to their studies in materials of many kinds. In historical studies they should be introduced to newspapers and journals in library archives which supply background information about local life in earlier times.

S   **Journals** of one kind and another now come within the scope of many children. They should learn that at least one journal or magazine which covers the area of each of their central interests is likely to be published, and that libraries subscribe to many of these. One way of keeping up to date in any interest is to follow periodical publications.

12. Using Supportive Media — Film, Radio, etc.

J   Children of this age are largely dependent on the teacher to locate films, filmstrips, and records relating to their current studies. However, they readily relate their normal TV viewing with current interests and classroom concerns. There is a certain immediacy and involvement engendered by TV which is valuable in the initial stages of developing an interest. Children are not likely to dismiss as irrelevant something which they have recently seen represented on TV, although it may have been difficult to arouse any sense of reality or concern beginning from comparatively cold and distant print.

M   Planned listening and viewing on a selective basis should be encouraged at this stage. Make a study of programme projections with the children, selecting programmes that are likely to further current classroom work. Children of this age are quite capable of using a filmstrip library, setting up and operating the machine independently after a short period of instruction. A few of the brighter children may be able to use catalogues to order films, records, or filmstrips from various libraries. The same children may undertake the task of pre-viewing, taking notes, and making oral or written reports to the teacher regarding content, level, suitability, quality, etc. **Records** and **tapes**, in particular, should be used much more frequently than is current practice: they bring the liveliness of the human voice into the literature programme.

S   Follow up suggestions at previous level — children should become quite independent in locating and evaluating audio-visual materials. Have selected children record what they have learned from a given programme and evaluate whether or not such learnings were important.

Encourage the children to use supportive media in presentations of their own topic studies.

13. Vocabulary of Criticism: Talking about Books

The following lists provide an extensive sampling of words which may be used in talking about books. No attempt has been made to assign these words to each of the three age levels. Teachers should use their discretion in introducing only those words which are intelligible to the children. See Section 1.1 esp. Level S; Section 2.1; and note where special vocabulary is called for in other Sections.

Emphasis has been given to the simple vocabulary of ordinary life which is accessible to the children and most appropriate to the discussion of literature at any level. Technical and literary language should aid and refine ordinary language, not replace it.

The four columns of Section 13.1 below reflect the following emphases:

A. Reality — realism and relevance to life.
B. Affect — emotional response
C. Coherence — logical, cognitive and academic qualities
D. Humanity — moral value and sensitivity

13.1 Qualities of writing

a. Truthfulness

A Reality	B Affect	C Coherence	D Humanity
true	candid	characteristic	open
realistic	frank	typical	honest
real	delicate	exact	pure
actual	fine	correct	sincere
certain	faithful	rigorous	just
accurate	perfect	sophisticated	right
natural	excellent	exaggerated	scrupulous
untrue	double-faced	misrepresented	reliable
mistaken	cunning	erroneous	trustworthy
faulty	sly	false	satirical
artificial	careless	unsound	wrong
unreal	clumsy	illogical	dishonest
plausible	boorish	inaccurate	insincere
	sentimental	incorrect	deceitful
	false sentiment	hasty	faked
		doubtful	forged
			mock
			axe to grind

b. Clarity

A Reality	B Affect	C Coherence	D Humanity
clear	stark	logical	plain-speaking
simple	candid	intelligible	frank
obvious	transparent·	comprehensible	unfeigned
plain	bold	unambiguous	undisguised
positive	concealed	obscure	evasive
direct	hidden	loose	illusory
forthright	veiled	indefinite	delusory
effective	reserved	unintelligible	insidious
sharp	mysterious	incomprehensible	double-dealing
distinct	feeble		
vivid	muddy		
vague	plausible		
covert			

c. Relevance to life

A Reality	B Affect	C Coherence	D Humanity
realistic	down to earth	significant	genuine
life-like	matter of fact	intelligible	no-nonsense
candid	full blooded	topical	inclusive
direct	lively	complicated	fake
actual	brief	meaningless	hollow
typical	vigorous	biased	phoney
puzzling	sunny	spurious	euphemistic
blind	tough	evasive	hypocritical
vague	trivial	pretentious	unjustified
distorted	sentimental	esoteric	improper
twisted	slippery	unwarranted	rhubarb
phoney	shifty	preposterous	unseemly
inappropriate	lifeless	trivial	
fictitious	uninteresting	circuitous	
	unimportant		

d. Author's point of view

A Reality	B Affect	C Coherence	D Humanity
sensible	sound	valid	fair
genuine	sincere	reasonable	just
realistic	assured	learned	good
natural	sympathetic	educated	wise
unbiased	upright	expert	sensitive
open-minded	kind	careful	compassionate
with-it	gentle	impartial	high-brow
commonplace	excitable	astute	low-brow
tuned in	amused	clear-headed	shrewd
square	optimistic	official	profound
true-to-life	ridiculous	tentative	humane
modern	foolish	dissenting	balanced
recent	stupid	dogmatic	sane
popular	puerile	absurd	healthy
objective	silly	illogical	arrogant
purposeful	smart	senseless	unjust
pragmatic	mad	rambling	unfair
sound	giddy	ignorant	jaded
blind	flighty	uninformed	soured
empty	shallow	pedantic	diseased
ignorant	self-satisfied	partial	corrupt
narrow	smug	bookish	cruel
blinkered	rude	hackneyed	selfish
twisted	one-eyed		
prejudiced	sly		
	pessimistic		
	old-fashioned		
	mean		
	sentimental		
	trite		

f. Vocabulary of formal discussion

See Section 16, esp. Scientific method of inquiry and committee procedures; and Section 17.2.

e. Tone and Manner

A Reality	B Affect	C Coherence	D Humanity
realistic	talkative	descriptive	fine
natural	fluent	narrative	profound
informed	chatty	poetic	elegant
candid	colloquial	figurative	graceful
direct	windy	explanatory	delicate
objective	smooth	expository	gentle
meticulous	persuasive	interpretive	noble
exact	neat	educational	cool
sensible	confident	academic	strong
plain	cheerful	thoughtful	ideal
explicit	energetic	considered	corrosive
earthy	exciting	witty	satirical
varied	fast	studious	ironic
magnificent	boisterous	orderly	refreshing
groovy	funny	tidy	polished
strange	cheery	theoretical	humane
fictitious	gay	hypothetical	humble
fabulous	merry	conjectural	enlightened
legendary	hilarious	clever	original
subjective	rollicking	concise	perceptive
imaginary	fantastic	sharp	creative
extravagent	quaint	cautious	amusing
far-out	solemn	easy	happy
queer	exalted	simple	devout
crazy	slow	low-brow	reverent
wild	sober	hard	sentimental
weird	sad	difficult	cheap
harsh	dreamy	complicated	high-sounding
careless	melancholy	awkward	pompous
uninformed	tragic	wordy	corrupt
nonsensical	dramatic	dry	insulting
twisted	curt	furtive	weak
spurious	abrupt	dogmatic	crude
artificial	harsh	roundabout	clumsy
biased	acidic	rambling	copied
eccentric	nasty	untidy	aping
prejudiced	irritable	disconnected	imitative
one-eyed	aggressive	ignorant	derivative
balderdash	pugnacious	idiotic	sick
bosh	horrible	ridiculous	irreverent
bunkum	oily	clumsy	profane
———	gawky	———	———
timid	repulsive	tedious	insipid
gloomy	dreary	silly	feeble
dull	tame	boring	monotonous

13.2 Elements of writing

g. About books as physical objects

cover	appendix	new edition	author
binding	bibliography	enlarged edition	manuscript
spine	index	illustrations	publisher

title page	author	footnotes	printer
table of contents	title	abbreviations	proofs
foreword	publisher	margins	binding
preface	date of publication	typeface	retailer
introduction	copyright notice	typographical	libraries
text	reprint	error	
	revised		

h. Kinds of writings

FICTION	HISTORY	CRITICISM	GENERAL
fairy tale	journal	discussion	scripts
fable	diary	commentary	writing —
legend	log	criticism	popular
parable	anecdote	essay	magazine
folk tale	memoirs	editorial	technical
allegory	autobiography	manifesto	scholarly
romance	journalism	leaflet	learned periodicals
novel	annal	tract	minutes
short story	chronicle	sermon	petition
DRAMA	EXPOSITION	satire	summary
monologue	report	GENERAL	precis
tragedy	article	fiction	abstract
comedy	manual	non-fiction	letter
farce	treatise	advertising copy	epitaph
spoof	lecture	advertisements	proverb
burlesque			parody
extravaganza			
musical			

i. The elements of structure in writing

content	style	middle	incident
form	point of view	climax	dialogue
mode	setting	anticlimax	slice of life
theme	plot	crisis	monologue
tone	sub-plot	crux	parody
mood	flashback	ending	satire
atmosphere	introduction	episode	symbol

j. Texture: the finer detail of the writing

abstract	VOCABULARY		USAGE
concrete	diction	emotive	grammar
general	common	sentimental	syntax
particular	formal	tired	context
literal	colloquial	overworked	tense
figurative	informal	cliche	number
metaphorical	slang	synonym	agreement
ambiguous	vulgarism	antonym	standard English
idea	euphemism	alternative	dialect
concept	technical	spellings	levels
notion	scholarly	derivation	register
generalization	Anglo-saxon	etymology	pronunciation
abstraction	Latinized	syllable	stress
dialogue	foreign	stem/root	intonation
punctuation	hip/mod	affixes	
setting		inflexion	

14. Surveying, Skimming and Adjusting Rate

Conventions:

Print hierarchies — size of print, bold, italic, indenting, underline, etc.

Tabulation hierarchies — simple, a.b.c. etc., subsumed, IV. B. 1.2.3. (Harvard outline form).

J In discussion before and after reading, through discussion of pictures, in finding textual support for the answer to a question, and in learning sound procedures for choosing books for personal reading, children should develop surveying and skimming techniques. Few children at this level are capable of adjusting rate and style to suit purpose, although much reading at recreational level will begin to produce a pleasure-reading-speed which is faster than speech. Children should be stimulated to form their own questions by such promptings as, *'What do we want to find out now?'*

M Surveying may be taught as an element of the SQ3R approach to study. Two factors in particular will induce versatility in rate and style:

a. The drive of interest or motivation in stretching reading to meet new needs.

b. Familiarity with material of different kinds and, in particular, with the organization of that material.

There is little evidence that direct physical or mechanical training aids efficiency — except in providing motivation. The production of appropriate and changing **set** towards materials and purpose seems a more fruitful line for teaching. The use of organizational cues is vital in this respect — see Section 2.2 and Section 3. In introducing a new piece of writing, ask the children to skim table of contents, headings, and topic sentences to obtain a preview of content. Often test at this point, discussing what information should be gained from using these procedures.

S Children should be able to determine organization rapidly and be responsive to a wide range of cue words, such as *finally* or *in summary*. They should understand **print hierarchies** (size, bold, italic, etc.) and **tabulation hierarchies** (I. A. 1.2.3. etc) as aids in determining the author's structure. More important than any other factor, they should have developed an aggressive, questioning attack on print, recognizing shallow or empty styles as suitable material to read at the speed of light, and stopping to savour the profound or the sensitive. Their style of reading should be responsive to their critical judgement of what they are reading.

15. Organizing Information — Note-taking

J Many of these skills begin at the level of listening and responding. Children follow the pattern of teachers' recapitulations to summarize and review. This task should be thrown over to the children increasingly, with guidance by careful questioning. Children should begin to condense statements. Activities involving **telegraphese** assist, e.g. sending telegrams to report on a lesson or topic. *Simple* numeration (i.e. 1. 2. 3. or a. b. c. but not 1a. 1b. etc.) should be used by the children independently.

M Have children make notes on a presentation and then discuss various versions, finally building up a model on the blackboard. Ask children to speak from *brief* notes. Have children use various types of numeration, particularly for main and subsidiary ideas. To teach recall, ask children to write a tabulation outline on one side of a card and the tabulation with completed items on the other. In review the children see how many items of the empty tabulation they can recall before checking the reverse of card. Repeat until learning is secure.

S Refine earlier procedures. Teach the children that the form and nature of an outline will be determined by the purpose of the study — begin by clarifying what questions to put to the material. (Relate to Section 14.) Have children leave a wide margin in notes for review summaries. Teach how to use concrete associational links as memory cues.

16. Carrying Out a Topic Study

16.1 Combining skills towards a specific study purpose.

J The organization and methods of the modern infant room are very suited to the development of sound topic study techniques — the procedures of developmental periods, centres of interest, and local field trips are too often abandoned in the upper school. The learning situations of the school should be such that it will become second nature for children to approach a subject in several different ways, actively questioning their materials and seeking a wide range of sources. Books are only part of the total process, although a vital one. The common factor which binds all activities together is thinking — inquiring, creative, critical attitudes.

M Having formulated a purpose, chldren should learn to follow through sound procedures independently — organizing, locating, surveying, skimming, formulating questions, reading, note-taking, checking with reference materials and library skills, discussing, formulating conclusions, and embarking on appropriate activities for expression or presentation. Such a series of activities is complex, and it is the work of many years to bring every part under independent control. By following themes relevant to the problems of personal development at any particular level, children may be helped to sustain effort, maintain clear purposes, and experience continuing satisfactions — all of which are vital to topic study.

The SQ3R Approach
During these years the children should be introduced to this technique.

Survey: Rapidly preview the material, especially organization (table of contents, headings, etc.) opening paragraph, and illustrations.

Question: Think of one or two questions about the topic which you expect the book to answer.

Read: Aided by the expectations based on S and Q, read the material to gain full and detailed comprehension. When studying a topic, note down main points.

Recite or Recall: Go over the main points in your mind with particular care to determine whether you have gained answers to earlier questions.

Review: Check your recall. When studying a topic, check against your notes, and refer to the text again where necessary. Make a condensed and clarified precis of your notes for later revision or presentation.

S As children undertake more and more studies of an academic and abstract kind, make sure that opportunities are given for many *topical* studies relevant to the children's immediate world and to their continuing and changing problems of personal development. For instance, a study of road safety and car design, or waste and pollution, will help children to see the relevance of intellectual activity, the complexity of real problems calling for varied techniques and ranging scholarship, and the great challenge of inertia and ineptitude in a modern world which pretends to have solved most of its problems. A study concerned with controlling emotions or understanding adults will display the richness of literature and the helpfulness of discussion in facing problems.

There should be growing understanding of the **scientific method of inquiry**:

A. Collect **data** — perhaps with certain hunches in mind but careful to see that the hunches do not dominate **selection** of the data.
B. Suggest hypotheses to explain the data — the **inductive** process. This results in the formulation of **rules** or **generalizations** or **principles**. If these are sound, they will apply to any individual case which falls under them, or to a statistically significant number of cases when group behaviour is being studied.
C. **Test** the hypothesis — the **deductive** and **experimental** processes. The hypothesis is now used deductively to **predict** that a particular state of affairs will fall out in a manner consistent with the hypothesis. Such a prediction is put to the test in an **experiment**. The hypothesis is strengthened if it helps to explain other phenomenon — if it simplifies (known as *Occam's razor*).
D. Retest with many different instances of as wide a variety as possible within the generalization. Control **variables**.
E. New data comes to light as a result of this process and there is a return to A.

EXAMPLE:

a. The egg-laying rate of hens seems to be seasonal. (A hunch)
b. Hens are sensitive to the daylight-darkness ratio. (An inductive structure)
c. If we artificially increase this ratio, we will increase the egg-laying rate of the hens. (A deductive structure) The hens do in fact lay more eggs or sustain laying. Strengthened by explaining high spring laying rate.
d. Could it be that the artificial lighting supplies greater heat? Control temperature. No change. Could it be that the hens can see to eat for longer periods? Control food intake. Little change.
e. What sensory or chemical agency is at work? Could we control this in a less expensive way than by illumination? Hormone additive to food? Breeding blind hens?

16.2 Working in a team towards clearly defined study ends.

Committee Procedures

a. Rule of the Chair.
b. The right to speak in strict order of request.
c. The right to be heard without interruption.
d. The right to question.
e. The right to silence — understanding that this implies assent.
f. The right to vote and to register dissent.
g. The willingness to accept decisions of the group within the context of group activity while maintaining the right to self-determination outside this context.
h. The ultimate right to dissociate from the group — the group is a voluntary association and there should be no captive members.

Vocabulary of formal discussion

chairman; secretary; agenda; minutes; constitution; motion; mover; seconder; resolution; amendment; point of order; vote; by voice; by hands; by ballot; majority; scrutineer; minority opinion; dissention.

J As children move out of the egocentric stage of infancy they should learn that common purposes may be fulfilled by corporate endeavour, division of labour, sharing of knowledge, using special talents, etc. Such an approach in the classroom is immeasurably more effective in the long run than an aggressively competitive spirit. Good habits of listening, of formulating questions, and of taking part in discussions are essential to team procedures. Children should learn to listen to other points of view even if they are not yet able to be tolerant, generous or discriminating.

M The foundations of team procedures are laid at this level. Children should learn the functions of **formal committee procedures** which protect the rights of each member of the group allowing him to make his maximum contribution, have his opinions heard, and participate in making an accurate consensus of opinion. It is essential that the extroverted and the withdrawn, the leader and the follower, the headstrong and the vacillating, the creative and the conforming *all* master the basic learnings of committee procedure, learn *from* them, and find *their own* way of functioning within them. Regardless of his personality type, **the gifted child** is likely to go through life unable to develop and express his giftedness unless he finds his own way of operating within a team. This does not imply any pressure for conformity or smothering of individuality — the creative individual will be much more effective if he learns how to handle, even manipulate, the group. More importantly, creativity is something which grows under discipline of the right kind, and blossoms in the service of human decency and concern. The group *is* often uncreative and conservative — this is one of the learnings involved in teamwork, especially for latent leaders. It is likely that the gifted individual will find it necessary to withdraw or become isolated at crucial points in his development, but if this withdrawal is to be fruitful, there must be a *return to people*. The gifted need to be taught how to make this return. A well-ordered classroom does not kill creativity in the interests of the group — it encourages independence and self-expression within a structure of human concern.

S Team procedures should function in a mature way by this stage. Every child should be able to fulfil the leadership role to some extent when the opportunity arises. Every child should know that he has a useful place in the wider functioning of the group, and that he may contribute without fear of ridicule or exclusion. He should be capable of working towards common purposes without competing for prominence and praise. He should be able to listen, to question, to consider, to contribute, and to share.

16.3 Keeping up to date

J Proper attention to newspapers and TV at this level will develop the idea that knowledge is changing rapidly and there is need to check recent findings in any field.

M Insights concerned with change and the expansion of knowledge should be developed. Converse insights are also important — today's discovery becomes tomorrow's mistake — and there is a need for tentativeness in accepting the latest ideas, at least as the last word.

S Children should check **date of publication** as an automatic procedure in dealing with factual material. Locating the sources of an author's material (using **footnotes** and **bibliography**) and checking the procedures he has followed to gather and interpret his information, are important skills for this age. Is the material first-hand or second-hand? What principles of selection has he used in organizing his material? If he is presenting the results of **research**, what methods has he used to gather his information, to see that his samples are typical, to verify his conclusions experimentally?

16.4 Presenting a study — representing the group

J Begin shaping up the spontaneous reports of young children by emphasizing sticking to the point, clear delivery, simple notes, supportive illustrations, etc. Less confident children should have the experience of addressing small groups rather than the class.

M At this stage, much reporting will be representative of team endeavour. Considering the nature of the audience begins to be a matter for attention. Have the children present reports outside the limitations of their own class — to younger or to older groups, to parents, to the headmaster, etc. Written reporting will begin to represent a larger proportion of presentations. Children need guidance in arranging displays, making charts, compiling magazines, etc.

S Emphasis will now be on the **form of the written report**:
    A. **Introduction** — a clear beginning stating scope of study, questions to be answered, organization to be adopted, etc.
    B. **Body** — clear organization following a single, major system where possible, e.g. time sequence, major areas, etc.
    C. **Conclusion** — summary emphasizing what the study claims to have shown, unanswered questions, and directions for further study.
Refinement of oral presentation should proceed, particularly in relationship to speaking from notes (Section 15) and the use of supportive media (Section 12).

    Children should combine to present experiences through drama, puppetry and mime. Variety of presentation through panel procedures, questioner and respondent, use of tape recorder, etc., should be encouraged.

17. Audience Reading

17.1 Preparation — without an audience
Preparation entails:
a. Solving all problems of word recognition and meaning free from pacing pressures.
b. Thinking about and practising ways of making the presentation more pleasing and audible to the audience.

Play reading:
Begin procedures which should be followed at all stages of development:
a. All children who are to participate read the entire play silently for enjoyment and understanding before casting takes place. This should often be handled as a normal guided silent reading lesson.
b. Discuss the play and suitable casting. Involve the children in the decisions of casting.
c. Each child prepares his or her own part, taking particular care to solve all problems of word recognition and meaning, to deepen understanding of the character involved, and to think about and practise ways of presenting the dialogue. See 17.2 below.
d. The cast come together for a first, practice oral reading, and discuss improvements with the producer.
e. The play is read to an interested audience, perhaps in a different class.

The diagnostic situation:
If a teacher wishes to obtain as clear a picture as possible of how a child operates in reading, he may have the child read to him in a diagnostic setting. An **Informal Prose Inventory** such as that provided in *Appendix A*, is useful for such a purpose.

Some important considerations:

a. There should be no audience other than the teacher.
b. The material should be read without preparation so that the teacher may observe something of the strategies used in solving different problems.
c. Put the child at ease and explain the purpose of hearing him read.
d. Begin at or below the child's estimated level of confidence.
e. Provide some oral introduction or *set* for each passage that is to be read so that meaning oriented skills may operate immediately.
f. Do not evaluate audience reading skills, such as fluency or phrasing, from evidence provided in this situation. Evaluate audience reading only after thorough preparation as outlined above.

For detailed notes on observation and interpretation of reading skills at different levels, see the introduction and the instructions for each test in *Appendix A*.

J Children should be encouraged to read favourite stories which they know very well to other children who have not heard the stories. Often these will be bed-time stories from home. They should be very clear about the purpose of the reading — to share enjoyment with others. Oral reading to the teacher should also be undertaken in this spirit — to share an enthusiasm or a success with an important adult.

   If the children read their own work, this also provides for adequate preparation. In all other cases where audience reading is required, the children should be given adequate opportunity to prepare, either silently or orally.

M Continue as above. There will be much reading in the presentation of topic studies. Preparation should now include looking up from the text and back — a very tricky eye manoeuvre. A large mirror is helpful to some children.

   The tape recorder and address system should be used to assist shy children. A puppet or a shadow theatre is also useful.

S Follow the same basic principles outlined above. Audience reading is a difficult, late developing skill. Many children will only now be reaching that proficiency and confidence in reading which makes oral reading a pleasure rather than an ordeal. Some children will never reach this degree of confidence: provided their silent reading skills are adequate and in line with expectations based on sound procedures, such children will not be greatly disabled by the lack of oral reading skill and should not be harried into performance.

17.2 Presentation — voice, volume, articulation, intonation; pace; pause and breathing; pre-scanning

J The control of such an array of skills in addition to those of normal reading presents a formidable developmental task usually covering many years. The very young are at a disadvantage in the thin tone and high pitch of their voices. Audiences should be kept as small as possible. If this means that the group is not under your control, make sure that the reader is not loaded with the additional task of keeping the group in order. One answer is to use a tape recorder in a quiet room and play back to the audience with some degree of amplification — especially of the lower pitch levels. Another is to train children to become used to a microphone and amplifier early.

   Audiences should be well trained in courtesy, and care should be taken not to put them in boring listening situations. This form of oral reading should be restricted to very short periods suited to the attention span of young children. Children should not be *forced* into audience reading at this stage: try to motivate all children by dramatic and other forms of presentation.

M There are so many skills to practise here that the first principle ought to be that children should not have to face problems of word recognition while attepting to control these other skills. Discuss and practice one skill at a time and don't overwhelm the children with points to attend to in a number of skills simultaneously. Remember that these skills will gradually come under automatic systems of control as they mature, and it is therefore highly unnatural to expect a child to give *conscious* attention to all of them at once.

First, perhaps, deal with **volume**. Practise holding book and head in the best position to throw the voice out, and breathe strongly to supply the additional energy required to increase volume. Practise in very short bursts of thirty to sixty seconds at first.

Now, perhaps, emphasize **pace**. Demonstrate the slower, more deliberate speed of audience reading which gives clearer articulation, better control of breathing, and more time to follow the print line ahead of the voice in phrase groups at first.

Intonation is usually more important in holding an audience than clear articulation, which is often over-emphasized at the expense of natural voice rhythms. Demonstrate and have children practise changes of **stress** within a given sentence such as, *Why do you think she did that?* Now do the same with **pitch**, e.g. *Oh yes?* ('You think so?') *Oh yes!* ('That's right!' or 'Of course — go on.') *Oh yes!* ('I couldn't agree more!' or 'Yes please!') Now do the same for **pause**, e.g. *Would-you-please-take-your-great hoof off my geraniums!* Discuss the way in which **punctuation** gives clues to intonation patterns.

Purposeful audience reading provides the ideal opportunity to concentrate on clear **articulation** for a period. Attend first to the most general deficiencies — slurred endings, devalued vowels, nasal speech, etc. Again, demonstrate the effects of laxity and the effects of a little attention. Tune children's ears to all that is delightful in the sounds of language.

S Most of the basic patterns of response should be almost automatic by this stage — now is the time for refinement. Drama and verse will provide ideal opportunities. Encourage those children who show promise in reflecting character through voice. Experiment with **dialect** and with different **registers** or **levels of language**. Have the children attempt the same utterance as if they were different people — a road labourer, a refined gentleman, a fussy old lady, a father, a teacher saying to a child, *Put that rubbish in the proper container*.

Arrange for older children to read to younger children regularly. This gives the older child the opportunity to bolster his sense of security by massive regression to the old favourites of his infancy — which he knows well, loves, and can read without any problems of word recognition. Conduct lively discussions about books, and encourage the children to exemplify the points they make by purposeful oral reading from the text.

18. Developing Satisfying Reading Habits as Part of a Life Style

18.1 Reading for pleasure

J   Unless the hundreds of hours of reading instruction over many years are largely pleasurable hours resulting in a will to read, the experiences of reading are likely to hinder personal development in many areas. A fundamental part of teaching reading is to use professional knowledge of children's books and of the children's current developmental needs to achieve a bond of relevance and satisfaction between reading and living. Even for young children there are always books available which deal with whatever current problem or interest or need presses in upon today. For those teachers who are unfamiliar with the wealth of literature at the level they teach there is always a knowledgeable children's librarian willing to advise or to assist. Reading aloud to children should be a prominent part of the reading programme at every level, but particularly in these beginning years great patience and ingenuity should be used to introduce children to books. If your programme has always been so crowded with instruction and organization that you have never quite got around to playing an active role in stimulating a wide interest in books, the time has come for some searching reflection on the nature and function of teaching.

M   The selection of books is a skill which must be learned: developing skills of choosing appropriate books is a vital task of this stage. Familiarity with a library should develop into a confident and knowledgeable use of library facilities.

S   Those children who have not developed reading as an essential part of daily living should be our greatest challenge at this level. Crash remedial programmes, repeated year after year, too often reinforce the non-reader's notion of reading as a cause of today's problems rather than as a relevant solution of them. For such children, in particular, print must be presented as a living voice with a highly personal message to those who learn to listen.

18.2 Using books appropriately — adapting rate and style of reading to suit purpose

J   Children should be introduced, often through listening, to the range of purposes which books may fulfil, and should lay the foundations for versatile reading.

M   Basic skills should be mastered to the point at which there is no technical impediment to meeting different needs through books. It is strong motive producing a drive towards self-seeking which stretches reading skills into new and more efficient patterns. Efficient reading cannot be produced by straining to perform special tasks on inane exercises. Here again the fundamental task of instruction is shown to be relevance and personal satisfaction through reading.

S   The mature reader cannot be described as a type. He is one who has for so long used reading to meet his life interests and needs that he has developed highly personal patterns and perception and response which reflect his own style of life.

Notes

1. The process of learning spoken language is so remarkably successful among all people that many linguists, led by Chomsky (1957), have postulated an innate language-learning faculty in man. The danger of this point of view is to regard spoken language as natural and written language as artificial — and to justify radically different conditions for the acquisition of literacy.

    In fact, learning spoken language is so like any other form of *developmental* learning that we must regard it as an *instance* of that successful body of learning. When the conditions for developmental learning are set up in a culture for quite new skills, such as riding a bicycle or bouncing a ball, they are mastered with the same high level of success. There can be no suspicion that these are innate faculties which allow mastery of bike riding or ball bouncing to be learned without instruction. Rather, we must look to the crucial conditions in the learning environments of developmental tasks to account for their remarkable efficiency — and for their lack of deliberate instructional intervention.

    Studies such as those of Durkin (1966), Clark (1976) and Butler (1979) tend to support the prediction that *if* the skills of literacy are modelled in a truly *developmental* environment, they are likely to be mastered with the same joyful ease as is learning to speak. Certainly we have no justification for claiming that any condition associated universally with mastering developmental tasks is educationally unsound. *That* would need to be proved — and I can imagine no experimental structure within which such proof would be possible.

    Literacy *can* be introduced as a developmental task, and there is increasing evidence that to the extent that the conditions of developmental learning are provided, to that extent learning is similarly successful, natural and joyful. I know of no research· which can be interpreted as contradicting this assertion. An increasing body of research points in the other direction. For a detailed discussion of these matters as they currently stand, see Holdaway (1979). See also notes 2, 3, 8, 14, and 18.

2. An obvious call on the responsible researcher *or* teacher is to study the conditions lying behind optimum learning of a skill and then to replicate those conditions as nearly as possible for sub-optimal learners. Sometimes, it may be impossible to set up those optimal conditions for sub-optimal learners — the crucial developmental stage has been passed; home conditions cannot be changed; the institutions of schooling have limits in flexibility, etc. This may entail compensating for sub-optimal conditions by highly skilled and informed teaching as in the Auckland University early

intervention programme (Clay 1980). However, such intervention is unlikely to be effective if it runs *counter* to the conditions prevailing for optimal learners. It is often necessary to devise *instructional* answers for environmental or other deficits and no doubt this is the role of most teaching. However the *ideal* model, when it is possible, is to set up optimal conditions patterned on the experiences of optimal learners.

This approach appears most irrelevant when we face extreme handicap or disability. However, it has been my experience that in designing programmes of behaviour management or precision teaching for handicapped children, not only is it necessary to keep optimal conditions in mind, but also *the precision programme, lovingly applied, tends to generate optimal conditions*. A marvellously documented instance of this tendency is described by Dorothy Butler in her moving account of the development of her handicapped grandchild, *Cushla and Her Books* (1979).

In the ten years of research and development in Auckland leading to the procedures which have come to be known as Shared Book Experience, this model was applied with manifest success. The replication of conditions as close as possible to optimal preschool literacy environments had markedly positive effects during the early years of schooling, especially on children who had experienced grossly sub-optimal conditions in terms of readiness for literacy-learning.

3. This can be said to be increasingly the case in remedial intervention as we move up the school system. Children who are failing in reading beyond their fifth year at school have been so denatured as learners that only expert teaching can help them. Much of this expertise, however, must be turned to the negative task of compensating for years of failure under *unnatural* conditions — failure that has been ground in grittily by competition, humiliation, and despair. It would be foolish to argue that these failure-induced effects can be overcome simply by restoring natural conditions — the damage has been done, and requires expert intervention in order to be undone. However, one important aspect of that expert intervention must be a movement towards more natural developmental conditions.

4. In contrast to other developmental tasks, learning to read is both difficult to model and badly modelled — especially by the school. If children saw literacy modelled in joyful and effective ways, they would want to be in the act, as with so many other things they learn 'naturally'. It has been reported that Sustained Silent Reading works best when the teacher *also* reads quietly and talks with enthusiasm about what he or she reads.

In reading *to* children on a regular basis, the teacher programmes himself or herself as a modeller of literacy. The covert and mysterious aspects of reading are made manifest, and the liveliness of personal response is breathed into the text.

Even in the content fields of the curriculum, children need to know just how a reader in *that* discipline goes about the task, and just what they get out of it. A teacher is to a large extent a manifester — and this applies particularly to a task like reading, which normally lacks overt, observable qualities. Above all, children need to see adults they respect engaging with enthusiasm and obvious relish in all modes of literacy.

5. Although communication is a crucial human activity, it is by no means the only or necessarily the major function of language. Halliday (1973) in his *Exploration in the Functions of Language* develops a multi-functional view of language, in which representational language — the major language of

schooling — is only one. The following is a summary of Halliday's language functions.

Instrumental	The 'I want' function.	Fulfilling needs.
Regulatory	The 'Don't do that' function.	Controlling
Interactional	The 'I love you' function.	Relating to others.
Personal	The 'This is me' function.	Defining self.
Heuristic	The 'What's that?' function.	Finding out.
Imaginative	The 'Let's pretend' function.	Making-believe.
Representational	The 'This is how it is' function.	Communicating about content

In explaining the significance of these functions Halliday says:

> Language is 'defined' for the child by its uses; it is something that serves this set of needs ... For the child, all language is doing something: in other words, it has meaning. It has meaning in a very broad sense, including here a range of functions which the adult does not normally think of as meaningful, such as the personal and the interactional and probably most of those listed above — all except the last, in fact. But it is precisely in relation to the child's conception of language that it is most vital for us to redefine our notion of meaning; not restricting it to the narrow limits of representational meaning (that is, 'content') but including within it all the functions that language has a purposive, non-random, contextualized activity (pp. 17-18).

We could add to this the peculiar language of thinking which itself fulfils many functions in planning, problem-solving, dreaming, fantasizing and so on. The functional richness of language needs to be explored thoroughly in the literacy programme if it is to have anything like its full impact. (Britton 1970.)

6. Children programme themselves in developmental tasks to have a nice relationship between successful activity, risk taking, and failure. They seldom resent their failures — after all, they are aware that they have caused them. Instead, they tend to *learn* from them. This is in great contrast to the failures that are *forced* on them from outside, and there is no agency in life which does more of that than the school. This is another reason for encouraging independence and self-regulation, both of which tend to make failure a point of learning. Clay (1972a pp. 124-6) comments on this tendency for successful learners both to make mistakes and to profit from them.

    On the positive side of reinforcement, children learning a developmental task set up patterns of intrinsic reward which sustain them in learning even in the absence of extrinsically rewarding adults. This occurs naturally in healthy reading at all levels: readers who are self-regulating monitor their own understanding and their moment-by-moment success; they take sensible risks and rapidly learn from their mistakes; they operate in an almost continuous flow of intrinsic reinforcement.

    Furthermore there is increasing evidence that intrinsic rewards are more effective — especially in the long term — than extrinsic rewards. Donaldson (1978 pp. 115-120) and Deci (1975) also draw attention to evidence suggesting that extrinsic motivation may be damaging — performance tends to fall when the rewards are withdrawn.

7. The following material on self-regulation, stages of reading development, and evaluation was presented in a similar form to the Fifth World Congress on Reading in Vienna during August 1974. The paper was published by the International Reading Association in the proceedings, *New Horizons in Reading* (1976).

8. Two misconceptions go hand-in-hand to cripple self-regulation: the notion, springing from 'hearing reading', that the task is a performance one rather than a thinking and responding one; and the belief that correction must come from outside. Most retarded readers are deeply misinformed in this way — they have abdicated from controlling their own behaviour while reading. One inevitable result of this abdication is a certain loss of semantic coherence. An equally crippling result is that they cannot read without being plugged into another person who assumes the abdicated role of corrector and controller. Hence the indispensable condition of learning to read — learning through reading — is denied to that child. Unfortunately the greater the retardation in reading, the more likely it is that self-regulation will be denied. Too many humane and supportive remedial programmes emphasizing the hearing (and correcting) of oral reading perpetuate or magnify dependence. The suggestions made in the chapter *Developing Reading Skills and Strategies* are intended as an antidote to the long-term toxins of dependence.

9. Book-loving infants role-play themselves as readers of their favourite books. They do not simply memorize and repeat the text in a rote manner; they *recreate* the text in their own syntax and vocabulary. They normally 'perform' without an audience, and unasked. In this closed setting they monitor their own output in self-corrective ways. They have learned the most fundamental strategy of the real reader.

    Detailed examples and discussion of this behaviour may be found in Holdaway (1979) pp. 38-63.

10. Confirmation, or the feedback process of reading, uses two major channels: one turns inwards to check semantic and syntactic coherence; the other turns outwards to visual detail in an act which checks on letter or feature expectation. In terms of letter-sound relationships this latter type of perception is quite distinct from the letter-to-sound movement taught in phonics programmes; it moves in the opposite direction, from sounds clearly positioned in words proposed by sampling and prediction, to letters expected to be seen in an appropriate position in the printed word. The result of such perception is either a feeling, of 'Yes it is!' or a 'Whoops! No. Must be X' self-correction — which also ends in the 'Yes' feeling. This process, then, not only assures accuracy, but also mediates *reinforcement*.

    It is also more simple and natural than 'blending' in phonics, which operates from unknown bits to a hoped for whole word. Letter confirmation *starts* from an understood whole and checks constituent parts. Furthermore, because it operates out of meaningful wholes which do not decay from short-term memory, as meaningless parts do, the process can maintain attention for much longer periods without fatigue. This is in considerable contrast to the over-phonicated retarded reader who rapidly fatigues himself in a laboured cacophony (It wasn't the cough that carried him off but the cacophon they carried him off in — often.)

11. Attempting to operate at a higher stage in a developmental task when a lower stage has not been mastered is a dangerous undertaking full of insecurity. Retarded readers are often in just this situation. In particular, the learnings of the lowest stage, Emergent Reading, are likely not to have been mastered and the reader has been plunged into the Early Reading stage without the underpinning security of a well-formed literacy set. Even after many years of failure this may continue to be the case and remediation will need to include successful Emergent Reading experiences.

    For details see *Appendix C, Literacy Set,* and the chapter, *Levels of Operation and Stages of Development.*

12. Too often questions of accountability are sheeted through to the classroom teacher without reference either to the real welfare of children or the distorting influences of what I have called the Third Force. In a sound system of accountability there needs to be first of all some way of monitoring the knowledge, power, and effects of authority influences upon teachers and children. A system of passing the buck ultimately comes down with all its weight on under-achieving children who are already harmed or crippled by anxiety, punitive comparisons, humiliation, and despair. (Holt 1964).

13. Carter (1973) reported favourably on the effects of individualized reading at the Grade 4 level, especially in changing attitudes to reading and in revitalizing skills progress among slower readers. His attitude scale (Carter 1977) provides a useful instrument for monitoring this vital, but neglected, part of the reading process.

14. Of particular importance here is the experience of children failing at the Early Reading Stage at whatever age. Learnings at the earliest Emergent Reading Stage are often neglected and in consequence these children do not have the strategies to sustain them in the slow, meticulous processes of early reading. Often a return to emergent reading and the creation of a powerful literacy set are required before comfortable progress can be made at the next stage. See Note 11 for details. See also Clay (1979).

15. The way in which prediction operates in the total problem-solving process may best be illustrated by a cross-reference diagram. The following figures are taken from Holdaway (1979) pp. 95-6.

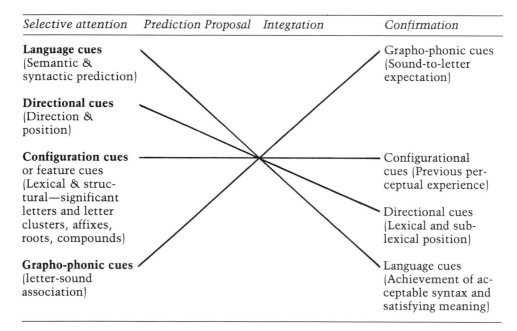

Selective attention Prediction Proposal Integration	Confirmation
Language cues (Semantic & syntactic prediction)	Grapho-phonic cues (Sound-to-letter expectation)
Directional cues (Direction & position)	
Configuration cues or feature cues (Lexical & structural—significant letters and letter clusters, affixes, roots, compounds)	Configurational cues (Previous perceptual experience)
	Directional cues (Lexical and sublexical position)
Grapho-phonic cues (letter-sound association)	Language cues (Achievement of acceptable syntax and satisfying meaning)

Prediction operates by bringing expectations from behind the eye to bear on a sampling of visual cues from what is in front of the eye. This narrows possibilities into probabilities and results in a proposal almost compulsively. The process is similar in efficiency to using both the horizontal and the vertical coefficients to find a street on a road map.

Suppose there are 20 horizontal coefficients and 20 vertical coefficients. If we were stupid enough to use only *one* set — like using a single word recognition skill — this would still reduce the searching task to one twentieth of the time. However, if we use *both* coefficients in cross-reference, we don't reduce the task additively to one fortieth — dramatically, we reduce the task by the square of the coefficients to *one four hundredth* of the searching time.

Suppose that I'm searching the verbal inventory in my brain for a word beginning with the letter p. There may be three thousand possibilities. But if we start to cross-reference:

Sample pr-   perhaps 200 possibilities
Sample a fairly long word (configuration)   perhaps 50 possibilities
Sample a noun following preposition 'from'   perhaps 10 possibilities
Sample a noun meaning a process in reading   perhaps 1 possibility
Total sentence supplying full semantic coherence and confirmation:

Ease and fluency in reading come from prediction. Of course, we would normally approach the sampling of graphic detail with an already developed semantic set of highly complex structure — what we bring to print from behind the eye — and this makes the process even more efficient.

The total process may be represented in the following four-phase analysis:

SAMPLE	PROPOSAL	TEST	RESOLUTION
Minimal observation of significant cues in relationship to ongoing meaning and sentence structure.	Possible slotfiller leaps to mind. One or more lexical items.	Checking newly significant cues. Weighing syntactic and semantic coherence.	Satisfaction Reinforcement Relaxation Restoration of faculties.
Emotional state: Pleasantly tense or anxious—tingling	Excited. Could it be . . .?	Calm and critical	Relaxed.
Example at 6 year level: 'Mother will *stay* at home.'			
'Mother will st--' —like 'stop' but different.	'stay'	Yes, 'stay at home'. Like 'day'. That's it!	Pleasure and relaxation. Readiness to proceed.
Example at 7 year level: 'The goat took a bite of *cactus*.'			
Texan goat—eats anything—but doesn't eat this— 'took a bite of cac---'	'cactus!'	Ends in '-us' Thought those things in the picture were potatoes.	Haha. That must've hurt. On we go.
Example at 8 year level: 'Wool makes fine hair and *whiskers*.'			
Making a mask? '. . . makes fine hair and w . . .' ◄— Like hair 'wisk---'	'wizzers' —— ➤No!—that 'k'! What's this? 'whiskers'	Right! There's the 'k' and the 'ers'	Of course—from animals like rabbits. I can do that.

Problem solving in reading . . . is fundamentally a hypothesis-test situation. We can distinguish four phases in such an operation, each with its own psychological style and emotional overtones. Under the influence of syntactic and semantic expectations, the reader makes a rapid and largely automatic sampling of the visual detail. Uncertainty is reduced by this sampling to the point where a proposal or hypothesis presents itself — usually automatically and compulsively without deliberation. Confirming occurs in light of newly significant visual detail within a framework of increasing semantic coherence. Reassured and momentarily rested, the reader moves on with sustaining energy. In analysing what is almost always a very rapid, automatic process we inevitably make it *look* more ponderous than it usually is. (The term *sample* derives from Ken Goodman's work quoted earlier. The term *proposal* refers to genuinely predictive processes — not to mere guessing (Smith 1978, p. 67). The term *test* refers to confirming processes, and the term *resolution* refers to the vital affective and organic outcomes.) p. 95.

16. There are three rather different uses of cloze (or prediction) in the classroom, each with its own characteristics:

a. Testing comprehension.

Here the deletion pattern in research has usually been 1 in 5 words after the first sentence, with each gap of equal length, and in a passage providing about 40 completions (200 plus words). Only exact replacements are scored as correct and a score of 45% exact replacements indicates good comprehension at that level. (Elley 1975.)

b. Readability.

Closely related to a. above is the use of cloze to determine readability of materials for a particular group. The deletion rate again should be 1 in 5 words after the first sentence, and 45% exact replacements indicates that the material is at Instructional Level for that child. This is a useful technique to determine the suitability of text books before an expensive purchase. (Elley 1975.)

c. Instruction.

Cloze procedures may be used in a great variety of ways to induce learning and healthy processing of print in oral, written, and read-along settings. Here the deletion should be between 1 in 10 words and 1 in 20 words since higher rates disturb fluency, confidence, and enjoyment. The level should always be a demonstrably *tolerable* one for all the children involved. Details of using cloze procedures in an instructional setting are outlined in the chapter *Group Teaching*.

17. See Note 15 for a more detailed exposition of the central hypothesis-test strategy. The term *Central Method of Word Attack* was coined many years ago as a simple introduction to the notion of a strategy rather than a skill. As described in this text it relates to the cross-referencing of skills in a hypothesis-test strategy.

18. Since the monitoring of oral reading remains the most popular way of teaching and checking reading, particularly in remedial settings, the nature of helpful and harmful intervention needs to be spelt out.

Helpful intervention induces the learner to be self-regulative and self-corrective. It does not put a high premium on fluency as such since the strategies of self-regulation often involve the sub-strategies, or minor strategies, of causing to think, sample and solve; re-running for syntactic and semantic coherence from the beginning of a phrase or sentence; and reading-on to probe context in forward reference before returning to re-run. Helpful intervention normally occurs at the end of sentences unless there has been a serious block on a word or a cumulative confusion — when intervention will suggest an appropriate minor strategy rather than asking for 'sounding out' or 'syllabification' in a meaning vacuum. Sometimes, helpful intervention will be no more than a warm and patient waiting — displaying no sign of tension. As Marie Clay (1972a) points out, it is often in fruitful silences that the child learns to solve problems independently. Our aim is to help the learner develop what Marie Clay calls 'a self-improving system'. (Butler and Clay 1979.)

Harmful intervention raises tensions and drives the child into more and more dependent habits. It leaves no room for proper pauses and problem-solving and destroys rather than sustains meaning. It focuses on accuracy at the expense of understanding and often insists on applying single skills or rules when only combined skills will work. It interrupts mid-sentence and *locates* the child's errors, so hindering the growth of healthy self-correction and confirmation.

For simple and helpful ways of intervening, see the section, *Guidelines in Word Recognition* in the chapter, Developing Reading Skills and Strategies.

19. The techniques of oral cloze provide powerful ways of inducing sound central functioning. The following are a few such procedures:
    a. Teacher has a book of normal size from which he or she reads in a manner which captures attention. By stopping at a suitable word with rising voice intonation he or she cues the children to predict. Crucial grapho-phonic detail may then be written on the blackboard. In this setting almost all responses may be received positively — they are not right or wrong.
    b. Teacher uses enlarged text — printed on card, paper, or over-head transparencies, or uses slide or filmstrip projector, or epidiascope. Children tune in and out depending on the difficulty. As the story develops, the teacher reads less and less. Some of the words or parts of them, may be covered by a flap mask to induce prediction and produce the opportunity for confirmation by letter detail.
    c. Use of a progressive exposure mask on the overhead projector as described in the chapter, *Group Teaching*.
    d. Use of read-along tapes as also described in that chapter.

References and Bibliography

Arbuthnot, May Hill. (1972) *Children and Books*. Chicago: Scott, Foresman and Co.

---- (1968) *Reading in the Home*.Chicago: Scott, Foresman and Co.

Barbe Walter B. and Abbott Jerry L. (1975) *Personalized Reading Instruction*. West Nyack, N.Y.: Parker Publishing Company, Inc.

Bormuth, J. R. (1969) 'Factor Validity of Cloze Tests as Measures of Reading Comprehension Ability.' *Reading Research Quarterly*, Vol. 4, 358-367.

Britton, James. (1970) *Language and Learning*. Harmondsworth: Penguin Books.

Burmeister, L. E. (1974) *Reading Strategies for Secondary School Teachers*. Reading, Mass.: Addison-Wesley.

Butler, Dorothy. (1979a) *Cushla and Her Books*. Auckland: Heinemann Educational.

----- and Clay, Marie M. (1979b) *Reading Begins at Home*. Auckland: Heinemann Educational Books.

Carter, Garry C. (1977) 'Assessing and Improving the Affective Dimensions of Reading'. In *Literacy for Life*, eds A. Ridsdale and J. Horan. Melbourne: Australian Reading Association.

Chambers, Dewey W. (1971) *Children's Literature in the Curriculum*. Chicago: Rand, McNally & Co.

Chambers, Marjorie. (1968) *Introduction to Dewey Decimal Classification for British Schools*. London: Forest Press Inc.

Charles, C. M. (1976) Individualizing Instruction. St. Louis: The C. V. Mosby Co.

Chomsky, Noam. (1957) *Syntactic Structures*. The Hague: Mounton.

Clark, Margaret M. (1976) *Young Fluent Readers: What Can They Teach Us?* London: Heinemann Educational Books.

Clay, Marie M. (1972a) *Reading: The Patterning of Complex Behaviour*. Auckland: Heinemann Educational Books.

----- (1972b) *The Early Detection of Reading Difficulties: A Diagnostic Survey*. Auckland: Heinemann Educational Books.

----- and Butler, Dorothy. (1979) *Reading Begins at Home*. Auckland: Heinemann Educational Books.

----- (1980) *Early Detection of Reading Difficulties: A Diagnostic survey with Recovery Procedures*. Auckland: Heinemann Educational Books.

Dale, Philip S. (1976) *Language Development: Structure and Function*. New York: Holt, Rinehart & Winston.

Deci, E. L. (1975) *Intrinsic Motivation*. New York: Plenum Press.

de Lacey, Philip (1974) *So Many Lessons to Learn*. Blackburn, Victoria: Penguin.

de Leeuw, Manya and Eric (1965) *Read Faster, Read Better*. Harmondsworth: Penguin.

Doake, David B. (1976) 'Comprehension and Teaching Strategies.' In *New Horizons in Reading*, ed. John E. Merritt, pp. 125-140. Newark, Delaware: International Reading Association.

Donaldson, Margaret. (1978) *Children's Minds*. Glasgow: Fontana/Collins.

Durkin, Dolores. (1966) *Children Who Read Early: Two Longitudinal Studies*. New York: Teachers College Press.

Elley, W. B. and Read, N. A. (1969) *Progressive Achievement Tests: Reading Comprehension and Reading Vocabulary*, Teacher's Manual. Wellington: New Zealand Council of Educational Research.

----- (1975) *The Problem of Readability*. Auckland: International Reading Association.

Fader, Daniel (1969) *Hooked on Books*. London: Pergamon Press.

Gilliland, John. *Readability*. London: Hodder and Stoughton.

Goodman, Kenneth (1976a) 'Behind the Eye: What Happens in Reading'. In *Theoretical Models and Processes of Reading*, eds H. Singer and R. B. Ruddell, pp. 470-496. Newark: International Reading Association.

------ (1976b) 'Reading: A Psycholinguistic Guessing Game'. In *Theoretical Models and Processes of Reading*, eds H. Singer and R. B. Ruddell, pp. 497-508. Newark: International Reading Association.

Goodman, Yetta M., and Burke, Carolyn (1972) *Reading Miscue Inventory*. New York: Macmillan.

Halliday, M. A. K. (1973) *Explorations in the Functions of Language*. London: Edward Arnold.

Harris, L. A. and Smith, C. B. eds (1972) *Individualizing Reading Instruction: A Reader*. New York: Holt, Rinehart & Winston.

Haviland, Virginia, ed. (1973) *Children and Literature: Views and Reviews*. Glenview, Illinois: Scott, Foresman and Co.

Herber, H. L. (1970) *Teaching Reading in Content Areas*. New Jersey: Prentice-Hall Inc.

Hittleman, Daniel R. (1978) *Developmental Reading: A Psycholinguistic Perspective*. Chicago: Rand McNally.

Holdaway, Don. (1976) 'Self-Evaluation and Reading Development'. In ed. John E. Merritt, *New Horizons in Reading*. pp. 181-192. Newark: International Reading Association.

----- (1979) *The Foundations of Literacy*. Sydney: Ashton Scholastic.

Holt, John (1964) *How Children Fail*. London: Pitman Publishing Co.

----- (1967) *How Children Learn*. London: Penguin Books.

Huck, Charlotte S. and Kuhn, Doris. (1976) *Children's Literature in the Elementary School*. New York: Holt, Rinehart and Winston.

Johnson, Barbara (1979) *Reading Appraisal Guide*. Melbourne: Australian Council for Educational Research.

Jones, Richard M. (1968) *Fantasy and Feeling in Education*. Harmondsworth: Penguin Books.

Kennerley, Peter, ed. (1979) *Teenage Reading*. London: Ward Lock Educational.

Kirk, S. A. and McCarthy, J. J. (1961) 'The Illinois Test of Psycholinguistic Abilities: An Approach to Differential Diagnosis'. American Journal of Mental Deficiency, 66.

Kohl, Herbert (1973) *Reading, How To*. New York: Dutton and Co.

McCracken, Marlene and Robert. (1979) *Reading, Writing & Language: A Practical Guide to Primary Teachers*. Winnipeg: Peguis Pub. Ltd.

MacKinnon A. R. (1959) *How DO Children Learn to Read?* Vancouver: Copp Clark.

McNeil, David (1970) *The Acquisition of Language: The Study of Developmental Psycholinguistics*. New York: Harper & Row.

Martin, Bill and Brogan, Peggy. (varied) *The Sounds of Language* series, Teacher's Editions. New York: Holt, Rinehart, Winston.

Merritt, John E. (1972) 'Reading Failure: A Re-Examination'. In *Literacy at All Levels*, ed. Vera Southgate, pp. 175-184. London: Ward Lock Educational.

Neville, Mary H. and Pugh, A. K. (1976) 'Context in Reading and Listening: Variations in Approach to Cloze Tasks.' *Reading Research Quarterly*, Vol. 12, No. 1, pp. 13-31.

Opie, Iona and Peter (1959) *The Lore and Language of School Children*. London: O.U.P.

----- (1969) *Children's Games in Street and Playground*. London: O.U.P.

Otto, Wayne; Peters, Charles W.; and Peters, Nathaniel. (1977) *Reading Problems: A Multidisciplinary Perspective*. Reading, Mass.: Addison-Wesley Publishing Co.

Pulvertaft, Anne (1978) *Carry on Reading*. Sydney: Ashton Scholastic.

Ruddell, Robert B. (1970) 'Psycholinguistic Implications for a System of Communications Model'. In *Theoretical Models and Processes of Reading*, eds H. Singer & R. Ruddell, pp. 452-469. Newark, Del.: International Reading Association.

Sartain, Harry (1971) *Individualized Reading: An Annotated Bibliography*. Newark, Del.: International Reading Association.

Smith, Frank (1973) 'Twelve Easy Ways to Make Learning to Read Difficult'. In *Psycholinguistics and Reading*, ed. Frank Smith, pp. 183-196. New York: Holt, Rinehart & Winston.

----- (1975) *Comprehension and Learning*. New York: Holt, Rinehart & Winston.

----- (1978a) *Understanding Reading: A Psycholinguistic Analysis of Reading and Learning to Read*. Second Edition. New York: Holt, Rinehart & Winston.

----- (1978b) *Reading*. Cambridge: Cambridge University Press.

Townsend, J. R. (1971) *A Sense of Story: Essays on Contemporary Writers for Children*. London: Longmans.

Veatch, Jeanette (1959) *Individualizing Your Reading Program*. New York: Putman's Sons.

----- (1966) *Reading in the Elementary School*. New York: Ronald Press.

----- (1968) *How to Teach Reading with Children's Books*. New York: Citation Press.

INDEX